Prohibition of Sexual Exploitation of Children Constituting Obligation *Erga Omnes*

Prohibition of Sexual Exploitation of Children Constituting Obligation *Erga Omnes*

Farhad Malekian and Kerstin Nordlöf

CAMBRIDGE
SCHOLARS
PUBLISHING

Prohibition of Sexual Exploitation of Children Constituting Obligation *Erga Omnes*,
by Farhad Malekian and Kerstin Nordlöf

This book first published 2013

Cambridge Scholars Publishing

12 Back Chapman Street, Newcastle upon Tyne, NE6 2XX, UK

British Library Cataloguing in Publication Data
A catalogue record for this book is available from the British Library

F.Malekian.In.Crim.L@telia.com and Kerstin.Nordlof@oru.se

ISBN (10): 1-4438-4766-6, ISBN (13): 978-1-4438-4766-7

... for the enforcement of the rights of children...

TABLE OF CONTENTS

Appendices

ABSTRACT

Whilst the value of human integrity within the laws of individual states and the documents of international human rights is being increasingly consolidated and will become, sooner or later, the primary concern of the law, severe breaches of this value are indeed still widespread. In particular the sexual exploitation of children constitutes one of the most serious questions of national, regional, transnational and international law. According to international records, every fifteen seconds a child is raped in Africa alone. Almost half of the cases heard by the ICTY concern the sexual exploitation of women and children during armed conflict. More or less similar conclusions may be reached regarding the ICTR or the SCSL. In Rwanda alone, 500,000 females were raped. Almost 200,000 females and children have been the victims of cruel forms of sexual violence during the conflicts in Congo. Sexual abuse of children by priests cannot any longer be ignored in Australia, Belgium, Canada, Germany, France, Ireland, Mexico, the United Kingdom, and the United States, although it is ignored in most Islamic countries. The sexual exploitation of children is also widely practised in many other countries. Regrettably, 79% of all world trafficking is for sexual exploitation.

The principal subject matter of this book is the legal etymology of sexual exploitation governing minors. The aim is to identify and analyse *jus cogens* and obligation *erga omnes* in relation to the sexual exploitation of children and to evaluate the international responsibility of states in relation to the elimination or prevention of the crime, and the prosecution and punishment of offenders.

PREFACE

Whilst the value of human integrity is increasingly developing into the primary concern of the laws of individual states and the documents of international human rights law, severe violations of these laws, provisions, norms, conventions and documents remain commonplace and widespread. A particularly grievous example is the trafficking in persons, which constitutes one of the most serious questions for national and international law. The term "trafficking in persons" does not only deal with the sexual exploitation of females and males, but also applies to the position of persons who have, by one means or another, lost the potential to control their personal integrity through working under conditions of forced labour or services, slavery or practices similar to slavery, or servitude, and extraction of organs, or tissues. Although defining sexual exploitation minutely is a challenging task, it broadly means to impose the interests of a person or persons or an organized group onto the body of the victim who has no right to choose but only to serve her or his master. This is what is also called prostitution, with *forcibly* given consent being typically characterized as rape.

The principal subject matter of this book is sex trafficking, with a particular concentration on the situation of young females. Unfortunately it has not been possible to produce anything comparable on the situation of boys. The reason for this is that most relevant documents deal with the position of women and girls, while documents dealing with the questions of the sexual exploitation of boys are very few in number. In any case, the sexual exploitation of children is one of the important concerns of the book. The intention is to identify and analyse the existing documents in the field of trafficking and see whether their provisions, norms and principles can be considered under *jus cogens* norms and consequently obligation *erga omnes*, which constitute the unavoidable international norms that have to be protected by the legal authorities of governments within the national, transnational and international arenas. Based on this aim, the theoretical understanding of the subject from the point of view of positive law is exhaustively investigated. With this in mind, the chapters of the book present a large number of norms and principles constituting an integral part of the body of international legislation concerning the prohibition of all forms of sex trafficking in children. It is however true that the law applicable to the trafficking in women and children is a significant part of international human rights law instruments and cannot be studied in isolation. This means that the law governing trafficking should be examined in conjunction with a considerable number of principles of human rights law which have a dominant role within international legal community as w whole.

Since the subject matter of the book falls broadly within the field of international law and particularly international criminal law, the function of this branch of jurisprudence is also one of its fundamental concerns. Throughout the work, we will concentrate on various definitions of the law governing sex trafficking, particularly as it applies to children. The book therefore explores the definitions of sex trafficking which are adopted at a regional and international level. The aim is to examine these different systems and to see whether there are any differences between them. But since the national rules are essentially supposed to be in accordance with regional rules and the latter should not legally be in conflict with international norms and principles, this means that there are certain strong connections between these three systems and that they ought to follow one another in form, phrasing and principles. This is what is required for the fulfilment of the principle of cooperation. By way of introduction, the chapters of the book emphasise the fundamental duties and responsibilities of states to face their international obligations.

Briefly, several principles of criminal law which are also an integral part of international criminal law are examined in scope. These include *inter alia* the principle of *de lege lata, de lege ferenda, ex post facto law, nullum crimen sine lege, nulla poena sine lege, mens rea* or 'mental elements', *ne bis in idem* and individual criminal responsibility. These are internationally recognized as an integral part of criminal systems within the legislations of different states.

One important orientation of the subject will be on the progressive development of the law governing the sex trafficking in persons within the law of different international criminal tribunals/courts. These include the Nuremberg Charter, the International Criminal Tribunal for the Former Yugoslavia, the International Criminal Tribunal for Rwanda, the Special Court for Sierra Leone and, most importantly, the Statute of the International Criminal Court in The Hague.

Our hope is that the work opens a window onto a vast array of legal materials which are not only today a part of national, regional, and international legislation, but are also an integral part of customary international criminal law, all of which have to be respected by all states regardless of their political, economic, military, cultural and religious situations. This does not only include Western states, but also those states which, while claiming to implement Islamic law and its principles, are seriously violating international law by misinterpretation and mistreatment of its jurisprudence. The main argument throughout the book is to emphasise the primary responsibility of governments, individually and together, for the prevention of sexual exploitation of children within and outside their territories. The book argues that the exploitation constitutes one of the heinous national, international, and transnational *erga omnes* crimes, the perpetrators of which should be prosecuted under the principle of universality of jurisdiction.

Farhad Malekian
Kerstin Nordlöf
Carolina Rediviva Library
Uppsala, Sweden
May 2013

CHAPTER ONE

THE EMERGENCE OF OBLIGATION *ERGA OMNES* IN INTERNATIONAL CRIMINAL LAW

Introduction

The very rapid development of global sex trafficking and its serious infringements of the provisions of international human rights law have raised basic questions regarding the relationships between the laws of individual states, regional law and international criminal law as a whole.[1] This is because an examination of various international conventions, agreements, treaties and other documents concerning sex trafficking in human beings proves that they have, in one way or another, some connection with the system of international criminal law, and almost none of these instruments applicable to trafficking may be treated without a proper examination of the systems of regional and national law. This is particularly significant in the case of provisions governing children who are subject to comparatively differing statutes under various national systems. Although one cannot deny that the system of international criminal law strongly protects the rights of children through various international conventions such as the Convention on the Rights of the Child, the position of the child is relatively unstable due to the policy of most states of the world, and the child is one of the most vulnerable subjects of sex trafficking under international social or economic systems.[2]

---

[1] Human trafficking has long existed within human civilization but has not until recently been identified as a crime.

[2] Farhad Malekian, Kerstin Nordlöf., *Confessing the International Rights of Children* (2012).

In this section we are focused on the foundations of the system of international criminal law with particular consideration of the question of sex trafficking. The purpose is here to analyse the relevant laws and to see to what extent the system prevents, prohibits, eliminates, prosecutes and punishes acts concerning sex trafficking with a special focus on children. We have therefore taken into examination various developments in international criminal law, including the statutes of the *ad hoc* tribunals, and the ICC. Certain practices of the *ad hoc* tribunals have been focused on with the intention of emphasizing the development of the principle of obligation *erga omnes*. This section includes, therefore, a discussion on the legal validity of the principle of *jus cogens* in the system of international criminal law and its effect concerning the position of the principle of obligation *erga omnes*. The section will stress the role of governments in the prevention, elimination, application and prosecution as well as punishment within the law of trafficking in persons.[3] The principle of obligation *erga omnes* is also of vital importance in laying the groundwork for all other sections of this book. They will discuss various legislations on trafficking issued by different regional and international instruments constituting an integral part of *jus cogens* or general international law and therefore obligation *erga omnes*. In addition, both principles – *jus cogens* and obligation *erga omnes* – are integral to the structure of all sections of this book. The purpose is to examine their validity within the relevant instruments applicable to the trafficking in persons and, particularly, children.

[3] The European Convention uses the terminology "human beings" instead of "person". See Convention on Action Against Trafficking in Human Beings adopted by the Council of Europe in 2005 and entered into force in 2008.

What Is International Criminal Law?

The system of international criminal law has been defined differently.[4] All of these definitions agree that the system has several functions which cannot be isolated from its nature. Thus, the definition of the term "international criminal law" has to be examined with its functions. This is because any law has to have a particular function; otherwise its legal validity will be weakened. That is why we have different laws with different functions. Examples include civil law, criminal law, procedural law, tax law or medical law. In fact, the functions of a law demonstrate the limits of its applicability. In this regard, the functions of international criminal law are criminalization, protection, prevention, prohibition, elimination, extradition, implementation, prosecution, jurisdiction, rehabilitation and also implementation of judgment. Consequently, the system of international criminal law is an integral part of public international law which aims at the deterrence of criminal conduct. This

---

[4] In order to approach to different definitions of international criminal law consult: Georg Schwarzenberger, 'The Problem of an International Criminal Law,' 3 *Current Legal Problems* (1950)263; Edward M. Wise, 'Prolegomenon to the Principles of International Criminal Law,' 16 *New York University Law Review* (1970) 562; Farhad Malekian, *International Criminal Law: The Legal and Critical Analysis of International Crimes* (2 vols. 1991); Farhad Malekian, *Principles of Islamic International Criminal Law: A Comparative Search* (2011); Farhad Malekian, *The Monopolization of International Criminal Law in the United Nations: A Jurisprudential Approach* (2 ed, 1995); M. Cherif Bassiouni (ed.), *International Criminal Law* (3 vols., 1999); Farhad Malekian, *International Criminal Responsibility,* in M. Cherif Bassiouni (ed.), *International Criminal Law*, (1999) 153; Michael Bachrach, 'The Protection and Rights of Victims under International Criminal Law,' 34(1) *The International Lawyer* (2000); M. Cherif Bassiouni, 'International Recognition of Victims' Rights,' in Bassiouni (ed.), *International Criminal Law,* vol. III, 635-701 (2008); Boas Gideon and William A. Schabas (eds.), *International Criminal Law Developments in the Case Law of the ICTY* (2003); Yoram Dinstein, *'International Criminal Law,'* 20 *Israel Law Review* 206 (1985); Robert A Friedlander, 'The Foundations of International Criminal Law: A Present-Day Inquiry,' 15 *Case Western Reserve Journal of International Law*13 (1983); M. Cherif Bassiouni, *Introduction to International Criminal Law* (2003); M. Cherif Bassiouni, 'The Discipline of International Criminal Law,' in M. Cherif Bassiouni (ed.), *International Criminal Law*, vol. 1 (2008) pp.3-40; M. Cherif Bassiouni, 'The Subjects of International Criminal Law: Ratione Personae' in M. Cherif Bassiouni (ed.), *International Criminal Law*, vol. 1 (2008) pp.41-70; Robert Cryer, 'The Doctrinal Foundations of International Criminalization,' in *International Criminal Law*, Vol.1 (M. Cherif Bassiouni, ed. 2008) pp. 107-128.

means that the whole body of law deals with criminal matters and what comes under its framework is generally called "international crime". Therefore, the key focus of international criminal law is crime/offence and its scope of definition. These include offences such as aggression, genocide, war crimes, crimes against humanity, piracy, crimes against internationally protected persons, terrorism, hijacking, unlawful medical experimentation on human subjects, slavery, prostitution, narcotic offences, postal offences, and for our purposes here, trafficking in persons, including sex trafficking relating to the child. This is a person who is under 18 years, although, we may encounter different age limits for the recognition of the child. There may still be legislations that do accept a higher and lower age limit for the protection of the state of childhood.

It must however be stated that the term "prohibition of sex trafficking" may fall within two different legal systems which have basically the same aim and purpose for the prevention of trafficking. Thus, prevention of sex trafficking may not only be carried out under international criminal law, but also under the provisions of transnational criminal law. While the former is a broader aspect of the international criminal law system, the latter may fall into the legal capacity of the former. The core reason is that the international criminal system is a legal system which has the capacity to deal with most criminal systems and their regulations. In other words, international criminal law is empowered with different theories of national criminal law and therefore most criminal provisions have some connections with international criminal law. Consequently, when we speak of international criminal law we also speak of transnational criminal law which has similar functions to the former, with several functions *inter alia* with the intention of prevention of trafficking in persons.

Transnational criminal law is a legal system which applies to criminal activities which are committed within and/or over national borders. The criminal conducts may be carried out with the complicity, assistance or direct engagement of the perpetrators in the commission of the crime. Transnational crimes are committed by an organized group or by several persons. Therefore, trafficking of humans for slavery or the like constitutes a transnational criminal enterprise which is typically carried out in countries suffering from poverty, corruption of law enforcement and weakness of government.[5] Those engaged in these crimes entice vulnerable

---

[5] However, the crime is also a problem in countries which have relatively strong economies and well-organized legislation. For example, "Sweden is a destination, source, and, to a lesser extent, a transit country for women and children subjected to sex trafficking and a destination country for men, women, and children subjected to forced labour. Women, men, and children are subjected to forced

women, men, and children with promises of good jobs, education and social stability. Thus, human trafficking may be in the form of domestic servitude, involuntary servitude, forced debt bondage, and, perhaps most serious of all, sex slavery. In the case of children, human trafficking includes child sex tourism, various child services, and sex services combined with heavy labour.

One chief difference between transnational crimes and international crimes is that the former are more often committed by private individuals while the latter are committed by governmental or non-governmental bodies or groups of individuals. Crimes coming under the framework of transnational crime include narcotic offences, trafficking in persons, or terrorism. Crimes coming under the scope of international crime include war crimes, crimes against humanity and genocide. It is yet to be asserted that there are also certain crimes the nature of which overlaps with the nature of transnational or international crimes. Such is the legal characterization of sexual abuse of children, child pornography and child sex services which may vary from case to case depending on war or peacetime.

International crimes denote the criminalization of an internationally wrongful conduct which is recognized as a crime by the international legal community as a whole. These are crimes recognized as such within conventions, treaties, agreements, declarations, arrangements, protocols, pacts, covenants and any other legal instrument. A particular recognition within these instruments is their criminalization of certain acts. It must however be stated that not all international crimes are based on the provisions of an international criminal convention. They may be found within other international conventions in which some aspects of

labour and forced criminal behaviour, including begging and stealing.... Foreign victims of sex trafficking originate from Central and Eastern Europe (Romania, Russia, Bulgaria, Hungary, the Czech Republic, the Slovak Republic, Albania, Estonia, Lithuania, and Armenia), Africa (Nigeria, Tanzania, Kenya, Ghana, Uganda, Sierra Leone, Gambia, Kenya), and Asia (Thailand, China, Uzbekistan, Kazakhstan, and Mongolia). Swedish girls were also vulnerable to sex trafficking within the country, which mostly occurs in apartments, houses, and hotels. Other sex trafficking victims are exploited in massage parlors. Both victims and perpetrators of forced begging and stealing originate primarily in Romania, Belarus, and Bulgaria." See UNHCR | Ref world | 2012 Trafficking in Persons Report - Sweden, www.unhcr.org/refworld/country,SWE,4562d8b62,4fe30c91c,0.html; See also Sex Trafficking of Children in Sweden, ecpat.net/EI/Publications/Trafficking/Factsheet_Sweden.pdf. Since purchase of sex services is prohibited in Sweden, many individuals purchase sex services in Denmark which is legally permitted. Ibid.

international criminal law are regulated, such as the Universal Postal Union conventions, which in certain articles deal with the prohibition of sending of certain materials such as weapons, narcotics, or obscene materials, in particular pornographic representations of children.[6]

The provisions of the system of international criminal law may also be examined within the principles of customary international criminal law. This means that all provisions of the law are not necessarily based on a conventional approach. They may be rules of customary law that, because of certain important functions for the maintenance of humanitarian or other laws, have been integrated into the system of international criminal law. It is also possible that the same rules of conventional international criminal law may be found within the rules of customary international criminal law or the contrary. This is because those two sources of the law complement one another and may adopt rules from each other. A customary rule may enter into the provisions of an international convention and a conventional rule because of its very important and significant effect may become a part of customary international criminal law. For instance, a considerable number of provisions of international humanitarian law of armed conflict may be found within both sources of international criminal law. At the same level is the prohibition of trafficking in persons which is not only a part of conventional law, but is also, a significant part of customary international criminal law which has been developed steadily since the start of twentieth century.[7]

Yet, certain provisions of conventional international criminal law may because of their very high value for the maintenance of international peace, equality, justice and security of humankind shift into the provisions of customary international criminal law. For instance, the provisions of the international Convention on Genocide are today an integral part of customary law. Other clear examples are the provisions of international

[6] Moreover, in the United States, it is a federal crime to send obscene material to a child who is under age 16. This is under condition that the sender knows that the child is under 16. Federal Law, 18 U.S.C. § 1470 (2008). § 1470. Transfer of Obscene Materials: "Whoever, using the mail or any facility or means of interstate or foreign commerce, knowingly transfers obscene matter to another individual who has not attained the age of 16 years, knowing that such other individual has not attained the age of 16 years, or attempts to do so, shall be fined under this title, imprisoned not more than 10 years, or both."

[7]*See* Prosecutor v. Kunarac, Kovac &Vukovic, Case No. IT-96-23-T, Judgment, ¶ 520 (Feb. 22, 2001). For the development of the customary prohibition, see also M. Cherif Bassiouni, *Enslavement as an International Crime*, 23 New York University Journal of International Law and Politics, 445 (1991).

criminal conventions applicable to the crimes of apartheid, discrimination, slavery and also the sex trafficking and sexual exploitation of women and children.[8] International criminal law has fundamentally been created and permitted to evaluate many internationally wrongful conducts which are seriously destructive of the international relations of states and may jeopardize political or legal agreements between states.

Sources of the Law

In order to prove the thesis of this book, namely that sex trafficking falls under the principle of obligation *erga omnes*, we have to examine the sources of the law to see in which sources the concept of sex trafficking is prohibited within the national, regional and international legal community. Sources of public international criminal law may be found within the provisions of Article 38 of the International Court of Justice. The relevant article refers to the following sources: international conventions; international customary law; decisions of national, regional and international courts; decisions of international arbitration tribunals; general

[8] It should be stated here that trafficking in persons is somewhat different from people smuggling. This is because human trafficking is a typical modern form of slavery. It concerns the illegal exploitation and trade in persons through the use of force or coercion, including threats, fraud, deception and debt bondage. As such, it inflicts upon the victim(s) the deprivation of liberty, the violation of social or economic integrity and the total deprivation of both natural and positive rights. The chief difference between people smuggling and trafficking in persons is that in the former case the person who is being smuggled has given his/her consent and has often paid a large amount of money in order to enter another country's borders. Therefore, human smuggling denotes the illegal transportation or facilitation of transportation of persons from one county to another. In addition, it often involves the presentation of false documents to cross an international border. However, the trafficking in persons almost always involves acts of force and the victim does not necessarily need to express consent or present any authorized papers. It violates all human rights conventions or declarations. Nevertheless, it must be stated that in particular situations a person who is being smuggled may also be recognised as the victim of human trafficking if she/he is then forced or coerced into working in degrading or exploitative conditions. However, this argument is much stronger in the case of persons who are under 18 years of age and are treated under the provisions of international conventions governing the rights of the child. The legal status of minors broadly differs from that of adults in the case of smuggling or trafficking. In both cases minors are the victims of people smuggling or trafficking in persons. This means that they should be treated differently and should not be considered as guilty of the commission of transnational crimes because of their illegal crossing of an international border.

principles of law; the opinion of publicists and also certain resolutions of the United Nations. Although the article does not specifically enumerate all of these sources they are generally understood from its content.[9]

Thus, in order to understand the legal characterization of the prohibition of sex trafficking and its prevention one has to examine the above sources and to see whether these sources have particular rules, regulations, principles, norms, provisions or other instructions applicable to the conduct in question which also simultaneously criminalize the relevant conduct. In short:

International conventions are those rules or regulations which have been formulated into written instruments and are signed and ratified by states parties. Examples are the conventions applicable to slavery, trafficking in persons, discrimination, and the suppression of sexual slavery, as well as support for the victims of crime and the establishment of the rights of children. These can be seen within the provisions of the Convention on the Rights of the Child which is formulated to recognize and enumerate the rights of children. The Convention strongly condemns the exploitation of children for various purposes including their employment as soldiers, sexual objects, slaves, or in other inhuman and degrading labour. One chief difference between international conventions and other sources of the law is that the provisions formulated into those agreements constitute *pacta sunt servanda*. They have, therefore, a binding effect on contracting parties and should be respected in their various national or international relations. This is because the merit of *pacta sunt servanda* is to demand the implementation of conventional provisions and this is regardless of the authority of the parties. That is to say the principle of *pacta sunt servanda* creates a legal obstacle against parties who do not respect the established norms of international law and violate them. International criminal conventions or treaties should therefore be considered as the most effective source for the prevention of trafficking in

---

[9] The Statute of the ICC, article 38 reads that "1. The Court, whose function is to decide in accordance with international law such disputes as are submitted to it, shall apply: a. international conventions, whether general or particular, establishing rules expressly recognized by the contesting states; b. international custom, as evidence of a general practice accepted as law; c. the general principles of law recognized by civilized nations; d. subject to the provisions of Article 59, judicial decisions and the teachings of the most highly qualified publicists of the various nations, as subsidiary means for the determination of rules of law. 2. This provision shall not prejudice the power of the Court to decide a case *ex aequoet bono*, if the parties agree thereto."

persons and the enforcement of *jus cogens* law and the principle of *erga omnes*.

International customary law sets forth rules, provisions, principles and norms that are not written within an international instrument but because of long and systematic duration in the practice of states have received the status of custom. Examples are provisions regarding the prevention of sexual slavery. The two most recognized components in international customary law are uniform and consistent state practice as well as evidence of *opinio juris*. State practice demands the presentation of state consent to the given rule. This requires the engagement of the state in constant and uniform conduct characterizing its behaviour. The *opinio juris* which presents the second component demands that the conduct of states has been based on a legal obligation. The rules of customary international criminal law have without doubt encouraged the prohibition of trafficking in persons and therefore create obligations on states to accept international legal standards regarding the prohibition of sex trafficking and the sexual exploitation of children, men and women.[10] Customary law also helps to clarify the significant values of conventional international criminal law governing the implementation of an international system which can prevent states, groups and individuals from engaging in trafficking or avoiding effectively preventing the relevant international crime.

General principles of law are those rules that may generally be found within the law of most states, such as provisions regarding the prevention of violations against women and children or provisions governing rape as

---

[10] In *Prosecutor v. Kunarac, Kovac & Vukovic*, the Trial Chamber of the International Criminal Tribunal for the former Yugoslavia specified charges of "enslavement as a crime against humanity" by quoting the international definition of slavery within customary international law. The court stated that the definition formulated in the 1926 Convention applies to enslavement under customary international law. "Enslavement as a crime against humanity in customary international law consist[s] of the exercise of any or all of the powers attaching to the right of ownership over a person." Prosecutor v. Kunarac, Kovac & Vukovic, Case No. IT-96-23-T, Judgment (Feb. 22, 2001), para. 539. The Court defined enslavement as "the exercise of any or all of the powers attaching to the right of ownership over a person." *Kunarac*, Case No. IT-96-23-T, para. 540 According to the Trial Chamber, the following reasons are examined in correctly deciding whether enslavement was carried out. These are such as "control of someone's movement, control of physical environment, psychological control, measures taken to prevent or deter escape, force, threat of force or coercion, duration, assertion of exclusivity, subjection to cruel treatment and abuse, control of sexuality and forced labour." *Kunarac*, Case No. IT-96-23-T, paragraphs 542–43.

a serious crime. The provisions of general principles of law simplify the recognition of certain rules of law that have achieved national recognition within the internal laws of most nations and have long been consolidated. This means that "general principles of law" help in the prohibition of sex trafficking through their recognition as being obligation *erga omnes.* Although there may be some controversy about what does and does not constitute a general principle of law, this cannot and should not inhibit the legal effect of general principles of law in the prevention of sex trafficking by the legal authorities of states. Therefore, the role of this source is to minimize the gap between different cultures and find certain rules and provisions which are similar to one another within the structure of most civilizations in the world. For example, the illegality of the sexual abuse of children is a principle that can be found within all civilizations of the world.

Decisions of courts refers to the judgment of national, regional, and international courts which may be considered appropriate for the settlement of a conflict or may be regarded as the creation of certain new norms within different schools of jurisprudence. These are rulings such as the decisions of International Criminal Tribunal for the Former Yugoslavia (ICTY) and the International Criminal Tribunal for Rwanda (ICTR) concerning rape as an international crime or the strict prohibition of violence against women during wartime. However, it must be underlined that the decisions of all courts cannot have a legal effect on the prevention of sex trafficking and cannot create binding effects on different states. This is because the applications of most decisions of national courts are limited to certain cases and territories and therefore the scope of their applicability is restricted. However, certain decisions of national, regional or international courts which make reference to international rules and standards of law may be recognized as effective and significant. Thus, decisions of regional Human Rights Courts, decisions of national courts which deal with international cases and international regulations may be used for the prevention of sex trafficking in persons and demand the implementation of the principle of obligation *erga omnes*.

Resolutions of the General Assembly or the Security Council of the United Nations may be vitally significant for the development of the rules of law. Some of the resolutions are therefore considered an integral part of sources of public international law and are therefore authoritative. This source of the law is not only important in the consolidation of the system of international customary law, but also, for the provisions of conventional international criminal law. Examples of these resolutions are those of the General Assembly which refer to the prohibition, elimination, prevention, prosecution and punishment of trafficking in persons or sex trafficking. A clear example is the resolution called the United Nations Global Plan of Action to Combat Trafficking in Persons.[11] This resolution condemns trafficking in persons with particular emphasis on women and *children*. However, it must be added that there are rules concerning the recognition of certain relevant resolutions of the General Assembly as authoritative sources of law. The functions of those rules are to identify the relevant resolution as an authentic source of law.[12] Despite this, most relevant resolutions of the General Assembly extensively contribute to the development of rules preventing trafficking in human beings and the prohibition of various types of slavery.

National law constitutes another source of law. This means that the provisions of different legal systems within different states have a very significant effect in the recognition of acts of sex trafficking or sex slavery. Regulations within national criminal systems may also create a representation of regional and international understandings of sex trafficking in human beings. They are also bound to fulfil the provisions of international human rights documents, otherwise, they may be asked to formulate those provisions within their legal system by the regional authorities, i.e., the European Commission and the European Court of Human Rights. For example, the European Court of Human Rights in its judgment of the case of Rantseva who was sexually exploited and died after jumping from a balcony concluded that the principles of human rights law had, on several occasions, been violated by Cyprus and Russia.[13] The decision of the Court was a historic decision concerning the duties of states regarding the provisions of their national laws.

The teaching of publicists may be considered to be a source of international law. There is no special condition for this. Article 38 of the Statute of ICJ speaks about highly qualified publicists but does not give any definition of what is meant by qualified. This means that the level of qualification may vary from country to country. The opinion of one person which is accepted in his/her country may be rejected by the legal and political authorities in another country. That is why the opinion of jurists of international law is considered as being a secondary source which may be helpful in certain circumstances. This does not mean that the opinions

---

[11] Resolution of the General Assembly 64/293.

[12] For recognition of these rules see Farhad Malekian, The Monopolization of International Criminal Law in the United Nations: A Jurisprudential Approach (1995).

[13] See Opinion No. 6/2010 - On the Decision of the European Court of Human Rights in the Case of Rantseva v. Cyprus and Russia.

of publicists are not effective in the recognition of trafficking in persons and the very question of *jus cogens* and obligation erga *omens*.

Yet, the problem is also a matter of understanding language and its interpretation. For instance, the fact that the works of a very highly qualified publicist in China, Japan or Persia may not have been translated into other languages does not diminish his position as a highly qualified writer. While one has to exercise a considerable degree of caution regarding the recognition and the effect of this source in international legal cases, this source has been effective in the formulation of new provisions relating to trafficking in persons and in the creation of international criminal courts.

It must be admitted that the most powerful source of law prohibiting the trafficking in human beings is conventional and national law and this is based on the fact that their provisions are codified and cannot easily be dismissed by those who are engaged in trafficking in persons for sexual exploitation. This is especially important when considering the position of children who are the most vulnerable victims of sex trafficking.

Jus Cogens

Normative Function

Within the provisions of the systems of public as well as international criminal law there are certain principles or norms which are important and essential foundations. They have received a wide recognition within the framework of international justice and human morality and consequently occupy a fundamental position in the body of the law.[14] In other words, the international legal community as a whole and international human rights law consider the full respect of certain norms as comprising norms from

---

[14] The very important position of *jus cogens* norms for the protection of human rights or protection of men, women and children from unlawful human rights violations can even be examined in the provisions of Articles 55 and 56 of the United Nations Charter. It is for this reason that the organization has the purpose of promoting human rights based on multilateral conventions such as the Convention on the Prevention and Punishment of Crime of Genocide (1948), the International Convention on the Elimination of All Forms of Racial Discrimination (1965), the International Covenant on Economic, Social and Cultural Rights (1966), the International Covenant on Civil and Political Rights (1966), the Convention on the Elimination of All Forms of Discrimination Against Women (1979), the Convention Against Torture and Other Cruel, Inhuman or Degrading Treatment or Punishment (1984), and the Convention on the Rights of the Child (1989).

which no derogation is permitted. This means that the values of these norms cannot be devalued or ignored by the provisions of law-making treaties. The 1969 Vienna Convention, which is considered one of the most important instruments in the field of the international law of treaties, recognizes these norms of the system of general international law under the term "peremptory" norms. It reads that "A treaty is void if, at the time of its conclusion, it conflicts with a peremptory norm of general international law." It further continues that "For the purposes of the present Convention, a peremptory norm of general international law is a norm accepted and recognized by the international community of States as a whole as a norm from which no derogation is permitted and which can be modified only by a subsequent norm of general international law having the same character."[15] In the practice of the system of public and international criminal law these norms are acknowledged by the term "*jus cogens*".

Superiority

The provisions of conventional international criminal law are enforceable as long as they have not been modified or terminated by another international convention. This element is however rather restricted concerning certain norms that have peremptory function. This is because with the peremptory function we mean those norms that have achieved a certain high level of recognition and are considered essential *a)* for the maintenance of peace, *b)* for the implementation of justice, *c)* for the application of the principle of human rights law, *d)* for the recognition of equality between men and women, *e)* for the elimination of discrimination and f) for the prevention of various forms of violation. It is for these and many other reasons that the *jus cogens* norms or the peremptory norms of general international law have superiority over other provisions of the systems of the international legal community.

In general, superiority applies to certain values and interests which have legal, political, economical and social priority over other principles. This means that when we speak about the prohibition of sex trafficking of children in conjunction with the norms of *jus cogens* or those peremptory norms of general international law, we simply mean that they have come to a certain stage of characterization that cannot be ignored by giving priority to other principles of law. They should always be accorded the

---

[15] The Vienna Convention was signed in 1969 and came into force in 27 January 1980.

highest privilege by the relevant authorities of states. In other words, the prohibition of sex trafficking of children should not be interpreted differently or be subordinated to certain cultural norms. This means that even countries in which the law permits a marriageable age as low as 9, cannot dispute internationally recognized norms regarding the age of majority.

Precedence over National Law

The normative function of the system of *jus cogens* norms creates for them precedence over the provisions of national law. This means that the legislative authorities within a state have to give a clear recognition to the *jus cogens* norms within the national legal system and whenever they are formulating or enacting a law should take all due consideration that the new legislation, not only does not conflict with the *jus cogens* norms, but also, takes precedence over those new regulations. In other words, states should not and cannot pass legislation which violates one of the norms of *jus cogens*. Hence, the sovereignty of states is practically limited by the normative principle of *jus cogens* law.

Precedence over International Law

Since *jus cogens* norms or the peremptory norms of general international law protect the most important provisions of the system of the international legal community, they have, in all circumstances, precedence over international regulations. This means that states of the world should not and cannot regulate mutual, multilateral and unilateral conventions by which certain peremptory norms of international law are limited, ignored or abolished. Even assuming that states do regulate certain provisions contrary to the legal characterization of *jus cogens* norms, these new rules of individual states are practically invalid.[16] This is due to the very high international legal validity of *jus cogens* norms and their automatic virtue of applicability. Those norms invalidate all international treaties that are in contradiction with the normative force of *jus cogens* law. In other words, the international legal personality of states is seriously limited by the norms of *jus cogens,* in so far as they may act against normative principles

[16] However, one cannot deny the fact that there may be many rules under national legislations that are essentially against *jus cogens* norms. For instance, although marriage of girls who are nine years old is against all human rights norms, is practically permitted in some of the Islamic states.

of international law. For instance, even if states have not ratified international conventions governing the suppression of sexual slavery, the slave trade, and trafficking in persons, or the conventions relating to the protection of children from various forms of sexual exploitation, they may not, even so, write a valid international convention that may permit organized criminality, trafficking in persons, sex trafficking, and most significantly from our point of view, the sexual exploitation of children by various means including their participation in sex pornography or their sale. All these acts are certainly against all sources of the law and international human rights law, even though, we may not have specific regulations within positive international law. The reason is that they are against the customary and general principles of law or those consolidated values of human civilization in the world such as the protection of women and children, protection of family unity, protection of the child and various other humanitarian protections.

Characterization

The question is always: what is the nature of the characterization of *jus cogens* norms? To explain it simply, they are norms that are internationally recognized as vital and have the value of natural or positive. Thus certain fundamental values are integrated into their nature and these have been acknowledged by states of the international legal community within the provisions of some of the international legal sources. The *jus cogens* norms are not a particular general source of international law, but together constitute a normative source which integrates the most important principles of different sources of international law within a single source. This means that the value of the legal characterization of the *jus cogens* norms is not essentially based in the signature or ratification of a treaty by all states of the world, but, on the significant function of certain norms which are also called the peremptory norms of general international law.[17]

[17] For instance, it is generally accepted that it is a consolidated norm of national and international law that the death penalty should not be imposed upon those who at the time of the commission of a crime were under eighteen years of age. This principle constitutes today an integral part of *jus cogens* norm. This was proved in a case concerning juvenile offenders. Accordingly, Micheal Domingues was sentenced to death when at the time of his commission of the murder of two persons he was 16 year old. The case was brought before the Inter-American Commission of Human Rights. The United States claimed that there was not a *jus cogens* norm prohibiting capital punishment for minor persons. The Commission ruled that, on the contrary, there was a "*jus cogens* norm not to impose capital

Categories

There are different categories of *jus cogens* norms.

One category consists of norms that are an integral part of general conventional international law such as certain regulations concerning open seas/high seas.

Another category consists of norms of international conventional criminal law such as regulations governing slavery, the slave trade, the prohibition of the sexual abuse of children, and the prohibition of child labour.

The third category is based on the most important principles of customary international law such as the principles of the Declaration of Human Rights.

The fourth category is based on the provisions of customary international criminal law such as prohibition of armed attack on hospitals and schools and prohibition of the use of children in armed conflicts.

The fifth category acknowledges the most important principles of international human rights law such as social, economic and political equality.

The sixth category is based on some of the most recognized general principles of law, such as the prohibition of rape and violence against women and children, and the principle of legality, *nullum crimen sine lege* and, *nullum poena sine lege*.

The seventh category of *jus cogens* norms are those which are emphasized within the law of international courts or tribunals such as the interpretation of the genocide convention by the ICJ or judgments of the ICTY, the ICTR, the Special Court for Sierra Leone and also the permanent International Criminal Court (ICC).

Although, all these categories have an independent character from one another, they may in certain circumstances come within two or more categories. This means a definition of a *jus cogens* norm may be recognized as important within several categories. Consequently, the categorization of *jus cogens* norms is *solely* for their legal recognition and has nothing to do with their level and degree of effectiveness. This is because there is not any privileging of *jus cogens* norms except for when the application of one such principle becomes necessary for the international legal community.

---

punishment on individuals who committed their crimes when they had not yet reached 18 years of age." The Michael Domingues Case: Report on the Inter-American Commission on Human Rights, Report No. 62/02, Merits, Case 12.285 (2002).

Criteria of Recognition

There is not any special condition in international law stating which parts of the international system may come under *jus cogens* norms and which do not. For this reason, one has to refer to certain criteria for the recognition of *jus cogens* norms. These are *inter alia* the following:

a) If the norm has received a wider international recognition in the international legal community as a whole.
b) If the norm can be found within the provisions of a number of international conventions.
c) If the norm is incorporated into multilateral treaties and is according to the provisions of those treaties prohibited from derogation.
d) If the norm is repeatedly stated within the decisions of national courts.
e) If the norm is considered important within the judgment of most international courts or tribunals.
f) If the norm is one of the significant principles within international public order.
g) If the norm is considered an integral part of international human rights law.
h) If the norm is given priority within most international criminal conventions.
i) If the norm is repeatedly stated within the resolutions of the General Assembly of the United Nations.
j) If the norm is an integral part of the content of most resolutions of the Security Council.
h) If the most widely acknowledged doctrines of international law refer to the existence of a particular norm.
l) If the practice of states denotes its existence.
m) If the norm is a pillar for the existence of particular principles.
n) If the norm is a repeatedly acknowledged part of customary law.
o) If the norm has a determinative function for the existence of ethical, cultural, social and religious factors.
p) If the elimination of the norm conflicts with general principles of civilization.
q) If the norm is repeatedly stated within different international instruments supporting the existence of the rights of minors.
r) If the violation of the norm constitutes discrimination against either sex.
s) If the norm is consistently stated within the legislations of most states of the world.
t) If the elimination of the norms is against the principles of democracy.

Jus Cogens Crimes

Jus cogens crimes concern the high value of certain norms of the international community as a whole and those which must be respected by all states without due regard to their ratification of certain international conventions or the provisions of their national legislations. Due to the existence of different criteria, some of the most recognized crimes within the system of *jus cogens* norms which are relevant are the following:

Piracy is a crime which is committed in the high seas (open seas). Since it is the subject of widespread prohibition over centuries and strong condemnation, the crime comes under the category of *jus cogens* crimes. The crime is often treated under the principle of universality.

War Crimes regulations have to be respected and cannot be ignored or violated by other provisions. They are also an integral part of the international humanitarian law of armed conflict.

Crimes against humanity are crimes that have long been recognized as such and states should not engage in the commission of these crimes. The latest developments within international conventions imply that sex trafficking is also a crime against humanity and can thus be examined in the law of the international criminal tribunals or the ICC.

Aggression has long been recognized as one of the most serious international crimes and rules prohibiting it are binding on all states.

Genocide may not be permitted by any provision in the international system. This crime is prohibited in accordance with conventional and customary international criminal law.

Slavery was a habit of most nations in the world. It has for a long period of time been abolished under the auspices of the League of Nations and most importantly by the United Nations. Any other forms of slavery, such as involuntary servitude, are also strongly prohibited. Sex trafficking is fundamentally identified as having the conditions of slavery. This is also true in the case of sex pornography and any other sexual abuse of children.

The practice of apartheid which is permitted by the provisions of any legislation is a serious violation of international rules. Trafficking for sexual exploitation of women and children, may also be considered as giving priority to one race over another, and therefore it may, in certain situations, be identified as the practice of apartheid against minors.

Non-discrimination and particularly the principle of racial non-discrimination are two of the most recognized principles within almost all national and international instruments. Sex trafficking may be considered a very grave form of discrimination against women and children.

Torture is one of the clear forms of *jus cogens* crimes. As a whole, it is rejected by the international legal system and states should prevent or eliminate such criminal behaviour. Sex trafficking is also assimilated to torture and it is by the victim considered a perpetual torture. This is especially tangible in the case of minors who have been subjected to sex trafficking or similar forms of abuse.

Trafficking in persons is recognized as a serious international crime in a considerable number of applicable international and regional conventions. This recognition is also entered into the provisions of customary international criminal law and also the laws of individual states. It deals with matters of prohibition, prevention, elimination, prosecution and punishment. The Statutes of the ICC, the ICTY, the ICTR and the Special Court for Sierra Leone recognise trafficking in persons/enslavement as the commission of crimes against humanity.[18]

Obligation *Erga Omnes*

Function

A *jus cogens* norm is based on a general norm of international law that is recognized by individual states and accepted by the international community of states as a norm from which no derogation is permitted. In other words, with the recognition of certain norms as *jus cogens* norms, the international legal community wants to underline the existence of certain norms that are common to most states of the world and it is expected that all states want to respect them. Thus, the principle of obligation *erga omnes*[19] expresses the recognition of certain norms as *jus cogens* norms, and therefore calls upon the immediate responsibility of states to prevent certain conducts that are commonly accepted to be internationally wrong or serious crimes.[20] These crimes are such as aggression, genocide, slavery, and discrimination. According to one opinion, they include at least five common elements. These are:

> (1) all four examples relate to narrowly defined obligations outlawing of ... aggression rather than, more broadly, the illegal use of force; outlawing of genocide rather than, more broadly, crimes against humanity; protection from slavery rather than, more broadly, all kinds

---

[18] See the relevant section below.

[19] For this principle see Christian J. Tams, *Enforcing Obligations Erga Omnes in International Law* (2005).

[20] Ibid., p.144.

of unlawful restrictions on freedom; protection from racial discrimination rather than, more broadly, all kinds of discrimination);

(2) while two out of the four examples are expressed in terms of the 'outlawing' of certain practices, and the two others in terms of the 'protection from' certain other practices, all four examples are essentially those of negative obligations (or prohibitions), rather than positive obligations;

(3) all four examples are those of 'obligations', or 'duties', in the strict sense (i.e. what 'one ought or ought not to do'), to the exclusion of other fundamental legal conceptions;

(4) all four examples are those of obligations deriving from rules of general international law belonging to *jus cogens* and codified by international treaties to which a high number of States have become parties; and

(5) all four examples are those of obligations instrumental to the main ... political objectives of the present time, namely the preservation of peace and the promotion of fundamental human rights, which in turn reflect basic goods (or moral values), first and foremost life and human dignity.[21]

Thus, the principle of obligation *erga omnes* protects the fundamental rights of men, women and children from various serious violations which may be committed by individuals, groups or states. The principle establishes therefore an international obligation and duty for all individuals, organs and states not to commit actions against the common interests or values of the international community as a whole and prevent others from committing violations against those interests.

Definite Implementation

Obligation *erga omnes* is one of the consolidated principles of national and international criminal law. It refers to the position of certain rules, provisions, regulations, principles or norms, the implementation of which are vital because they are *jus cogens* norms. The principle of obligation *erga omnes* applies, therefore, to the necessary duties of states to protect the victims immediately, without any time delay, when certain commonly recognized and accepted principles of general international law are violated. For instance, it is a compulsory legal duty of states to prevent genocide, torture, crimes against humanity, apartheid, war crimes, aggression and sex trafficking, in particular that of children. The reason is that these crimes are an integral part of *jus cogens* crimes and should not

---

[21] Maurizio Ragazzi., *The Concept of International Obligations* Erga Omnes (2000).

be ignored at any stage. Thus, the international legal and political responsibility of states is called upon, which arises from their membership of the international legal community. The purpose is to stop grave violations of the norms of international law and of *jus cogens*. The responsibility of a state to prevent certain serious violations of international norms constitutes a duty which it is impossible to abrogate.[22] Consequently, the maintenance of *jus cogens* norms are in the interests of all states. As the ICJ states:

> 33. When a State admits into its territory foreign investments or foreign nationals, whether natural or juristic persons, it is bound to extend to them the protection of the law and assumes obligations concerning the treatment to be afforded them. These obligations, however, are neither absolute nor unqualified. In particular, an essential distinction should be drawn between the obligations of a State towards the international community as a whole, and those arising vis-a-vis another State in the field of diplomatic protection. By their very nature the former are the concern of all States. In view of the importance of the rights involved, all States can be held to have a legal interest in their protection; they are obligations *erga omnes*.

---

[22] For instance, the Nigerian government was recognized responsible by the Community Court of Justice of the Economic Community of West African States for the violation of the international rights of one of its citizens by allowing her to be under the conditions of slavery. In 2008, the Court cited the *Kunarac* Appeal case (ICTY). According to it "the law does not know of a 'right of ownership over a person'. Article 1(1) of the 1926 Slavery Convention speaks more guardedly 'of a person over whom any or all of the powers attaching to the right of ownership are exercised.' That language is to be preferred. … [T]he question whether a particular phenomenon is a form of enslavement will depend on the operation of the factors or indicia of enslavement identified by the Trial Chamber. These factors include the "control of someone's movement, control of physical environment, psychological control, measures taken to prevent or deter escape, force, threat of force or coercion, duration, assertion of exclusivity, subjection to cruel treatment and abuse, control of sexuality and forced labour. Consequently, it is not possible exhaustively to enumerate all of the contemporary forms of slavery which are comprehended in the expansion of the original idea; this Judgement is limited to the case in hand." Prosecutor v Dragoljub Kunarac, Radomir Kovac and Zoran Vukovic, Judgment, IT-96-23, paras.118-119. See alsoDuffy, Helen., 'HadijatouMani Koroua v Niger: Slavery Unveiled by the ECOWAS Court', *Human Rights Law Review* (2008), pp.1-20; see also Piotrowicz, Ryszard., 'States' Obligations under Human Rights Law towards Victims of Trafficking in Human Beings: Positive Developments in Positive Obligations', Vol. 0, No.0 *International Journal of Refugee Law*, pp. 11-12.

> 34. Such obligations derive, for example, in contemporary international law, from the outlawing of acts of aggression, and of genocide, as also from the principles and rules concerning the basic rights of the human person, including protection from slavery and racial discrimination. Some of the corresponding rights of protection have entered into the body of general international law; others are conferred by international instruments of a universal or quasi-universal character.[23]

The ICJ does not however clarify the obligations of a state towards the international community as a whole. But it lists some of these obligations by stating that those "obligations derive, for example, in contemporary international law, from the outlawing of acts of aggression, and of genocide, as also from the principles and rules concerning the basic rights of the human person, including protection from slavery and racial discrimination. Some of the corresponding rights of protection have entered into the body of general international law.[24] ... others are conferred by international instruments of a universal or quasi-universal character."[25] As we will discuss later, the statements of the ICJ are today an integral part of the Statue of the ICC and these obligations of states towards the international legal community may also be found within the statutes of other international criminal tribunals such as the ICTY and the ICTR. However, we do not deny the fact that opinions vary from writer to writer and government to government depending on political persuasion. Accordingly, the principle of obligation *erga omnes* still belongs to the legislation of the "ought" [26] rather than that of the "is"[27]. Although these

[23] Barcelona Traction, Light and Power Co. Ltd. (Belg. v. Spain), 1970 I.C.J. 3, 32 (Feb. 5), (*Reservations to the Convention on the Prevention and Punishment of the Crime of Genocide, Advisory Opinion, L.C.J. Reports 195I*, p. 23).

[24]*Reservations to the Convention and Punishment of the Crime of Genocide, Advisory Opinion, I.C.J. Reports 1951*, p. 23).

[25] Barcelona Traction, Light and Power Co. Ltd. (Belg. v. Spain), 1970 I.C.J. 3, 32 (Feb. 5).

[26] Maurizio Ragazzi., The Concept of International Obligations *Erga Omnes* (2000), p.216. According to Ragazzi, "Today, it would be inaccurate to suggest that the concept of obligations *erga omnes* already has all its 'molecules' and 'layers'. At the same time, it would be equally inaccurate to infer, from the absence of several of these 'molecules' and 'layers', that the concept itself is not yet well established." Ibid. However, "one should avoid putting 'too much strain' (and too many expectations) on the law, as the use and abuse of the concept of obligations *erga omnes* is essentially a political question." Ibid, p.216.

[27] Cf. B. Simma., 'Does the UN Charter Provide an Adequate Legal Basis for Individual or Collective Responses to Violations of Obligations Erga Omnes?,' in Jost, Delbrück (ed.), *The Future of international Law Enforcement: New Scenarios*

opinions are rather strong, the principle of obligation *erga omnes* is now considered as a cornerstone of modern international law, international criminal law, international humanitarian law, transnational criminal law, and human rights law. This means that there is a widespread acceptance of the principle in case law, international practice, and academic literature.[28]

A clear example of this is the engagement of the European Parliament (Eruoparl or EP) which is an elected parliamentary institution of the European Union, in the Cambodian case of sexual exploitation of children.[29] This is known as the European Parliament resolution on trafficking of women and children in Cambodia (2005).[30] According to the resolution exploitation of children or sexual exploitation of children constitutes a crime of *erga omnes* and therefore relevant to all states. It declares that:

> ...
> F. whereas trafficking in human beings is increasing because of poverty, unemployment, the vulnerability of women and children, deteriorating social conditions in the countries of origin, the high profits and low risks experienced by traffickers, and the demand for women and children for purposes of prostitution and other forms of sexual exploitation,
> G. whereas efforts still need to be made in the fight against organised crime and trafficking in human beings,
> ...
> 1. *Denounces the sexual exploitation of minors as a crime "erga omnes" and an attack on the fundamental rights of children which must be fought at all levels;*[31]
> 2. Stresses its preoccupation with child prostitution in Cambodia and with the trafficking in human beings both to and from Cambodia, with the objective of using them for forced labour, prostitution and begging and in illegal adoptions;
> 3. Recalls the principles of the Charter of Human Rights and especially the rights of girls, in the case of sexual exploitation of minors in Asia and in the rest of the world.[32]

– *New Law?* proceedings of an International Symposium of the Kiel Institute of International Law, March 25 to 27, 1992 *(1993),* p.125.

[28] But, see also Brownlie, Ian, Principles of Public International Law (1979), pp.514-515.

[29] For the whole case see http://www.humantrafficking.org/updates/20.

[30] Official Journal 247 E , 06/10/2005 P. 0161 – 0163.

[31] Emphasis added.

[32] For the whole resolution see the appendix.

In fact, the principle of *erga omnes* permits all states bring a claim against another state which has violated an international obligation essential for the protection of fundamental interests of children of international community as a whole.[33] These interests can, for example, be found on the UN Convention on the Rights of the Child, the Convention on the Elimination of All Forms of Discrimination against Women, the UN Protocol to Prevent, Suppress and Punish Trafficking in Persons, especially Women and Children, and the UN Convention against Organised Crime.

Differences

There is a basic difference between the term "obligation *erga omnes*" and the term "*jus cogens*". The former refers to the juridical propositions arising from the legal characterization of the crimes constituting *jus cogens* norms. In other words, it concerns the implementation of the juridical validity of certain norms having the nature of an international non-derogative character. The latter refers to those parts of the law which have achieved the highest level of recognition in the international legal community as a whole. More specifically, *jus cogens* norms are the basic values of certain rules of the international community. For instance, when we speak about the prohibition of sex trafficking or pornography perpetrated against children, we mean that the nature of this prohibition has the character of *jus cogens* and cannot be dismissed by any state, because of its significant legal and moral function.

Due to the different function and scope of both legal terms, all peremptory obligations are part of obligation *erga omnes* but all

[33] However, it is also asserted that the principle of erga omnes is a clear case of retaliation by one state or several states against another. Accordingly "an erga omnes norm exists when other states retaliate against a violation of a norm that injures a particular state. In effect, the transgressor's act, though apparently injuring only one state, in fact injures multiple states, so a multi-state reaction can be expected. The injury is indirect, or at least not as clearly visible, but it is still real. The free-riding problem limits the likelihood of such a multi-state reaction, but it will nonetheless occur when individual states, or a small group of states, have enough at stake. The states with the most at stake—the highest benefits and lowest costs from intervention—will take the lead and sometimes even act alone." Posner, Eric A., Erga _Omnes Norms, Institutionalization, and Constitutionalism in International Law 1 (The Law School, the University of Chicago, 2008), Johan M. Olin Law and Economics Working Paper No. 419 (2d Series), Public Law and Legal Theory Working Paper No.224, Electronic copy available at: http://ssrn.com/abstract=1211424. Visited on 18-04-2013.

international obligations are not peremptory norms.[34] Although, one cannot deny the fact that both terms refer to the same matter with different explanations, they have essentially different functions. In other words, obligation *erga omnes* which calls upon the immediate responsibility of a state in order to prevent certain criminally wrongful conducts, may not be resorted to as long as the norms of *jus cogens* are not violated. But, the *jus cogens* norms may increase in number without having necessarily any need to fulfil the principle of obligation *erga omnes*. That is to say one is based on the element of fulfilment of obligations while the other on the element of recognition and acceptance. Thus, when we say that norms of sex trafficking constitute *jus cogens*, we mean that they already exist and simultaneously have the nature of obligation *erga omnes*, i.e., they specify the responsibility of the state to fulfil these obligations and prevent violations of internationally recognized norms. Consequently, the principle of obligation *erga omnes* constitutes also an integral part of *jus cogens* norms, but is not used as long as these norms are respected.

Enforcement

Obligations of obligation *erga omnes* are enforced in different ways. When the norms of *jus cogens* are violated, states may act *a)* regionally, *b*) internationally, and *c*) individually. All these depend on the level and stage of violations.

States act *regionally* when they react against certain violations of the norms of *jus cogens* from a regional point of view. They may formulate a regional policy for the elimination of the conduct. The policy is a part of the principle of obligation *erga omnes* and aims to guarantee the basic values of certain norms of the region.

The General Assembly may act *internationally* when states react together against certain violations of the norms of *jus cogens*. This reaction is most often expressed by the adoption of different sanctions. An example is when the states of the world adopted a considerable number of sanctions against the apartheid regime in South Africa. All these sanctions aimed at the prevention and elimination of apartheid in South Africa. The sanctions also considered apartheid as a crime against humanity. According to the resolutions of the General Assembly, all policies of racial discrimination and apartheid were against the principles of international

[34] It is also very doubtful which obligations states accept as an integral part of *erga omnes*. Karl Zemanek,, 'The New Trends in the Enforcement of Erga Omnes Obligations,' 6 *Max Planck Yearbook of United Nations Law* (2000), 1-52, at 4 see in www.pdf-search-engine.com/jus-cogens-and-erga-omnes-pdf.htm -70k.

law and the purposes and principles of the Charter of the United Nations. They also considered apartheid a serious threat to international peace and security. Other examples are the resolutions of the General Assembly relating to the prevention and prohibition of trafficking in persons. Most of the provisions of these resolutions have the character of *jus cogens* norms and are therefore binding upon all states. The merit of these resolutions is based on the fact that they have been adopted by the majority of states in order to prevent certain violations *of jus cogens* norms that have seriously been infringed in the practice of states or because of their failure to act.

In addition, the Security Council may by its decisions implement the norms of international law and *jus cogens* when they are violated. This means that the Council may take an effective measure for the prevention of certain acts which are considered serious violations of international peace and security. The Council may therefore react by adoption of resolutions or also take decisions according to which it may take military measures against the state which violates norms of *jus cogens*. However, the problem of the Security Council decision is that it may represent the political interests of the permanent members. Thus, it may apply different policies according to the circumstances of the case and violations. For instance, although the Security Council is aware that the trafficking of human organs from executed prisoners in China is one of the serious problems concerning violations of international norms and the fundamental principles of human rights law, it has done nearly nothing about this trafficking. The political relations between the permanent members and their authorities on the one hand, and the existence of illegal markets on the other hand, help the situation get more and more serious and insecure.[35] Thus, the principle of obligation *erga omnes* may not be enforced and trafficking continues. However, we do not deny the fact that the Security Council members have had a unanimous policy regarding the prevention of trafficking in persons and the prevention and prohibition of sexual abuse or pornographic representation of children. Again, the decision of the Security Council concerning violations of the *jus cogens* norms under the apartheid regime in South Africa was divided, since the United States, the United Kingdom and Israel were against any resolution which condemned the apartheid system. This was based on the fact that all three states had significant economic interests in the region.

A state may *individually* take responsibility for the restoration of justice and the violations of the norms of *jus cogens*. This is when the state

[35] China acts on Prisoners Organs Scheme, The Independent, 23 March 2012. www.independent.co.uk/.../china-acts-on-prisoner-organ-scheme-7582914.html, visited on 25/10/2012.

considers it to be its own individual responsibility to put an end to particular violations within its own territory and, more rarely, in other territories. This may be carried out with different sanctions emanating from its legislations, such as serious border control for prevention of sex trafficking and particular programs for the protection of children. It must be admitted that it is here the principle of obligation *erga omnes* which calls upon the responsibility of the state for the fulfilment of its obligations.[36] Thus, concerning certain violations of the system of international criminal law, such as genocide or other similar crimes, different actions of states, such as decisions not to send or buy certain goods to or from the violator state, do not constitute intervention and are simply the protection of fundamental norms of *jus cogens*. But concerning the question of the sex trafficking of women and children, it is mostly the actions of groups of individuals or organized groups who carry out transnational organized crimes such as trafficking in persons, particularly children, and not necessarily the state. However, a state may require that another state fulfil the principle of obligation *erga omnes* for the prevention of transnational crimes and for the respect of *jus cogens* norms.

---

[36] The principle of obligation *erga omnes* is also considered of essential importance for the fulfilment of certain positive obligations of states that should not be ignored in the international legal and political communities. A clear example of this is protection and maintenance of the principle of self-determination. In fact, protection of this principle is considered by the International Court of Justice as a duty of all states. For instance, the Court in the case relating to the Legal Consequences of the Construction of a Wall in the Occupied Palestinian Territory concerning the relation between the principles of *obligation erga omens* and self-determination stated that "As to the principle of self-determination of peoples, the Court points out that it has been enshrined in the United Nations Charter and reaffirmed by the General Assembly in resolution 2625 (XXV) cited above, pursuant to which 'Every State has the duty to refrain from any forcible action which deprives peoples referred to [in that resolution] . . . of their right to self-determination.' Article 1 common to the International Covenant on Economic, Social and Cultural Rights and the International Covenant on Civil and Political Rights reaffirms the right of all peoples to self-determination, and lays upon the States parties the obligation to promote the realization of that right and to respect it, in conformity with the provisions of the United Nations Charter. The Court recalls its previous case law, which emphasized that current developments in "international law in regard to non-self-governing territories, as enshrined in the Charter of the United Nations, made the principle of self-determination applicable to all [such territories]", and that the right of peoples to self-determination is today a right *erga omnes*." www.icj-cij.org/docket /files/131/1677.pdf -.

The International Criminal Court or the *ICC*, which will be studied later, has also certain duties for the implementation of *jus cogens* norms. This is because the Court has an independent international legal personality which means it creates for the Court international legal capacity to act when certain fundamental values of the international community as a whole are violated. These norms are such as those relating to genocide, war crimes, aggression and crimes against humanity. Due to the provisions of the Court, sex trafficking and sexual exploitation of children constitute an integral part of crimes against humanity. This means that the Court, as an international authorized legal person, has to fulfil the requirements of the principle of obligation *erga omnes*.[37] The purpose is to bring the perpetrators of trafficking in women and children under the jurisdiction of the Court.

International Law Commission

The notion of obligation *erga omnes* has also been developed by the work of the International Law Commission of the United Nations General Assembly.[38] This can particularly be examined in the work of the Commission relating to the concept of international responsibility of states. The Commission in its draft articles on responsibility of states emphasises that "every internationally wrongful act of a State entails the international responsibility of that State."[39] The wrongdoer state may have a twofold responsibility towards the injured states. One may be the responsibility of the state towards the victim state and the other the international community of states as a whole. One of the most relevant articles of the draft concerning the invocation of responsibility by an injured State provides that:

> A State is entitled as an injured State to invoke the responsibility of another State if the obligation breached is owed to:
> (a) That State individually; or

---

[37] For further consideration consult *infera.*

[38] The Commission is one of the subsidiary organs of the General Assembly. The Commission works for the codification of international law.

[39] Article 1 of the Draft Articles on Responsibility of States. Text adopted by the International Law Commission at its fifty-third session, in 2001, and submitted to the General Assembly as a part of the Commission's report covering the work of that session (A/56/10). The report, which also contains commentaries on the draft articles, appears in the *Yearbook of the International Law Commission, 2001*, vol. II, Part Two, as corrected.

(b) A group of States including that State, or the international community as a whole, and the breach of the obligation:
(i) Specially affects that State; or
(ii) Is of such a character as radically to change the position of all the other States to which the obligation is owed with respect to the further performance of the obligation.[40]

The provisions of Article 42 should be read in conjunction with the provisions of Articles 46 and 48 of the draft articles on responsibility of states. Whilst Article 42 concerns mainly an injured state, more than one state may still be injured by an internationally wrongful act and other states may therefore be entitled, in accordance with the provisions of articles 46 and 48, to invoke responsibility of the state which has committed the internationally wrongful act.[41] Article 46 provides that: "Where several States are injured by the same internationally wrongful act, each injured State may separately invoke the responsibility of the State which has committed the internationally wrongful act." This means that the obligation *erga omnes* norms provide third states, rather than just the injured or victim state, the right to bring legal claims against the state that violate the established international norms.

Article 48 concerns the concept of invocation of responsibility by a state other than an injured state. It clarifies that:

1. Any State other than an injured State is entitled to invoke the responsibility of another State in accordance with paragraph 2 if:
(*a*) the obligation breached is owed to a group of States including that State, and is established for the protection of a collective interest of the group; or
(*b*) the obligation breached is owed to the international community as a whole.
2. Any State entitled to invoke responsibility under paragraph 1 may claim from the responsible State:
(*a*) cessation of the internationally wrongful act, and assurances and guarantees of non-repetition in accordance with article 30; and
(*b*) performance of the obligation of reparation in accordance with the preceding articles, in the interest of the injured State or of the beneficiaries of the obligation breached.

---

[40] Article 42.
[41] Draft articles on Responsibility of States for Internationally Wrongful Acts, with commentaries, *Yearbook of the International Law Commission* (2001), vol. II, Part Two, p.116.

3. The requirements for the invocation of responsibility by an injured State under articles 43, 44 and 45 apply to an invocation of responsibility by a State entitled to do so under paragraph 1.

The provisions of Articles 42, 46 and 48 relate to any breach of an international obligation of whatever character. They are also, without doubt, closely related to the concept of obligation *erga omnes* norms in international law. This is because the relevant provisions deal also with the obligations belonging "to the international community as a whole" from which no derogation is permitted in international law. In other words, the provisions of the articles deal with obligations arising under international law from whatever sources and are not restricted to particular form of obligations. Some of these obligations have a *jus cogens* character and are therefore obligation *erga omnes* or create rights for all states to demand the prevention of certain internationally wrongful conduct occurred by the wrongdoer state or a group of individuals in its territory. A clear example is the prohibition of sexual exploitation of women, men or children in international criminal law or transnational criminal law.

It is not therefore without reason that Article 19 of the draft articles on responsibility of states takes into serious examination the concept of criminal responsibility of states and condemns the breach of certain international obligations which are basically essential for the protection of fundamental interests of the international community as a whole. It deals with international crimes and delicts such as genocide, aggression, apartheid, duties of safeguarding the right of self-determination of peoples, and prohibition of massive pollution of the atmosphere or of the seas. It reads that:

1. An act of a State which constitutes a breach of an international obligation is an internationally wrongful act, regardless of the subject-matter of the obligation breached.
2. An internationally wrongful act which results from the breach by a State of an international obligation so essential for the protection of fundamental interests of the international community that its breach is recognized as a crime by the community as a whole constitutes an international crime.
3. Subject to paragraph 2, and on the basis of the rules of international law in force, an international crime may result, inter alia, from:

(a) a serious breach of an international obligation of essential importance for the maintenance of international peace and security, such as that prohibiting aggression;

(b) a serious breach of an international obligation of essential importance for safeguarding the right of self-determination of peoples, such as that prohibiting the establishment or maintenance by force of colonial domination;

(c) a serious breach on a widespread scale of an international obligation of essential importance for safeguarding the human being, such as those prohibiting slavery, genocide and apartheid;

(d) a serious breach of an international obligation of essential importance for the safeguarding and preservation of the human environment, such as those prohibiting massive pollution of the atmosphere or of the seas.

4. Any internationally wrongful act which is not an international crime in accordance with paragraph 2 constitutes an international delict.

As it is shown, paragraph 4 refers to the concept of an internationally wrongful act which is a delict. A delict has not the character of an international crime. It is a negligent act which gives rise to a legal obligation of the wrongdoer state towards the injured state. As the International Law Commission explains, the legal consequences of delicts are less problematic and constitute a more familiar subject. According to Ago, the Special Rapporteur of the International Law Commission who was later counsel for Spain in the Barcelona case, "denial of justice committed against a particular person is not a kind of crime towards the international community as a whole or towards each one of its members; it is an international delict committed by a State towards the State to which the person in question belongs."[42] Yet, the wisdom of this approach is questionable due the fact that all significant norms of international law have not the character of crime. This means that obligation *erga omnes* norms may also be found within international rules which deal with negligent.[43] The reason is that all states or a majority of states may be

---

[42] I.C.J. Pleadings, Barcelona Traction, Light and Power Company, Limited (New Application: 1962), ii, p. 212. Ago was counsel for Spain for the new application.

[43] However, it is important to mention that civil law countries have different degrees of recognition for the concept of delict. For countries such as Belgium, France, Switzerland and Denmark, a delict is less serious than a crime while for Italy and Spain, a delict is a most serious crime. In addition, common law countries deal with the concept of tort and not delict. Such is the Great Britain. Tort law in these countries arises from case law and divided into many types of torts. Tort law concerns with civil wrongs as distinguished from criminal wrongs. In civil law counties like German, tort law emphasises the rights of civilians such as the right to life, personal liberty, health, physical integrity, and the right to property. These rights are the starting point for compensation in German courts. See Van Dam Cees, *European Tort Law* (2007).

injured by a delict pursuant to the provisions of Article 40(2)(e,f).[44] For instance, a state may breach a provision relating to human rights law or fundamental freedoms under general international law or a multilateral treaty. Article 40 (2) (e), does not require that the obligation should have been "of essential importance" or such a breach should have serious nature.[45] It is, for example, enough that a breach of an obligation be regarded as a part of systematic failure to grant refugee status to particular culture or nationality. That is why the International Court of Justice stated in its judgment that the rules regarding the basic rights of individuals are *erga omnes* obligations.[46]

---

[44] First report on responsibility of states by Mr. James Crawford, Special Rapporteur, UNGA, A/CN.4/490/Add.1 (1998), p.5.

[45] Article 40 (part II) of the draft articles on responsibility of states clarifies that "injured State" means: "(a) if the right infringed by the act of a State arises from a bilateral treaty, the other State party to the treaty; b) if the right infringed by the act of a State arises from a judgement or other binding dispute settlement decision of an international court or tribunal, the other State or States parties to the dispute and entitled to the benefit of that right; (c) if the right infringed by the act of a State arises from a binding decision of an international organ other than an international court or tribunal, the State or States which, in accordance with the constituent instrument of the international organization concerned, are entitled to the benefit of that right; (d) if the right infringed by the act of a State arises from a treaty provision for a third State, that third State."

[46] *Barcelona Traction* Case, [1970] ICJ *Reports*, paras. 33, 34.

CHAPTER TWO

BASIC PRINCIPLES OF CRIMINALIZATION OF TRAFFICKING IN CHILDREN

Introduction

This section deals with those basic principles of criminalization which are necessary for the recognition of the sex trafficking and sexual exploitation of women and children. Whenever one discusses the criminalization of certain conducts in law, national, regional or international criminal law, one is obliged to prove that certain conducts are recognized as crimes, and are therefore against the given laws. This is a principle that constitutes the cornerstone of the application of the concept of criminal responsibility to certain persons for the commission of certain acts against children who are the victims of transnational or international crimes. Consequently, the section deals with the principle of *de lege lata, de lege ferenda, ex post facto law, nullum crimen sine lege, nulla poena sine lege, mens rea* or mental element, *ne bis in idem*, including individual criminal responsibility. The study of these principles helps in the identification of sexual crimes against children and in the methods of prevention, as well as in their criminalization on a national, regional or international level.

De Lege Lata

The principle of *de lege lata*, which is also called *lex lata*, constitutes one of the most important principles of law in general and criminal law in particular. Thus, the principle has a valuable function within civil and criminal law. The principle implies the law as it exists. This means also, *inter alia*, that for the recognition of certain conducts as wrong, the existing body of law must contain certain provisions for the recognition of the relevant conducts. *De lege lata* implies also the scope of the recognition of certain acts within national, regional, or international legislation. *De lege lata* is consequently the contemporary law, or the law which is already accepted in the practice of different courts. The principle of *de lege lata* is also used as opposed to the principle of *de lege ferenda*.[1]

The principle of *de lege lata* is also considered important for the protection of social structure and for the protection of the accused persons. The reason is that the principle outlines certain limitations for the machinery of justice. This is in order not to apply law, rules or provisions that have not already been formulated within the legislations of the relevant state. Reference to the principle of *de lege lata* was mostly employed during the proceedings of the International Military Tribunal in Nuremberg in 1945, and later in connection with other international courts. The principle aims to prevent anarchy or lawlessness within different jurisdictions. Examples of legal documents implying the principle of *de lege lata* are the constitution of the European Union, the Charter of the United Nations, and the Statute of the permanent International Court in The Hague. A national example is the Swedish constitution.[2] Relating to criminal matters one can refer to a considerable number of international criminal laws identifying certain acts or conducts as crimes.

It is on the principle of *de lege lata* that the whole content of this volume is based and its argument is developed with reference to certain international instruments applicable to sex trafficking and the sexual exploitation of women and children. The whole theory of *de lege lata* contributes to the better understanding of the law and effective realization of international conventions relevant to the subject of sex trafficking. This principle simultaneously helps victims and witnesses of sex trafficking to achieve their rights according to the norms of justice. The principle is also particularly necessary for the recognition of sexual crimes against children. This is based on the fact that the position of children may, to some extent, differ from that of adults and require a precise definition of who is the child and how she/he understands the sexual offence, pornography and the like. The principle has therefore a decisive function for the elimination, prevention, restoration, and punishment of crimes.

De Lege Ferenda

The principle of *de lege ferenda* or *lex ferenda,* which comes from the Latin language, refers to the position of rules, regulations or provisions that have not yet been granted legal power and are, in other words, laws for the future. This means that the principle speaks about what the law

---

[1] See sub-section below.

[2] For the Swedish constitution see RF Chapter 1 Section 1 and 3rd paragraph.

should be. The principle is therefore opposed to the principle of *de lege lata*. The principle of *de lege ferenda*, even if it exists, is not and cannot be applied at the present time. It is reserved for the future relations of individuals or the future international conduct of states. Thus, formulation and recognition of various acts as sexual crimes against children under this principle does not establish any legitimate concept of crime.

That is why, in the process of international courts, one of the duties of judges is to distinguish between the principles of *de lege lata* and *de lege ferenda*. Due to this important matter, the provisions of any draft proposal by the United Nations or any other international body concerning sex trafficking and sexual exploitation of children may only be considered as the law for the future. This means that for their enforcement certain provisions have to be adopted, signed as well as ratified due to the requirements of the new instruments. Yet, an agreement may be ratified, but still fall under the decree of *de lege ferenda* based on the fact that it comes into force only after a certain period of time, e.g., three years.

In short, the principle of *de lege ferenda* contains in a legal context what the law ought to be from a juridical point of view, as opposed to the weaknesses of the law as it currently exists. Thus, the principle is used in the context of draft legislation in order to create, modify, strengthen or abolish certain rules or regulations. This process of the development of the law of trafficking relating to the sexual exploitation of women and children in war or peacetime can be examined within the provisions of many international conventions and documents.

Ex Post Facto Law

The principle of *ex post facto* law or retroactive law also constitutes one of the principles of legislation. The principle implies the fact that a conduct which was not recognized as wrong at the time of the performance of the conduct cannot be recognized as wrong at the present time. The purpose of *ex post facto* law is to retroactively modify the legal consequences that existed prior to the adoption of certain rules. *Ex post fact law* may therefore criminalize actions that have not previously been recognized as crimes and were therefore legal. The principle may even call for more severe penalties for acts which were previously recognized under a different classification of offences. Therefore, the use of the principle is often avoided or rejected by the accused.

It must also be noted that the function of the principle is not always to increase the severity of the penalty. On the contrary, it may mitigate the punishment. The principle may therefore be a strong reason for a more lenient punishment of the defendant in a criminal case. Thus, a specified time of imprisonment may be imposed when the penalty would have been life imprisonment. The Statute of the ICC also speaks about *non-retroactivity ratione personae* and its positive consequences. It says that "In the event of a change in the law applicable to a given case prior to a final judgement, the law more favourable to the person being investigated, prosecuted or convicted shall apply."[3] Here, the Statue makes it clear that although the application of a penalty is significant for the implementation of judgment, it is nevertheless of secondary importance for the exercise of justice.

With reference to the principle of *ex post facto* law, the Universal declaration of human rights law states that "No one shall be held guilty of any penal offence on account of any act or omission which did not constitute a penal offence, under national or international law, at the time when it was committed. Nor shall a heavier penalty be imposed than the one that was applicable at the time the penal offence was committed."[4] The Statute of the ICC concerning the *non-retroactivity ratione personae* reads that "No person shall be criminally responsible under this Statute for conduct prior to the entry into force of the Statute."[5] Similar content is to be found in the constitutions of many states.[6]

However, there are different views concerning the application of retroactive law and its use in the procedures of justice. Generally, states which have a written constitution or have based their legislations on the International Bill of Human Rights, i.e., the Universal Declaration of Human Rights, the International Covenant on Economic, Social and Cultural Rights, and the International Covenant on Civil and Political Rights and its two Optional Protocols, do not apply the principle of *ex post facto* law and rely heavily on the principle of *de lege lata*. The principle may only be employed where it reduces the level of punishment against the accused or condemned. Thus, the principle does not help the victim if, at the time the crime was committed, the act was not identified as a crime and was permitted. The principle therefore creates some controversies for and against criminal justice and its subjects, especially when they are mostly children.

---

[3] Article 24 (2).

[4] Article 11 (2).

[5] Article 24 (1).

[6] For example see the Swedish legal system: RF Chapter 2 Section 10. In the application of this principle there are no differences between Swedish citizens and foreigners. RF Chapter 2 Section 22 paragraph 5.

Nullum Crimen Sine Lege

The principle of *nullum crimen sine lege* is widely established within the legal system of most states of the world. The principle also constitutes one of the important principles for the protection of the freedom and integrity of all individuals. The principle guarantees that no act may be recognized as a crime as long as it has not been regulated by law. The principle is also used in conjunction with the principle of *nulla poena sine lege*. This principle like the former principle demands no punishment without a previous penal legislation.

After serious criticisms of the Charter of the Nuremberg Tribunal, the principle has become internationally one of the most recognized principles of criminal law. The important function of this principle has also been entered into the provisions of a number of international courts, in particular the ICC. The Statute of the ICC under the section "general principles of criminal law" spells out the value of this principle. It reads that "A person shall not be criminally responsible under this Statute unless the conduct in question constitutes, at the time it takes place, a crime within the jurisdiction of the Court."[7] In other words, the principle of *nullum crimen sine lege* specifies the necessity of the criminalization of certain conducts within the provisions of national or international legislation.

The philosophy behind the principle of *nullum crimen sine lege* is also strengthened within the European Convention on Human Rights. The Convention therefore prevents the application of any principle which may violate the theory of prior criminalization and punishment. This means that the Convention gives full respect to the principle of prior sanction. It reads that "No one shall be held guilty of any criminal offence on account of any act or omission which did not constitute a criminal offence under national or international law at the time when it was committed. Nor shall a heavier penalty be imposed than the one that was applicable at the time the criminal offence was committed."[8]

The principle of *nullum crimen sine lege* also prohibits the application of any other principle based on analogy. This is because analogy may change or modify the scope of the application of the law and may finally end in unjust decisions in a criminal jurisdiction. The Statute of the ICC

---

[7] Article 22 (1).

[8] Article 27 (1). Sub-section 2 of the same article provides that "This article shall not prejudice the trial and punishment of any person for any act or omission which, at the time when it was committed, was criminal according to the general principles of law recognised by civilised nations."

also denotes this fact. The relevant section of the ICC concerning the principle of *nullum crimen sine lege* clarifies that "the definition of a crime shall be strictly construed and shall not be extended by analogy. In case of ambiguity, the definition shall be interpreted in favour of the person being investigated, prosecuted or convicted."[9] This means the creation of full guarantees for the implementation of human rights law for the accused person.[10]

The principle of *nullum crimen sine lege* constitutes today as an integral part of customary international criminal law.[11] This has been established in the practice of international criminal courts.[12] A short examination of the principle of *nullum crimen sine lege* implies that the principle constitutes one of the basic reasons for the application of justice. This has also to be respected in the case of the application of the provisions of the laws on sex trafficking and sexual exploitation of women and children. Although, one cannot deny that the principle may, in certain circumstances, limit the recognition of criminal actions because of the new methodological and technological developments in international communication, for example, new methods of sexual abuse of children through the internet, it represents fair and appropriate justice for the accused and the victim.

Criminal Responsibility

The principle of criminal responsibility constitutes one of the important principles of criminal law. In addition, the principle of "criminal responsibility" is often interchanged with the principle of "criminal liability". It calls upon the person or persons who have violated the

---

[9] Article 22 (2).

[10] The national laws of some states have clearly referred to the importance of the principle of prior sanction. In the Swedish legislation the principle of *nullum crimen sine lege* is to be found in the Penal Code specifying the principle by stating that "A crime is an act which is described in this Code or in another law or regulation and for with penalty, which is said below, is stated." BrB Chapter 1 Section 1. It is further developed in the Law of Introducing the Penal Code. It says that, if by the time of the judgment another law is applicable, the one which will result in freedom from penalty or a more lenient penalty will be applied. BrP Section 5.

[11] Lorenzo Gradoni., *Nullum crimen sine consuetudine:* A Few Observations on How the International Criminal Tribunal for the Former Yugoslavia Has Been Identifying Custom, at p.18. http://www.esil-sedi.eu/sites/default/files/Gradoni_0.PDF, visited on 24-04-0213.

[12] Ibid., pp.1-18.

provisions of the relevant law. Thus, the principle guarantees the implementation of the law according to the jurisdiction of a criminal court. This means that an accused person may bear no criminal responsibility, as long as his/her guilt is not proved by the procedure of a criminal court. The identification of the principle is particularly significant in the case of the recognition of the criminal responsibility of persons accused of committing trafficking in persons or sexual exploitation of women and children.

The principle of criminal responsibility may be classified under different levels. This is because the age of the suspect[13], the gravity of the crime, the value of the norm which is violated, and the degree of participation in the criminal conduct may have an effect on the level of attribution of the concept of criminal responsibility. This means that a person who has carried out a crime and a person who has attempted or assisted in the preparation of the same crime may receive different punishments. However, the degree of punishment does not necessarily mean that the position of a person may free her/him from criminal responsibility. Thus, the official capacity of persons who engage in the sexual exploitation of women, children, minors, and juveniles during an armed conflict, may not release them from their criminal liability by reference to their legal position. Similarly, the condition of war does not exclude the concept of the criminal responsibility of the accused. This is also clearly stated within the provisions of the Statute of the ICC. It says that it applies "equally to all persons without any distinction based on official capacity. In particular, official capacity as a Head of State or Government, a member of a Government or parliament, an elected representative or a government official shall in no case exempt a person from criminal responsibility under this Statute, nor shall it, in and of itself, constitute a ground for reduction of sentence."[14] It further continues that "Immunities or special procedural rules which may attach to the official capacity of a person, whether under national or international law, shall not bar the Court from exercising its jurisdiction over such a person."[15]

Thus, the conclusive task in the attribution of criminal responsibility within the law of sex trafficking is for the contracting parties to adopt appropriate measures within their legislations for the punishment of those

---

[13] According to the Statute of the ICC a person becomes criminally responsible at the age of eighteen. Article 26 (exclusion of jurisdiction over persons under eighteen). In the Swedish Penal Code criminal responsibility occurs at the age of fifteen. The Penal Code Chapter 1 Section 6.

[14] Article 27 (1).

[15] Article 27 (2).

who have, by one means or another, engaged in the commission of the offences. This is even more serious in the case of crimes committed against children who have been abused because of their fragile position as minors. It must be stated that the principle of criminal responsibility within the provisions of conventions applicable to sex trafficking is based on guilt. The principle expresses that the concept of criminal responsibility must be proven in a criminal court. This means that no form of strict liability is admitted within the provisions of international conventions.[16] This is because the policies of the conventions are to determine the degree of participation of the accused persons in the criminal conduct and not to find a person responsible for the criminal conduct caused by her/his engagement or omissions without due regard to the concept of intent or culpability. Thus, the concept of *mens rea* has a very important function within the policy of the conventions which deal in one way or another with sex trafficking. Naturally, the concept of criminal responsibility also facilitates the concept of the compensation of child victims. However, the existence of certain reasons, such as, e.g., reasonable defence and consent, may mitigate or completely wipe out the concept of criminal responsibility.[17]

---

[16] The use of strict liability within criminal law is not normal but is used in other connections. For example, product liability creates the responsibility of the perpetrators for the injuries those products cause the public. This includes, for instance, manufacturers, suppliers, distributors and retailers. In Swedish law, strict liability is applied to the owners of dogs and cats when they cause damage.

[17] Due to the provisions of Article 31 of the Statute of ICC dealing with grounds for excluding criminal responsibility: "1. In addition to other grounds for excluding criminal responsibility provided for in this Statute, a person shall not be criminally responsible if, at the time of that person's conduct:

(a) The person suffers from a mental disease or defect that destroys that person's capacity to appreciate the unlawfulness or nature of his or her conduct, or capacity to control his or her conduct to conform to the requirements of law;

(b) The person is in a state of intoxication that destroys that person's capacity to appreciate the unlawfulness or nature of his or her conduct, or capacity to control his or her conduct to conform to the requirements of law, unless the person has become voluntarily intoxicated under such circumstances that the person knew, or disregarded the risk, that, as a result of the intoxication, he or she was likely to engage in conduct constituting a crime within the jurisdiction of the Court;

(c) The person acts reasonably to defend himself or herself or another person or, in the case of war crimes, property which is essential for the survival of the person or another person or property which is essential for accomplishing a military mission, against an imminent and unlawful use of force in a manner proportionate to the degree of danger to the person or the other person or property protected. The fact that the person was involved in a defensive operation conducted by forces shall not

A considerable number of cautions must be exercised in the case of a child's consent. In fact the age of consent is a legal term which specifies the legal age at which one can consent to having sex. The discussion and its resolution is however very problematic concerning consent which is expressed by children. In the legal system of the European Union, the legal age of consent has been expressed as "the legal age for sexual activities." This means that engaging in sex trafficking in children not only constitutes an international crime but also violates the laws governing the age of consent. The purpose of the law is to protect children from criminal activities by those who would take advantage of their age. Thus, any consent expressed by children is subject to serious inquiry and does not in any circumstance release the traffickers from their criminal responsibility by resorting to appeal to the child's consent. It is to be emphasised that the age of marriage, which in some countries is lower than the age of consent, should not affect the concept of the criminal responsibility of traffickers.

Mens Rea

The principle of *mens rea* constitutes one of the most essential principles in the prosecution and punishment of those who have violated criminal law. The principle of *mens rea* refers to the guilty mind of the accused. The principle is also used in conjunction with the very well-known terms "mental element" or *actus reus* or "physical element". All these refer to the intention to commit a crime. This means that a court cannot find a person guilty unless it has not been proved beyond reasonable doubt that

---

in itself constitute a ground for excluding criminal responsibility under this subparagraph;
(d) The conduct which is alleged to constitute a crime within the jurisdiction of the Court has been caused by duress resulting from a threat of imminent death or of continuing or imminent serious bodily harm against that person or another person, and the person acts necessarily and reasonably to avoid this threat, provided that the person does not intend to cause a greater harm than the one sought to be avoided. Such a threat may either be: (i) Made by other persons; or (ii) Constituted by other circumstances beyond that person's control.
2. The Court shall determine the applicability of the grounds for excluding criminal responsibility provided for in this Statute to the case before it.
3. At trial, the Court may consider a ground for excluding criminal responsibility other than those referred to in paragraph 1 where such a ground is derived from applicable law as set forth in article 21. The procedures relating to the consideration of such a ground shall be provided for in the Rules of Procedure and Evidence." This may be compared with Chapter 24 of the Swedish penal Code which includes general reasons for freedom from criminal responsibility.

the person had the intention to commit the crime. Of course, this make the position of the court very difficult and the court has to examine all relevant evidence for the proof of the intention of the accused person. The problem gets more difficult, in the case of sex trafficking, when certain persons who have engaged in the crime do not admit that they had the intention to engage in trafficking. Carriers of victims from one territory to another or from one part of the world to another may raise such arguments and deny their intention or guilt. The position is more difficult when the victims come from different states and the offences are not committed within one jurisdiction. It is due to its transnational character that the principle of *mens rea* may open the possibility of escaping from criminal responsibility before a national or international criminal court.

Although, the principle of *mens rea* creates certain problems for the machinery of criminal justice and accused persons may successfully deceive the court because of the requirements of the principle, it is to be held that the principle is a guarantee for the application of appropriate justice. It ensures the respect of other principles such as *nullum crimen sine lege, nulla poena sine lege* and *de lege lata.* This is because the term "*mens rea*" refers to the criminal intention of the accused and this also guarantees that no one is condemned when she/he did not have a guilty mind. This is what is called *actus non facitreum nisi mens sit rea.*

The principle of *mens rea* guarantees also the application of the principles of human rights law. The reason is that human rights principles seriously protect the rights of the accused. The Optional Protocol to the Convention on the Rights of the Child on the Sale of Children, Child Prostitution and Child Pornography also states this fact.[18] According to it "Nothing in the present article shall be construed to be prejudicial to or inconsistent with the rights of the accused to a fair and impartial trial."[19] The rights of the accused can also be found under the civil and political rights which protect a person accused of committing a crime. These rights are applicable to the relevant person from the time of her/his arrest and the bringing of charges against her/him. It also protects the person even if she/he is acquitted or convicted. The whole theory is based on the maxim of innocent until proven guilty. Article 10 of the International Covenant on Civil and Political Rights states that:

[18] The Protocol was adopted and opened for signature, ratification and accession by General Assembly resolution A/RES/54/263 of 25 May 2000. It entered into force on 18 January 2002.
[19] Article 8.

1. All persons deprived of their liberty shall be treated with humanity and with respect for the inherent dignity of the human person.
2. (a) Accused persons shall, save in exceptional circumstances, be segregated from convicted persons and shall be subject to separate treatment appropriate to their status as un-convicted persons;
   (b) Accused juvenile persons shall be separated from adults and brought as speedily as possible for adjudication.
3. The penitentiary system shall comprise treatment of prisoners the essential aim of which shall be their reformation and social rehabilitation. Juvenile offenders shall be segregated from adults and be accorded treatment appropriate to their age and legal status.

However, the problem gets more serious when it comes to the question of criminal negligence, which means that a court without any need to prove the intention of the accused person stresses the principle of *mens rea* but with due regard to the consideration of wilful blindness. For instance, a person who has engaged in the transportation of victims of sex trafficking claims that she/he did not know about the illegal nature of trafficking and had no intention to commit the offence. But the court may insist that she/he was wilfully blind or was wilfully careless. This means that one has neglected to prevent criminal conduct. Here the question gets more complicated because the court has to measure the degree of culpability of the accused person and their indirect intention to engage in the commission of criminal conduct. The situation is however met by the provisions of the Statute of the ICC but in language which may be interpreted differently according to the given circumstances. The Statute concerning the "Mental element" reads that:

1. Unless otherwise provided, a person shall be criminally responsible and liable for punishment for a crime within the jurisdiction of the Court only if the material elements are committed with intent and knowledge.
2. For the purposes of this article, a person has intent where:
   (a) In relation to conduct, that person means to engage in the conduct;
   (b) In relation to a consequence, that person means to cause that consequence or is aware that it will occur in the ordinary course of events.
3. For the purposes of this article, "knowledge" means awareness that a circumstance exists or a consequence will occur in the ordinary course of events. "Know" and "knowingly" shall be construed accordingly. [20]

[20] Article 30.

The ICC Statute uses the principle of *mens rea* or mental element in connection with intent and knowledge but whether the accused was wilfully blind or careless is still subject to debate and may vary depending on the circumstances of each case.[21] The terms "wilful ignorance" or "ignorance of law" are also employed to express the term "wilfully blind" which implies the position of a person who tries to convince the authorities that he/she has not been told of criminal conduct and therefore they lack the requisite intent to violate the law. However, these arguments are not strong concerning child trafficking for the purpose of the prosecution of pornography. This is because one of the elements of criminal law expresses that the accused or "defendant should have known" about the criminal conduct and therefore the defendant cannot flee prosecution and punishment by expressing his/her non- awareness. Even were the arguments of the defendant to be accepted, the position creates the concept of criminal recklessness which also gives rise to the notion of criminal responsibility and does not therefore constitute a valid defence. In particular, courts should not let the principle of wilful blindness reduce the value of the general element that the "defendant should have known" in the case of the sexual trafficking of children and child pornography. The sexual exploitation of children in peace or wartime is a crime of such severity that it should not be neglected by any court.

Ne Bis in Idem

The principle of *ne bis in idem* constitutes one of the most imperative basic principles of criminal law. The function of the principle is to prevent a person who has already been punished from being punished again for the same action. The principle of *ne bis in idem* may therefore guarantee the position of a person who has been already punished for the same act under the jurisdiction of one state and who has been arrested under the jurisdiction of another state for the same offence. The intention of the principle is prevention of double punishment. This means that in the application of the provisions of the conventions relating to trafficking in

---

[21] According to the Swedish Penal Code, a person may only be found guilty if she or he had committed the crime with intent or with carelessness for certain stated crimes. Serious mental disorder does not release a person from criminal responsibility. Such a person may though not be condemned to imprisonment. If the court finds that any other punishment may not be applicable she/he will be free of punishment.[21] Concerning the crime of trafficking in human beings the Swedish Penal Code demands a guilty mind for criminal responsibility. BrB Chapter 4 Section 2.

children for sexual exploitation, one has to be very cautious concerning the prosecution and punishment of offenders in order not to find a person guilty for the same offence that has been prosecuted and punished in earlier court proceedings.

The problem which may arise here is that the jurisdiction of one state may not accept the judgment of another state and may be of the opinion that the offender has not sufficiently been punished for her/his criminal conducts. The problem is more controversial when there is no treaty of extradition between the contracting parties. Although one cannot deny that the relevant instruments relating to the prevention and elimination of sex trafficking call upon states to accept their provisions specifying the given crimes as extraditable between themselves, this does not in any way preclude the possibility of imposing punishment twice for the same offence. This is because, firstly, a treaty of extradition may not exist between the disputing parties. Secondly, the parties may not give any effect to the requirement of the relevant instruments concerning the extradition of criminals. Thirdly, the interested states may wish to try the accused under their own jurisdiction because of the victims being their own nationals. Fourthly, many other questions may arise which may make the position of already convicted persons more complicated.

This position has also been taken into consideration within the provisions of the Statute of the ICC which is the most modern method of juridical approach to the problem. Article 20 of the ICC which is entitled *ne bis in idem* points out that:

1. Except as provided in this Statute, no person shall be tried before the Court with respect to conduct which formed the basis of crimes for which the person has been convicted or acquitted by the Court.
2. No person shall be tried by another court for a crime referred to in article 5 for which that person has already been convicted or acquitted by the Court.
3. No person who has been tried by another court for conduct also proscribed under article 6, 7 or 8 shall be tried by the Court with respect to the same conduct unless the proceedings in the other court:
   (a) Were for the purpose of shielding the person concerned from criminal responsibility for crimes within the jurisdiction of the Court; or
   (b) Otherwise were not conducted independently or impartially in accordance with the norms of due process recognized by international law and were conducted in a manner which, in the circumstances, was inconsistent with an intent to bring the person concerned to justice.

Although the above article strongly supports the principle of *ne bis in idem* for the prevention of double punishment of an already convicted person, it opens a deep gap within the provisions in section 3. This is because it leaves the situation to the will of the states which are disputing the position of the convicted person. A state may easily claim that the jurisdiction of another state has not been impartial in the application of its rules or has acted on some vested interests. This means that there will always be the question of which state has the right to jurisdiction, in particular, when criminal proceedings on jurisdiction are already taking place in two different states for the same crime.

The seriousness of the position and the effect of the principle of *ne bis in idem* in criminal proceedings has also been one of the questions raised in the European Commission. According to the Green Paper of the European Commission, a logical "response to the problem of (positive) conflicts of jurisdiction would be to create a mechanism for allocating cases to an appropriate jurisdiction. Where prosecutions are concentrated in a single jurisdiction, an issue of *ne bis in idem* would no longer arise." It further states that "such a mechanism would complement the principle of mutual recognition, which provides that a judicial decision taken in one Member State is recognised and - where necessary – enforced by other Member States."[22] Accordingly, a common action based on Article 31 (1) (d) of the Treaty on European Union should be taken in order to include prevention of conflicts of jurisdiction between Member States. In certain situation, if deemed necessary by the members, the provisions of section C of Article 31 (1) could provide a complementary basis to guarantee compatibility in rules enforceable in the Member States as may be required to progress judicial cooperation. The following principles are suggested in order to reduce conflicts of jurisdiction between criminal proceedings. These are principles such as the obligation to exchange the relevant information between the parties; when the case is prosecuted in another member state, other member states should refrain from initiating a prosecution; identification and information of "interested parties"; consultation /discussion and dispute settlement/mediation.[23]

---

[22] www.network-presidents.eu/spip.php?article50 - 7k.

[23] According to one commentator, "The principle of legal certainty in a European judicial space needs to be bolstered by clear guidelines as to time limits on Member States' decisions as to whether or not to take proceedings in a given case. Such time limits could apply from the time when a Member State takes action and considers proceedings rather than from the time of the alleged commission of the offence as the notion of such time barring is not common to Member States' legal cultures and would be unacceptable in some Member States. There must, however,

The question of *ne bis in idem* has also been raised in the application of the Schengen agreement. It has resulted in several cases, some of which have been tried by the Court of the European Union.[24]

Article 4 of Protocol 7 of the European Convention has also dealt with the principle of *ne bis in idem.* It has to be read in conjunction with Article 6 of the Convention. According to Section 2 of Article 4,*ne bis in idem* may not prevent a new trial of the same case if new evidence or new circumstances exist or a serious mistake has been committed in the earlier procedure of the court. These exceptions may only be considered if they have had an effect on the outcome of the trial. The question of *ne bis in idem* has been tried by the European Court of Human Rights. Of six cases the court found one to be an insult to Article 4 of the European convention.[25] The significant merit of the principle has therefore been entered into the legislation of most European states.

In Swedish law the principle of *ne bis in idem* is to be found in the Code of Procedure. The fundamental provision says that a judgement has legal force when the time for appeal has expired and hereby the question has been concluded of which legal action has been taken. A question that has been concluded may not be tried again.[26] Concerning criminal cases it states further that when the time for appeal has ended, the question of the responsibility of the accused for the conduct which has been tried through the judgement could not be tried again.[27]

The question of *ne bis in idem* and extradition for proceedings in criminal matters is dealt with within the Swedish legal system in several laws. Of fundamental importance is the provision in the Penal Code that an accused may not be tried again if he has been already tried in a judgement that is being enforced and this has occurred where the criminal conducts took place or in a state which has ratified one of eight conventions concerning transferring on proceedings in criminal matters.[28] At the

---

be a definable end to the threat of proceedings in one or other Member States of the European Union. It is intolerable for a person to under a constant and real threat of continued proceedings indefinitely." www.eurowarrant.net/documents/cms_eaw_12_ 1_nebisinidemjustice.pdf.

[24]C-187/01 and C-385/01 Gözütok and Brügge; C 469/03 Miraglia, C-436/04; C-467/04 Gasparini; C-150/05 Van Straaten; C-288/05 Kretzinger; C-367/05 Kraaijenbrink.

[25] An insult was considered exist in Gradinger (1995) but not in Oliveira (1998), Ponsetti and Chesnel (1999), Göktan (2002), Zigarella (2002) and Nikitin (2004).

[26] RB Chapter 17 Section 11.

[27] RB Chapter 30 Section 9.

[28]BrB Chapter 2 Section 5a; The European Convention on the International Validity of Criminal Judgements, 12 May 1970; European Convention on the

international level and in accordance with the European Convention on the Transfer of Proceedings in Criminal Matters from 1976 which entered into force in 1978,[29]the Swedish legal system includes legislation on international cooperation concerning criminal proceedings. It is applicable to those who have ratified the above convention.[30] The question of extradition due to criminal conduct is further dealt with in particular by three laws of which one is limited to the Nordic countries and one to the European Union. Granting extradition has several aims, among which one can refer to humanitarian reasons. A person with Swedish citizenship may under certain circumstances be extradited to another Nordic country. A person may also be extradited to another state of the European Union if an order of arrest of that person has been issued with the purpose of bringing the person to trial.[31]

The disputes over the principle of *ne bis in idem* are indeed very serious and problematic. On the one hand, even if one allows that the European states within the European Union will solve the problem entirely and will not face the conflict of jurisdictions between various criminal proceedings, the seriousness of the question is still powerful because of serious development in the field of international criminal law and recognition of various crimes at an international level. On the other hand, the other states of the world are naturally not bound by the European measures. The question of the sexual exploitation of children of various nations and the need to protect the accused or convicted person from double punishment and jurisdiction will always face problems of justice, practice and morality.

The principle of *ne bis in idem* has also evolved in the jurisprudence of the courts of other European states, such as the courts in Luxemburg and Strasbourg. In addition, the principle of *ne bis in idem* has been effective

---

Transfer of Proceedings in Criminal Matters, 15 May, 1972; The Convention on the protection of the financial interests of the European Communities, 26 July, 1995; The First Protocol of 27 September 1996 to the Convention on the protection of the European Communities' financial interests; Convention of the 19 of June, 1990 implementing the Schengen Agreement of 14 June 1985; The Convention of 25 May 1987 between the EC Member States on double jeopardy; The Second Protocol of 19 June 1997 to the Convention on the protection of the European Communities' financial interests.

[29]CETS No.: 073.

[30]Lag (1976:19) om internationellt samarbete rörande lagföring för brott. See also Förordning (1978:108) om internationellt samarbete rörande lagföring för brott.

[31]Lag (1957:668) om utlämning för brott; Lag (1959:254) om utlämning för brott till Danmark, Finland, Island och Norge; Lag (2003:1156) om överlämnande från Sverige enligt en europeisk arresteringsorder. See also the Council Framework Decision of 13 June 2002 on the European arrest warrant and the surrender procedures between Member States 2002/584/RIF.

in cases brought before the Court of Justice of the European Union. The cases concerned matters from civil service disciplinary actions to competition proceedings. The principle has been interpreted differently and with different criteria. The principle is today considered as an important element in the protection of human rights in Europe.[32]

Transnational Organized Crime

Trafficking in children for sexual exploitation is widely recognised as an integral part of transnational organized crime. It is also a crime against humanity. The crime is stated to be not only against the personal integrity of a person but also the national security policy of the state and it is therefore very harmful to the interests and policies of different states. The problem of transnational organized crime was highlighted in the World Inter-Ministerial Conference on Transnational Organized Crime in Naples in 1994. However, it must not be put aside that all crimes coming under the title of transnational organized crimes do not necessarily have the pure nature of crime, as it is usually identified under national criminal law. They may be committed for political reasons or to force authorities to carry out certain acts, such as in the case of terrorist activities. Other organized crimes are *inter alia* money laundering; illicit trafficking or drug trafficking; human smuggling or trafficking; trading in weapons; trade in body organs; illegal immigration; trade in unlawful nuclear materials; pornography and prostitution; sale and purchasing of stolen property or art; piracy; hijacking or kidnapping of ordinary individuals or diplomatic staff.

The fight against transnational organized crime has been taken up more seriously by European Union institutions and other regional or international bodies. The question of transnational organized crime has also been taken into serious consideration by other international bodies such as NATO. In 1999, the New Strategic Concept of the North Atlantic Treaty Organization emphasised that the Alliance's security interests can be affected by organized crime. Nonetheless, apart from the arguments developed because of the provisions of Alliance interests concerning different questions of transnational organized crimes, it is evident that the organized sexual exploitation of children has led to the effective increase of its dangerous consequences for the future of the victims.

---

[32] J. Vervaele, "The Transnational *ne bis in idem* Principle in the EU: Mutual Recognition and Equivalent Protection of Human Rights", 1 *Utrecht Law Review* (2005), p.100.

Needless to say that organized crime in general and the sexual exploitation of children in particular constitute an increasing threat to national security and the international stability of human rights law. This exploitation can undermine processes for the proper establishment of the rights of the child as it is provided in the Convention on the Rights of the Child and is therefore harmful for the entire population of the world including the peaceful relations between states. In fact, the sexual exploitation of children has systematically conflicted with the state's interests. It has serious relevance to the classical concept of state sovereignty. This means that it violates the international legal personality of states because of its multifaceted character. In other words, since transnational organized crime involves the jurisdictional sovereignty of several states or is carried out within the territorial jurisdiction of different states, it naturally violates their independent international legal personalities and it is here that the states in question are responsible for taking serious measures against the crime. It is therefore according to this responsibility that states of the world have signed and ratified the International Convention on Transnational Organized Crime 2001.

The Convention on Transnational Organized Crime is one of the great achievements under the auspices of the United Nations Organization. The Convention aims to criminalize certain acts that are harmful to the interests of states and threaten international security, peace and justice. It is on this account that the contracting parties to the convention have accepted responsibility for cooperating with one another for the eradication of various transnational crimes which are seriously dangerous for their national security. Article 1 of the Convention clearly states that the "purpose of this Convention is to promote cooperation to prevent and combat transnational organized crime more effectively." Article 2 of the Convention defines and clarifies certain very important terms that have a significant function for the identification or prosecution of transnational organized crime. Selected terms which are relevant to this study are defined as follows:

(a) "Organized criminal group" shall mean a structured group of three or more persons, existing for a period of time and acting in concert with the aim of committing one or more serious crimes or offences established in accordance with this Convention, in order to obtain, directly or indirectly, a financial or other material benefit;
(b) "Serious crime" shall mean conduct constituting an offence punishable by a maximum deprivation of liberty of at least four years or a more serious penalty;

(c) "Structured group" shall mean a group that is not randomly formed for the immediate commission of an offence and that does not need to have formally defined roles for its members, continuity of its membership or a developed structure;
(d) "Property" shall mean assets of every kind, whether corporeal or incorporeal, movable or immovable, tangible or intangible, and legal documents or instruments evidencing title to, or interest in, such assets;
(e) "Proceeds of crime" shall mean any property derived from or obtained, directly or indirectly, through the commission of an offence;
(f) "Freezing" or "seizure" shall mean temporarily prohibiting the transfer, conversion, disposition or movement of property or temporarily assuming custody or control of property on the basis of an order issued by a court or other competent authority;
(g) "Confiscation", which includes forfeiture where applicable, shall mean the permanent deprivation of property by order of a court or other competent authority;
(h) "Predicate offence" shall mean any offence as a result of which proceeds have been generated that may become the subject of an offence as defined in article 6 of this Convention;
(i) "Controlled delivery" shall mean the technique of allowing illicit or suspect consignments to pass out of, through or into the territory of one or more States, with the knowledge and under the supervision of their competent authorities, with a view to the investigation of an offence and the identification of persons involved in the commission of the offence.

Another important article of the Convention is Article 3. It deals with the scope of applicability of its provisions. Here, the purpose of the legislators has been to ensure that the perpetrators of transnational organized crimes do not escape from prosecution for their criminal conduct by resorting to the inapplicability of the Convention to certain acts because of geographical or other reasons. The article describes therefore the scope of its applicability with the following words:

1. This Convention shall apply, except as otherwise stated herein, to the prevention, investigation and prosecution of:
   (a) The offences established in accordance with articles 5, 6, 8 and 23 of this Convention; and
   (b) Serious crime as defined in article 2 of this Convention; where the offence is transnational in nature and involves an organized criminal group.
2. For the purpose of paragraph 1 of this article, an offence is transnational in nature if:
   (a) It is committed in more than one State;

(b) It is committed in one State but a substantial part of its preparation, planning, direction or control takes place in another State;
(c) It is committed in one State but involves an organized criminal group that engages in criminal activities in more than one State; or
(d) It is committed in one State but has substantial effects in another State.

The Convention in Articles 5, 6, 8 and 23 lists and describes which acts should be considered as constituting transnational organized crime. Of particular interest is article 23 dealing with the criminalization of the obstruction of justice.[33] The article goes further and states that:

> Each State Party shall adopt such legislative and other measures as may be necessary to establish as criminal offences, when committed intentionally:
> (a) The use of physical force, threats or intimidation or the promise, offering or giving of an undue advantage to induce false testimony or to interfere in the giving of testimony or the production of evidence in a proceeding in relation to the commission of offences covered by this Convention;
> (b) The use of physical force, threats or intimidation to interfere with the exercise of official duties by a justice or law enforcement official in relation to the commission of offences covered by this Convention. Nothing in this subparagraph shall prejudice the right of States Parties to have legislation that protects other categories of public officials.

The provisions of the Convention were essential in enabling the creation of the Protocol to Prevent, Suppress and Punish Trafficking in Persons, Especially Women and Children, Supplementing the United Nations Convention Against Transnational Organized Crime.[34] Although the provisions of the Convention are appreciated for the criminalization of certain acts as constituting transnational organized crimes, the convention without doubt has been directed at the political interests of certain states. The Convention, for instance, aims to prevent and criminalise many acts under the title of terrorism. It is ambiguous whether this purpose of the Convention condemns the efforts of certain nations, individuals or groups to struggle for their right of self-determination. This is because not only the United Nations Charter, but also, the whole system of international law permits states support for groups or nations struggling for self-

---

[33] Other relevant articles of the Convention governing the criminalization of certain acts are studied in other parts of this book.

[34] G.A. res. 55/25, annex II, 55 U.N. GAOR Supp. (No. 49) at 60, U.N. Doc. A/45/49 (Vol. I) (2001).

determination. In addition, the principle of self-determination is also recognized as a general principle of law and enshrined in a considerable number international treaties including customary international law. The International Covenant in Civil and Political Rights is one of the clear examples denoting for the right of self-determination.

CHAPTER THREE

THE PROHIBITION OF SEX TRAFFICKING IN CHILDREN WITHIN THE GENERAL FRAMEWORK OF INTERNATIONAL HUMAN RIGHTS LAW

Introduction

Prohibition governing sex trafficking in persons and particularly children was originally developed within the general instruments of international human rights law which still constitute today the legal foundation for the prevention of trafficking. It is for this reason that most international conventions in the field of international human rights law have, by one means or another, referred to or stated the significant provisions of certain international conventions or agreements for the development of their principles. The aim of this chapter is to investigate some of the most important provisions of the basic instruments of human rights law governing the prohibition of trafficking in children for the purpose of their sexual exploitation.[1]

The Message of the United Nations Charter

One of the most central reasons for the development of the system of international human rights law is to be found in the Charter of the United Nations Organization which was adopted in 1945.[2] The Charter states that it was created in the pursuit of justice and peace for humanity.[3] In fact, one

---

[1] For the principle of *jus cogens* and obligation *erga omnes* see the relevant chapter.

[2] The Charter of the United Nations was adopted in San Francisco, on 26 June 1945 and entered into force on 24 October 1945. The Statute of the International Court of Justice remains an important part of the Charter.

[3] Although the promotion of human rights, justice and peace has been one of the most fundamental reasons for the establishment of the United Nations, these aims

of the significant principles of the Charter is to establish full respect for the integrity of human life and to eradicate discrimination among women, men and children. The Charter clearly states in its preamble that among the most basic obligations of member states are duties "to reaffirm faith in fundamental human rights, in the dignity and worth of the human person, in the equal rights of men and women and of nations large and small, and to establish conditions under which justice and respect for the obligations arising from treaties and other sources of international law can be maintained, and to promote social progress and better standards of life in larger freedom". This means that states of the world are under a recognized international responsibility to respect their obligations under the Charter.

Obviously, with the above provisions in the preamble, the Charter means *inter alia* that states parties are under an international obligation to prevent individuals from becoming involved in activities which are harmful and degrading to human beings of both genders. This includes sex trafficking in persons and therefore trafficking in children for the purpose of prostitution and other sexual activities. Needless to say, these obligations on the states parties under the provisions of the Charter are *pacta sunt servanda* which simply means that they have to be respected and fully implemented in the state's national and international affairs.

The obligations of the members of the United Nations stated in its preamble have particularly been strengthened within the provisions of Article 1, which deals directly with the purposes of the organization. The article vividly states the purposes of the United Nations. It reads that "To achieve international cooperation in solving international problems of an economic, social, cultural, or humanitarian character, and in promoting and encouraging respect for human rights and for fundamental freedoms for all without distinction as to race, sex, language, or religion; and ... To be a centre for harmonizing the actions of nations in the attainment of these common ends..." are the legal duties of the member states of the organization.

In particular, the above provisions of the United Nations have to be read in conjunction with the provisions of Article 2 of its Statute. The article specifically states that "All Members, in order to ensure to all of them the rights and benefits resulting from membership, shall fulfil in good faith the obligations assumed by them in accordance with the present

---

have not unfortunately been fulfilled. The United Nations has failed in achieving these principles and the occurrence of a considerable number of wars and violations of the rights of women and men, as well as the killing of millions of people, prove this unfortunate fact.

Charter."[4] One of the significant provisions in the above is that all members are under an obligation to "fulfil in good faith" their given obligations under the Charter. This means that in the application and interpretation of the Charter of the United Nations, states should be fair and just. Consequently, governments are, in accordance with the United Nations Charter, bound neither to engage in nor encourage, in one way or another, any activities within their own or other territories which may prejudice the integrity of woman, man or child or discriminate between them or give priority to one over another. This means that the prevention of sex trafficking or sexual exploitation of children is one of the important and basic duties of the member states based on the fact that it is also the duty of all members to prevent and refrain from all types of activities which end in discrimination between women, men and children.

It is worth mentioning that the term "human rights" has not only been referred to within the preamble of the Charter, but also within some other articles which promote respect for and development of the principles of human rights law.[5]

It is to be added that the Charter of the United Nations is signed and ratified by 191 states of the world. This means that the Charter is one of the most recognized international treaties to which all states of the world are signatory members. In other words, with strong reservations as to certain provisions of the Charter, the provisions regarding the equality between woman, man and children and non-discrimination between them constitute undoubtedly one of the consolidated principles of the international law of *jus cogens* and have therefore peremptory character. This means that states are principally responsible for preventing any form of sex trafficking relating to children within and outside of their territory based on the positive strength of the Charter and its intention to promote the welfare of men, women, and specifically children. In other words, the basic structure of the Charter should be regarded as the foundation for the development of international human rights law and the protection of

---

[4] Article 2 (2).

[5] These are Articles 1, 55, 56, 62, 68 as well as 76 of the Charter of the United Nations. Articles 55 and 56 of the Charter have also clearly stated the important value of the principles of human rights. In particular, Article 55 reads that "universal respect for, and observance of, human rights and fundamental freedoms for all without distinction as to race, sex, language, or religion.." is the duty of all members of the organization. According to Article 62 of the Charter, the Economic and Social Council "may make recommendations for the purpose of promoting respect for, and observance of, human rights and fundamental freedoms for all." Article 62 (2).

children including the prevention and elimination of any form of sexual abuse perpetrated against them.

The Value of the Human Rights Declaration

When the United Nations was established, it was supposed to create peace, justice, equality and respect for human rights principles. These were recognized as some of the fundamental duties of all members. It was in the pursuit of these principles that the Universal Declaration of Human Rights was adopted by the organization in 1948.[6] Although the Declaration is based on the resolution of the General Assembly of the United Nations and does not therefore create binding treaties, it has a very significant value within the system of international human rights law and is considered an integral part of the international law of *jus cogens* including customary international law. This is because the provisions of the Declaration are so significant and essential that they cannot be ignored within the provisions of other international instruments. For these reasons, the position of the Declaration as a resolution of the General Assembly does not decrease its legal value.

Moreover, it should not be forgotten that certain resolutions of the General Assembly may create *soft law*. This means that such resolutions should pass certain conditions that are necessary for their recognition as resolutions having the power of law. Yet, a large number of international documents governing the protection of human rights law are based on the resolutions of the General Assembly and have significant value within the framework of international human rights law. This is because, it is practically and politically almost impossible to formulate the contents of all the relevant resolutions of the General Assembly into treaties, conventions, agreements, arrangements, protocols, pacts, statutes and covenants.

It would practically also be impossible to convince the leading powers and many other states to ratify the content of those treaties which deal with international human rights law. The examples are many. For instance, although the international legal community created several important treaties concerning the apartheid situation in South Africa, almost none of the provisions of these international treaties were effective in the prevention and elimination of the apartheid regime in South Africa. The only way to realise the purposes of the United Nations Charter, the

---

[6]For a closer examination of the articles of the declaration see also section on Universal Declaration of Human Rights, p.120.

Declaration of Human Rights, the International Convention on the Prevention and Punishment of Apartheid and many other treaties was the resolutions of the General Assembly. It was indeed through the influence of these resolutions that the General Assembly succeeded in ending the practice of apartheid, although none of the relevant resolutions had the character of international treaties.[7]

Consequently, the significant effect of the Universal Declaration of Human Rights in the prevention and abolition of practices concerning the sex trafficking of children is difficult to deny. The Declaration has achieved this important aim by some of its key principles. It has specifically stated in its preamble that "the peoples of the United Nations have in the Charter reaffirmed their faith in fundamental human rights, in the dignity and worth of the human person and in the equal rights of men and women and have determined to promote social progress and better standards of life in larger freedom." The above provisions have obviously created a strong motivation for the prevention of acts which prejudice the integrity of women and children within national or international contexts or cause the exploitative trafficking of minors from one territory into another. It refers to social progress and better standards of life for women, men and children, which clearly implies that sex trafficking in persons is not compatible with the welfare and security of the citizens of a state.

In particular, the provisions of the Declaration in its preamble should be read in conjunction with its articles. The duties of governments to guarantee the personal integrity of women and children and to protect them within social relations can be seen within the articles of the Declaration. The Declaration has also strengthened the rights of women and children and their protection from any unlawful, unjustified and illegal measures. Based on this fact, rights and freedoms formulated in the Declaration should be carried out without distinction of any kind.

Needless to say, sex trafficking goes also against the provisions of Article 16 of the Declaration regarding the rights to marry and to found a family. This is because, clearly, sex trafficking of females and children strongly denies them their right to their own will and prevents them from exercising their choice to marry. It denies their liberty and causes the violation of their integrity. More obviously, a woman or child whose body has been sexually abused may be deprived of the capability of creating a family. This means that sex trafficking openly violates the provisions of Article 16 of the Declaration regarding free choice of family foundation.

---

[7] However, it must also be added that these resolutions of the General Assembly concerning prevention of apartheid in South Africa were voted against by the United States, the United Kingdom and Israel.

In addition to this, sexual interference against a woman or child also prevents the victim from exercising any other rights such as the right to engage in social activities, political activities, employment and the practice of her own beliefs. These and a considerable number of other rights which are integrated into the provisions of the Declaration of Human Rights are consequently without any practical function for those who are the subject of trafficking in persons or sexual exploitation. This can particularly be observed in the case of vulnerable and socially excluded children who fall victim to sex trafficking.[8]

The Legacy of the Vienna Declaration

One of the greatest achievements within the history of international efforts to define and protect human rights is the Declaration and Program of Action: World Conference on Human Rights in Vienna in 1993. This document clearly approaches *inter alia* to the protection of the rights of women in the world and is therefore one of the most important instruments in the prevention of all types of sex trafficking offences committed against women and female children. The Declaration specifically cites the Preamble to the Charter of the United Nations concerning the promotion of "fundamental human rights, in the dignity and worth of the human person, and in the equal rights of men and women and of nations large and small." For this reason the Declaration is deeply concerned with the various forms of discrimination against women or children. It also deals with violence against women, an issue which is not treated with equal seriousness within all states of the world.

The words of the Declaration challenge governments to fulfil their duties in the eradication of the exploitation of women and children. It significantly points to the fact that *a)* there is not any difference between human rights for men and women; *b)* the integrity of women has to be totally respected; *c)* principles of human rights which are applied to a female child should not be less substantial than those applied to a male child, *d)* women have equal rights to participate in social interactions; *e)* discrimination should not be permitted against women; *f)* national, regional and international law should respect the full rights of women within human rights law; *g)* the exploitation of women and children should be criminalized by all states; *h)* trafficking must be internationally condemned; *i)* cultural prejudice of all types which are directed against

[8] See also section on Universal Declaration of Human Rights, p.120.

women should be prevented; *j)* sexual harassment should not be allowed; *k)* the United Nations fully supports the equal rights of women; *l)* governments have responsibility for the protection of various rights of women including the prevention and prohibition of sex trafficking of women and female children; *m)* national institutions and intergovernmental institutions are also responsible for the prevention of various types of trafficking against women or children; *n)* non-governmental entities should also fight against the sex trafficking of females as required by the Declaration *o)* they should also struggle for the protection of children's rights against all types of sexual abuses or trafficking, including pornography and posing for naked photos.[9] The Declaration of the Conference has particularly defended the specific rights of children including those who are the victims of sexual exploitation with the following words:

> 21. The World Conference on Human Rights, welcoming the early ratification of the Convention on the Rights of the Child by a large number of States and noting the recognition of the human rights of children in the World Declaration on the Survival, Protection and Development of Children and Plan of Action adopted by the World Summit for Children, urges universal ratification of the Convention by 1995 and its effective implementation by States parties through the adoption of all the necessary legislative, administrative and other measures and the allocation to the maximum extent of the available resources. In all actions concerning children, non-discrimination and the best interest of the child should be primary considerations and the views of the child given due weight.

---

[9] The Declaration has specifically stated that: "18. The human rights of women and of the girl-child are an inalienable, integral and indivisible part of universal human rights. The full and equal participation of women in political, civil, economic, social and cultural life, at the national, regional and international levels, and the eradication of all forms of discrimination on grounds of sex are priority objectives of the international community. Gender-based violence and all forms of sexual harassment and exploitation, including those resulting from cultural prejudice and international trafficking, are incompatible with the dignity and worth of the human person, and must be eliminated. This can be achieved by legal measures and through national action and international cooperation in such fields as economic and social development, education, safe maternity and health care, and social support. The human rights of women should form an integral part of the United Nations human rights activities, including the promotion of all human rights instruments relating to women. The World Conference on Human Rights urges Governments, institutions, intergovernmental and non-governmental organizations to intensify their efforts for the protection and promotion of human rights of women and the girl-child."

> National and international mechanisms and programmes should be strengthened for the defence and protection of children, in particular, the girl-child, abandoned children, street children, economically and sexually exploited children, including through child pornography, child prostitution or sale of organs, children victims of diseases including acquired immunodeficiency syndrome, refugee and displaced children, children in detention, children in armed conflict, as well as children victims of famine and drought and other emergencies. International cooperation and solidarity should be promoted to support the implementation of the Convention and the rights of the child should be a priority in the United Nations system-wide action on human rights.

The declaration also supports other rights of women within its provisions.[10] This not only includes rights in peace but also in wartime and especially when women are victims of unlawful violations by governments.[11] The Declaration of the Conference especially condemns the elimination of the rights of females and their abuse as a tool of war. It openly "expresses its dismay at massive violations of human rights especially in the form of genocide, 'ethnic cleansing' and systematic rape of women in war situations, creating mass exodus of refugees and displaced persons. While strongly condemning such abhorrent practices it reiterates the call that perpetrators of such crimes be punished and such practices immediately stopped." Naturally, the term "systematic rape" of women within the provisions in the above is also applicable to sex trafficking of females or children. This is because the term "sex trafficking" does not necessarily refer to buying or selling women for the purpose of prostitution, but also refers to the abuse of the sexual organs of a woman or her entire body as an object of war. It is for this reason that the Declaration calls for the specific protection of females' rights, including those of the girl-child, against the violations of their integrity caused by sex trafficking in the form of rape.[12] The Declaration has therefore formulated two important sections (3 and 4) within its content concerning the protection of women and children.

---

[10] See paragraphs 23 and 28.

[11] Para. 29.

[12] "The World Conference on Human Rights is deeply concerned about violations of human rights during armed conflicts, affecting the civilian population, especially women, children, the elderly and the disabled. The Conference therefore calls upon States and all parties to armed conflicts strictly to observe international humanitarian law, as set forth in the Geneva Conventions of 1949 and other rules and principles of international law, as well as minimum standards for protection of human rights, as laid down in international conventions." Para.29 see also para. 30.

Section 3 of the declaration concerning *the equal status and human rights of women* reads as follows:

> In particular, the World Conference on Human Rights stresses the importance of working towards the elimination of violence against women in public and private life, the elimination of all forms of sexual harassment, exploitation and trafficking in women, the elimination of gender bias in the administration of justice and the eradication of any conflicts which may arise between the rights of women and the harmful effects of certain traditional or customary practices, cultural prejudices and religious extremism. The World Conference on Human Rights calls upon the General Assembly to adopt the draft declaration on violence against women and urges States to combat violence against women in accordance with its provisions. Violations of the human rights of women in situations of armed conflict are violations of the fundamental principles of international human rights and humanitarian law. All violations of this kind, including in particular murder, systematic rape, sexual slavery, and forced pregnancy, require a particularly effective response.

As a whole, section 3 of the declaration governing *the equal status and human rights of women* points out that national governments are the agents most responsible for the prevention and eradication of all types of sex trafficking offences against women. It puts a heavy emphasis on the principle of non-discrimination and encourages all states to fight for the inviolable rights of women. Accordingly, governments should provide the information necessary to enable women to make more effective use of their rights. It upholds the value of the mental and physical health of women during their life span. This means that the Declaration, by one means or another, condemns the unspeakable situation of women and girls who are the victims of sex trafficking and are forced to live in appalling conditions.[13]

Another significant condemnation of sex trafficking of all types may be examined within the provisions of section 4 of the Declaration governing *the rights of the child*. This section implies the value of protection of the rights of the child at a national, regional and international level. It has, like the previous section of the Declaration, recognized the duty of governments to work for the protection of children's rights by all means including prevention of sexual abuses and trafficking. It has especially called for immediate action against all types of exploitation of children using all available means. It states that "The World Conference on Human Rights urges all States, with the support of international

---

[13] Section 3, para. 41.

cooperation, to address the acute problem of children under especially difficult circumstances. Exploitation and abuse of children should be actively combated, including by addressing their root causes. Effective measures are required against female infanticide, harmful child labour, sale of children and organs, child prostitution, child pornography, as well as other forms of sexual abuse."[14] Obviously, the term "sexual abuse" refers here to all types of sexual intercourse with children. It is also axiomatic that with the phrase "to ensure the effective protection and promotion of human rights of the girl child", the Declaration insists on the prevention of sex trafficking and its damaging physical and psychological effects throughout the life of the child.[15]

It must be stated that one of the fundamental values of the 1993 Vienna Declaration and Program of Action: World Conference on Human Rights has been its particular emphasis on the prohibition of sex trafficking of women and female children. This is the general way of directing that the provisions concerning the protection of females and prevention of sexual exploitation of children constitute an integral part of customary international criminal law and have to be entered into the legislation of different states.[16] The provisions also highlight the legal responsibilities of states to prevent the sexual abuse of children.

The Origins of the Millennium Declaration

The United Nations Millennium Declaration is also one of the important instruments of international human rights law focusing *inter alia* on the protection of the rights of women and children and the eradication of sex trafficking of women and female children. In fact, the Millennium Declaration was adopted by the United Nations General Assembly in 2000.[17] One of the remarkable provisions of the Millennium Declaration deals with the divisions of the concept of responsibility. It has therefore categorized two types of responsibilities for the protection of the rights of

---

[14] Para.48.
[15] Para.49.
[16] Consult also Declaration on the Right and Responsibility of Individuals, Groups and Organs of Society to Promote and Protect Universally Recognized Human Rights and Fundamental Freedoms, 1998. See also the annex concerning the Declaration on the Right and Responsibility of Individuals, Groups and Organs of Society to Promote and Protect Universally Recognized Human Rights and Fundamental Freedoms.
[17] See Resolution 55/2 of 8 September 2000.

women. These are *a)* separate responsibilities devolving to our individual societies and *b)* a collective responsibility to maintain the principles of human dignity, equity and equality at the global level.

The purpose of these two divisions is to enlarge the scope of responsibilities between national and international boundaries and to underline that the children of the world are the cornerstone of the future international community and should, therefore, be protected properly by national and international legislation. The Millennium Declaration has further recognized the equal rights of women and men to be free from the fear of violence, oppression and injustice. It emphasises the promotion of the social and economic welfare of individuals in order to prevent and eradicate the extreme poverty which is a serious problem for a billion of the world's people. According to the Millennium Declaration the promotion of rights should also be related to the issue of gender inequality in order to eradicate this evil.

With this introduction the Millennium Declaration drives home the responsibility of the governments of the world in responding to one of the most serious problems of the world, namely, violence against women. Although it does not use the term "trafficking", it clearly identifies it as a danger for the equal integrity of women. It asks governments to fight against all kinds of violence directed against the integrity of women. The government should therefore work to "combat all forms of violence against women and to implement the Convention on the Elimination of All Forms of Discrimination against Women." Naturally the term "all forms of violence against" women, includes sex trafficking against women and female children. The aim of the Declaration is thus to underline that states should respect and fulfil their obligations concerning the equal rights of women and should not ignore violence against this sex. The message of the Millennium Declaration regarding the duty of governments to combat violence against women is clearly based on the general principle of the responsibility of states for civilians and those who are, for one reason or another, under their territorial jurisdiction.

CHAPTER FOUR

PROHIBITION OF THE SEXUAL EXPLOITATION OF CHILDREN WITHIN THE SPECIFIC FRAMEWORK OF INTERNATIONAL HUMAN RIGHTS LAW

Introduction

The system of the international legal community has a legacy of a large number of international provisions which have, by one means or another, prohibited the sexual exploitation of women and children. They have generally been directed at the illegal and unlawful nature of certain conducts constituting violations of the fundamental values of the international community of nations as a whole. These provisions may be found within different categories of international documents including conventions, declarations, resolutions, and sometimes in the form of the declaratory document of an international conference. One chief tendency of all these instruments is their policy of criminalization in order to prevent, prohibit or eliminate the given conduct. This section examines some of the provisions of the relevant instruments dealing with various forms of discrimination against women with particular focus on the sex trafficking of children.

Elimination of Discrimination against Females

How to achieve equal respect for the integrity of women has always been one of the serious questions of justice and the instruments of international human rights law. The Declaration on the Elimination of Discrimination against Women is one of these instruments aiming at the protection of the rights of women and the prevention of discrimination against them in national and international relations.[1] In fact, the Declaration was adopted by the General Assembly of the United Nations to fulfil the missing provisions of other instruments such as the Convention on the Political Rights of Women of 1952, the Convention on the Nationality of Married Women of 1957, the Convention on Consent to Marriage, Minimum Age for Marriage and Registration of Marriages of 1962, and the Recommendation on Consent to Marriage, Minimum Age for Marriage and Registration of Marriages of 1965.[2]

One of the articles of the Declaration concerns the prohibition of exploitation, trafficking and any other illegal act against women. It deals with several important principles concerning the prohibition of certain acts against women. It specifies that *a)* states should take appropriate measures for that end, *b)* they should take legislative measures within their national law, *c)* they should combat all forms of trafficking in women, and *d)* they should prohibit the exploitation of women caused by prostitution.[3]

The Declaration has, because of its Articles 6 and 10, become one of the most important instruments of human rights law concerning protection against inequality and discrimination affecting women.[4] However, these two articles have become very controversial so other subsequent international instruments do not refer to the body of the Declaration. Nevertheless, the relevant articles established certain rights between wife

---

[1] For the Declaration see General Assembly Resolution 2263(XXII) of 7 November 1967.

[2] All these were the works of the Commission on Human Rights but had not yet achieved their purposes.

[3] Article 8.

[4] Article 10 provides that: "1. All appropriate measures shall be taken to ensure to women, married or unmarried, equal rights with men in the field of economic and social life, and in particular: *(a)* The right, without discrimination on grounds of marital status or any other grounds, to receive vocational training, to work, to free choice of profession and employment, and to professional and vocational advancement; *(b)* The right to equal remuneration with men and to equality of treatment in respect of work of equal value; *(c)* The right to leave with pay, retirement privileges and provision for security in respect of unemployment, sickness, old age or other incapacity to work; *(d)* The right to receive family allowances on equal terms with men. 2. In order to prevent discrimination against women on account of marriage or maternity and to ensure their effective right to work, measures shall be taken to prevent their dismissal in the event of marriage or maternity and to provide paid maternity leave, with the guarantee of returning to former employment, and to provide the necessary social services, including child-care facilities. 3. Measures taken to protect women in certain types of work, for reasons inherent in their physical nature, shall not be regarded as discriminatory."

and husband and the right to equality of treatment in respect of work of equal value. Article 6 has, in particular, given a very high priority to the rights of children and their protection in all possible circumstances.[5]

Suppression of All Forms of Discrimination against Females

Whilst there have been a considerable number of international legal instruments which combat discrimination against women, none of these instruments have had a good enforceability policy. It was for this reason that the Convention on the Elimination of All Forms of Discrimination against Women was adopted by the General Assembly with the hope of putting an end to the policy of non-enforceability of the other instruments.[6] Thus, it aimed to emphasise effectively the rights of women against any kind of discrimination based on sex. The convention is, because of its very significant function in the establishment of equality between men and women, considered as an international bill of rights for the protection of women.

---

[5] Article 6 of the Declaration provides that "1. Without prejudice to the safeguarding of the unity and the harmony of the family, which remains the basic unit of any society, all appropriate measures, particularly legislative measures, shall be taken to ensure to women, married or unmarried, equal rights with men in the field of civil law, and in particular:
(a) The right to acquire, administer, enjoy, dispose of and inherit property, including property acquired during marriage;
(b) The right to equality in legal capacity and the exercise thereof;
(c) The same rights as men with regard to the law on the movement of persons.
2. All appropriate measures shall be taken to ensure the principle of equality of status of the husband and wife, and in particular:
(a) Women shall have the same right as men to free choice of a spouse and to enter into marriage only with their free and full consent;
(b) Women shall have equal rights with men during marriage and at its dissolution. In all cases the interest of the children shall be paramount;
(c) Parents shall have equal rights and duties in matters relating to their children. In all cases the interest of the children shall be paramount.
3. Child marriage and the betrothal of young girls before puberty shall be prohibited, and effective action, including legislation, shall be taken to specify a minimum age for marriage and to make the registration of marriages in an official registry compulsory."

[6] General Assembly Resolution 34/180 of 18 December 1979. The Convention entered into force on 3 September 1981.

The term "discrimination against women" is defined by the provisions of the Convention accordingly: it "shall mean any distinction, exclusion or restriction made on the basis of sex which has the effect or purpose of impairing or nullifying the recognition, enjoyment or exercise by women, irrespective of their marital status, on a basis of equality of men and women, of human rights and fundamental freedoms in the political, economic, social, cultural, civil or any other field."[7] It is upon this definition that the parties to the Convention have undertaken certain responsibilities to condemn all forms of discrimination within their national legislations.[8] Consequently, the Convention makes clear that the prohibition of sex trafficking is the duty of all governments and they should work for that end. This is stated in the provisions of Article 6 of the Convention. According to it, "States Parties shall take all appropriate measures, including legislation, to suppress all forms of traffic in women and exploitation of prostitution of women." As it can be seen, the article uses the term "suppress" which is a strong form of duty binding states concerning the prohibition of sex trafficking in women. The parties should not ignore the enforcement of legislation which in one way or another deals with the question of eliminating sex trafficking.

---

[7] Article 1.

[8] Article 2 of the Convention relates to this matter. It constitutes a cornerstone for the implementation of the provisions of the Convention. It has therefore special value within the documents applicable, in one way or another, to the rights of women in the international community as a whole. The article reads that states "condemn discrimination against women in all its forms, agree to pursue by all appropriate means and without delay a policy of eliminating discrimination against women and, to this end, undertake: (a) To embody the principle of the equality of men and women in their national constitutions or other appropriate legislation if not yet incorporated therein and to ensure, through law and other appropriate means, the practical realization of this principle; (b) To adopt appropriate legislative and other measures, including sanctions where appropriate, prohibiting all discrimination against women; (c) To establish legal protection of the rights of women on an equal basis with men and to ensure through competent national tribunals and other public institutions the effective protection of women against any act of discrimination; (d) To refrain from engaging in any act or practice of discrimination against women and to ensure that public authorities and institutions shall act in conformity with this obligation; (e) To take all appropriate measures to eliminate discrimination against women by any person, organization or enterprise; (f) To take all appropriate measures, including legislation, to modify or abolish existing laws, regulations, customs and practices which constitute discrimination against women; (g) To repeal all national penal provisions which constitute discrimination against women."

Despite the strong policy of the Convention for the protection of females, some of its provisions have caused serious problems for its implementation.[9] In fact, a considerable number of reservations due to the provisions of Articles 28 and 29 have reduced the legal effect of the Convention. In particular, Article 28 provides that:

> 1. The Secretary-General of the United Nations shall receive and circulate to all States the text of reservations made by States at the time of ratification or accession.
> 2. A reservation incompatible with the object and purpose of the present Convention shall not be permitted.
> 3. Reservations may be withdrawn at any time by notification to this effect addressed to the Secretary-General of the United Nations, who shall then inform all States thereof. Such notification shall take effect on the date on which it is received.

The legal effect of the provisions in the above can be examined in the content of the reservations of the states parties.[10] For instance, the reservation submitted by the Algerian government invalidates the effect and the value of the provisions of the Convention concerning the protection of children by referring to the Algerian Family Code. It also goes against the purpose of Article 9 of the Convention which provides that states parties "shall grant women equal rights with men with respect to the nationality of their children."[11]

Similarly, the reservation by the government of Bahrain has definitely invalidated the object of the Convention on the Elimination of All forms of Discrimination Against Women. This is based on the fact that the relevant government in two separate sections makes it clear that the implementation of the provisions of the Convention in Article 2 and others depend on the requirements of the regulations of Islamic law or *Shariah*.

---

[9] William A. Schabas, 'Reservations to the Convention on the Elimination of All Forms of Discrimination Against Women and the Convention on the Rights of the Child,' *3 William & Mary Journal of Women and the Law (1997),* 79-112.

[10] See Karl Zemanek, New Trends in the Enforcement of *Erga Omens* Obligations, Max Planck, UNYB 4 (2000) 1-52, www.mpil.de/shared/data/pdf/pdfmpunyb/zemanek_4.pdf.

[11] A child may receive the nationality of an Algerian mother when "the father is either unknown or stateless; the child is born in Algeria to an Algerian mother and a foreign father who was born in Algeria; moreover, a child born in Algeria to an Algerian mother and a foreign father who was not born on Algerian territory may, under article 26 of the Algerian Nationality Code, acquire the nationality of the mother providing the Ministry of Justice does not object.".

A similar view is expressed by the government of Egypt. It says that the "Arab Republic of Egypt is willing to comply with the content of this article, provided that such compliance does not run counter to the Islamic *Sharia*." Along the same lines is the reservation by the government of Brunei Darussalam. It declares that the government "expresses its reservations regarding those provisions of the said Convention that may be contrary to the Constitution of Brunei Darussalam and to the beliefs and principles of Islam, the official religion of Brunei Darussalam and, without prejudice to the generality of the said reservations, expresses its reservations regarding paragraph 2 of Article 9 and paragraph 1 of Article 29 of the Convention." Other Islamic states such as Iraq, Kuwait, Libya, Malaysia, Maldives, Mauritania, Morocco, Oman, Pakistan Saudi Arabia, Syrian Arab Republic, and Yemen have, more or less, stated similar views. There have been a considerable number of objections to the reservations made by the Islamic states. According to these objections, the relevant reservations by the Islamic countries contribute to undermining the basis of international treaty law and consequently lead to the non-application of international provisions at national, regional and international levels.

Elimination of Violence against Females

The Declaration on the Elimination of Violence against Women is a further instrument of human rights which applies to violations of the rights of women and aims to protect these rights.[12] The Declaration recognizes that the term "violence" includes physical, sexual and psychological harm and threats, as well as coercion against women in public or private. Its preamble reaffirms many of the instruments of human rights including the Universal Declaration of Human Rights, the International Covenant on Civil and Political Rights, the International Covenant on Economic, Social and Cultural Rights, the Convention on the Elimination of All Forms of Discrimination against Women and the Convention against Torture and Other Cruel, Inhuman or Degrading Treatment or Punishment.

The Declaration came into force in order to work against various illegal acts directed against women and their integrity. This can be seen within the words of the Declaration. It recognizes that "violence against women is a manifestation of historically unequal power relations between men and women, which have led to domination over and discrimination against women by men and to the prevention of the full advancement of

[12] It was adopted by the United Nations General Assembly Resolution 48/104 of 20 December 1993.

women, and that violence against women is one of the crucial social mechanisms by which women are forced into a subordinate position compared with men."

The Declaration also states that there is "a need for a clear and comprehensive definition of violence against women, a clear statement of the rights to be applied to ensure the elimination of violence against women in all its forms, a commitment by States in respect of their responsibilities, and a commitment by the international community at large to the elimination of violence against women," and that this is a basic responsibility of states. According to the Declaration, the following acts are considered serious violations of women's rights:

> Violence against women shall be understood to encompass, but not be limited to, the following:
> (a) Physical, sexual and psychological violence occurring in the family, including battering, sexual abuse of female children in the household, dowry-related violence, marital rape, female genital mutilation and other traditional practices harmful to women, non-spousal violence and violence related to exploitation;
> (b) Physical, sexual and psychological violence occurring within the general community, including rape, sexual abuse, sexual harassment and intimidation at work, in educational institutions and elsewhere, trafficking in women and forced prostitution;
> (c) Physical, sexual and psychological violence perpetrated or condoned by the State, wherever it occurs.[13]

Within the above provisions, the Declaration has taken into account several important aims which have, more or less, increased the level and degree of legislative force directed towards violence against women. These are violations such as psychological violence occurring within the general community, including rape or "physical, sexual and psychological violence perpetrated or condoned by the State, wherever it occurs". This last statement is particularly aimed at those sexual violations which occur due to the activities of state machinery. It applies certainly to the underlying political system of a state which permits the infringement of the rights of women. It has therefore opened a new door for the protection of the rights of those who are the victims of sex trafficking under the auspices of the state. Needless to say that many of the acts mentioned in the Declaration overlap with one another, clear examples of this are forced prostitution and rape.

---

[13] Article 2.

It must be asserted that although the provisions of the Declaration on the Elimination of Violence against Women like the provisions of the Convention on the Elimination of All Forms of Discrimination against Women do not specifically refer to children in their contents, the word "women" applies generally to females of all ages. This means that most of their provisions are applicable to female children. Otherwise, it would be a serious mistake to accept that the relevant instruments are solely applicable to those females who are above 18 years and do not govern females who are under this age.

Struggles for the Equality of Females

The Beijing Declaration and Platform for Action, Fourth World Conference on Women: Action for Equality, Development and Peace was the gathering of representatives of governments for the prevention of certain unlawful actions against women.[14] The significant function of the Beijing Declaration has also been stated by the resolution of the General Assembly. It encourages the implementation of the Declaration. According to it, the content of the Declaration should be promoted by "an active and visible policy of mainstreaming a gender perspective at all levels, including in the design, monitoring and evaluation of all policies, as appropriate, in order to ensure effective implementation of the Platform".[15]

The Beijing Declaration aims *inter alia* at the prevention of sex trafficking and sexual exploitation of women and children. It particularly aims at the condemnation of rape during times of war or peace. This purpose of the Declaration was in particular welcomed in the Conference due to the consideration of the use of systematic rape during the former Yugoslavian states' conflicts.[16] The Declaration condemns the sexual

---

[14] The declaration was also endorsed by the General Assembly Resolution 50/203 of 20 December 1995.

[15] Follow-Up to the Fourth World Conference on Women and Full Implementation of the Beijing Declaration and the Platform for Action, G.A. res. 50/203, U.N. Doc. A/RES/50/203, 1995).

[16] According to it "The end of the cold war has resulted in international changes and diminished competition between the super-Powers. The threat of a global armed conflict has diminished, while international relations have improved and prospects for peace among nations have increased. Although the threat of global conflict has been reduced, wars of aggression, armed conflicts, colonial or other forms of alien domination and foreign occupation, civil wars, terrorism and extremist violence continue to plague many parts of the world. Grave violations of the human rights of women occur, particularly in times of armed conflict, and

abuse of women and girls as a weapon of war.[17] By the same token, it condemns any other measures which infringe the rights of women in times of war or peace. The Declaration goes even further and condemns various forms of sexual exploitation of women and children which have increased globally because of war and the associated movements of families.[18] It also specifically focuses on the protection of children and condemns their abuse in various forms of exploitation. According to a very specific passage:

> The girl child of today is the woman of tomorrow. The skills, ideas and energy of the girl child are vital for full attainment of the goals of equality, development and peace. For the girl child to develop her full potential she needs to be nurtured in an enabling environment, where her spiritual, intellectual and material needs for survival, protection and development are met and her equal rights safeguarded. If women are to be equal partners with men, in every aspect of life and development, now is the time to recognize the human dignity and worth of the girl child and to ensure the full enjoyment of her human rights and fundamental freedoms, including the rights assured by the Convention on the Rights of the Child, universal ratification of which is strongly urged. Yet there exists world-wide evidence that discrimination and violence against girls begin at the earliest stages of life and continue unabated throughout their lives. They often have less access to nutrition, physical and mental health care and education and enjoy fewer rights, opportunities and benefits of childhood and adolescence than do boys. They are often subjected to various forms of sexual and economic exploitation, paedophilia, forced prostitution and possibly the sale of their organs and tissues, violence and harmful practices such as female infanticide and prenatal sex selection, incest, female genital mutilation and early marriage, including child marriage.[19]

Without doubt, the whole Beijing Declaration constitutes an integral part of positive international law, even though it does not have the character of an international convention. This is based on the fact that the basic principles of the Declaration may be found within most instruments in the field of international human rights law. In fact, the Declaration represents the integration of the provisions of many international agreements within one single instrument. Moreover, the Declaration does

---

include murder, torture, systematic rape, forced pregnancy and forced abortion, in particular under policies of "ethnic cleansing". (No.13 of the Declaration).

[17] Nr. 14 of the Declaration.

[18] No. 38 of the Declaration.

[19] No. 41 of the Declaration.

not develop the basic principles of human rights law, but it simply introduces them in specific and practical contemporary language.

Prevention and Punishment of Violence against Women

Another valuable instrument condemning sex trafficking or other exploitation of women is the Inter-American Convention on the Prevention, Punishment and Eradication of Violence against Women which was adopted in 2004.[20] The Convention has in general aimed at the prohibition of crimes against women, including sex trafficking. According to the provisions of the Convention, the term "violence against women" has been defined as follows: it "shall be understood as any act or conduct, based on gender, which causes death or physical, sexual or psychological harm or suffering to women, whether in the public or the private sphere." This means that the Convention covers both public and private violations of the rights of women.

Article 2 of the Convention relates to the perpetration of violence against women within the family and community. According to it, violence has several features which may include physical, sexual and psychological violence. One form of violence is when it "occurs within the family or domestic unit or within any other interpersonal relationship, whether or not the perpetrator shares or has shared the same residence with the woman, including, among others, rape, battery and sexual abuse". The other is when it "occurs in the community and is perpetrated by any person, including, among others, rape, sexual abuse, torture, trafficking in persons, forced prostitution, kidnapping and sexual harassment in the workplace, as well as in educational institutions, health facilities or any other place." The Convention has also recognized a third form of violence against women which occurs under the legal and political auspices of the state. This third form of violence "is perpetrated or condoned by the state or its agents regardless of where it occurs". Thus, according to a soft interpretation of these provisions, violence due to the acts of a state is not limited to a specific place. It may occur in private places or it may be carried out in public. According to the Convention, all women have the right to be free from violence in both public and private spheres.[21]

---

[20] The convention was adopted at the twenty fourth regular session of the General Assembly, at Belém do Pará, Brazil on 9 June 1994. It came into force on 5 March 1995. See also 33 I.L.M. 1534 (1994).

[21] Article 3.

Some important provisions of the Convention relate to the criminalization of acts. It is the duty of all the contracting parties to take the necessary legislative measures for the condemnation of violence and the prosecution and punishment of the perpetrators. Thus, as is provided in the passage below, the enforcement and respect of the provisions of the Convention depends essentially on the strength of the state's legislation. The Convention has thus focused on the obligations of the contracting parties and says that:

> The States Parties condemn all forms of violence against women and agree to pursue, by all appropriate means and without delay, policies to prevent, punish and eradicate such violence and undertake to:
> a. refrain from engaging in any act or practice of violence against women and to ensure that their authorities, officials, personnel, agents, and institutions act in conformity with this obligation;
> b. apply due diligence to prevent, investigate and impose penalties for violence against women;
> c. include in their domestic legislation penal, civil, administrative and any other type of provisions that may be needed to prevent, punish and eradicate violence against women and to adopt appropriate administrative measures where necessary;
> d. adopt legal measures to require the perpetrator to refrain from harassing, intimidating or threatening the woman or using any method that harms or endangers her life or integrity, or damages her property;
> e. take all appropriate measures, including legislative measures, to amend or repeal existing laws and regulations or to modify legal or customary practices which sustain the persistence and tolerance of violence against women;
> f. establish fair and effective legal procedures for women who have been subjected to violence which include, among others, protective measures, a timely hearing and effective access to such procedures;
> g. establish the necessary legal and administrative mechanisms to ensure that women subjected to violence have effective access to restitution, reparations or other just and effective remedies; and
> h. adopt such legislative or other measures as may be necessary to give effect to this Convention.

The policy of the Convention governing criminalization of the acts under the legislation of states is considered to be one of the progressive developments in the recognition of violence against women including forced prostitution, sexual abuse and rape. Its provisions are also considered to present an integral and essential part of international law at the level of *jus cogens*. This means that there are certain duties of states to enforce its provisions and also to exercise their criminal jurisdiction over those who violate the given international provisions.

Globalization of Commitment on HIV/AIDS

The dreadful and shocking increase of the problem of AIDS and HIV has demonstrated that the world has to put, in one way or another, an end to the problem of sex trafficking and sexual exploitation of women and girls. The reason is that this transnational and international crime has also created other serious problems such as health problems. Yet, although it is true that the trafficking is causing serious health problems and medical dependency for the carriers of HIV/AIDS, many medical companies in the world have increased their profits due to the consequences of the crime of the sex trade in children and women, sexual exploitation, pornography and sex trafficking. This means that questions surrounding legality and morality are confusingly scandalous concerning the sexual exploitation of women, and in particular minors.

The Declaration of Commitment on HIV/AIDS, which was adopted by the General Assembly of the United Nations, constitutes therefore a major landmark governing their response to the disease. The most serious provision of the Declaration is that it clearly states that the sexual abuse of girls and women, sexual exploitation and sex trafficking constitute a "Global Crisis" requiring "Global Action". This means that the aforementioned crimes are seriously infringing the values of the international community as a whole. The Declaration requires immediate cooperation between states of the world in order to effectively deal with the questions posed by the spread of HIV/AIDS and its treatment.[22]

The Declaration describes how the "global HIV/AIDS epidemic, through its devastating scale and impact, constitutes a global emergency and one of the most formidable challenges to human life and dignity, as well as to the effective enjoyment of human rights." It asks, therefore, that governments take effective and necessary measures for the prevention of sex trafficking, prostitution, sexual abuse and sexual exploitation. It reads that states should by "2005, ensure development and accelerated implementation of national strategies for women's empowerment, the promotion and protection of women's full enjoyment of all human rights and reduction of their vulnerability to HIV/AIDS through the elimination of all forms of discrimination."[23] They should also prevent "all forms of

---

[22] General Assembly Resolution S-26/2 of 27 June 2001.

[23] Declaration (no. 61).

violence against women and girls, including harmful traditional and customary practices, abuse, rape and other forms of sexual violence, battering and trafficking in women and girls."[24] The Declaration has obviously stressed the issue of sex trafficking as a key factor in the development of the HIV/AIDS crisis.[25]

The Declaration particularly deals with the health problems of those children who are the victims of sex trafficking and who have, by one means or another, been handed to the traffickers. It considers the governments responsible for giving priority to these victims and seriously attempting to prevent or eliminate different forms of sex trafficking. According to it, children orphaned and affected by HIV/AIDS need special assistance. This matter should be given special care by the states of the world. It says that by 2003, states should develop and by 2005, states should implement domestic strategies and various policies to build and make stronger governmental, family and community capacities in order to offer "a supportive environment for orphans and girls and boys infected and affected by HIV/AIDS, including by providing appropriate counselling and psychosocial support, ensuring their enrolment in school and access to shelter, good nutrition and health and social services on an equal basis with other children."[26] They should also "protect orphans and vulnerable children from all forms of abuse, violence, exploitation, discrimination, trafficking and loss of inheritance."[27]

A close examination of the provisions of the Declaration will show that it obviously implies the condemnation of various forms of sex trafficking in the world. The Declaration clearly, without any need for further improvement within conventional international law, consolidates the question of effective implementation of the instruments preventing and

---

[24] *Ibid.*

[25] At the same line in the above, the Declaration reads that "By 2003, in order to complement prevention programmes that address activities which place individuals at risk of HIV infection, such as risky and unsafe sexual behaviour and injecting drug use, have in place in all countries strategies, policies and programmes that identify and begin to address those factors that make individuals particularly vulnerable to HIV infection, including underdevelopment, economic insecurity, poverty, lack of empowerment of women, lack of education, social exclusion, illiteracy, discrimination, lack of information and/or commodities for self-protection, and all types of sexual exploitation of women, girls and boys, including for commercial reasons. Such strategies, policies and programmes should address the gender dimension of the epidemic, specify the action that will be taken to address vulnerability and set targets for achievement." (no.62).

[26] Declaration (no.65).

[27] *Ibid.*

eliminating sexual abuse of women and children. Although the policy of the Declaration has been warmly welcomed as upholding fundamental values of the international community, the states of the world have not been successful in preventing sex trafficking.

As will subsequently be demonstrated, the question is neither the matter of law nor the matter of obligation *erga omnes*, but to what extent, if any, states are seriously ready to put all their resources towards combating various forms of sex trafficking in the world. Even though medical science has been successful in providing some improvements for the victims, the underlying problem has remained intractable. Those who have unknowingly been infected by HIV/AIDS because of blood transfusions are also the victims of sex trafficking. This is just one side of the problem and the question of the elimination of sex trafficking of women and children is itself another feature of the response to HIV/AIDS.

CHAPTER FIVE

PROHIBITION OF SEX TRAFFICKING IN CHILDREN WITHIN THE REGIONAL HUMAN RIGHTS LAWS

Introduction

The prohibition governing sex trafficking has almost its own separate chapter within the regional documents governing international human rights law. These documents are accordingly divided into several categories recognizing sex trafficking as a national, transnational or international crime. The word categorization does not necessarily mean different levels of law but also different regions in which the relevant governments have formulated and adopted certain provisions that may prevent various forms of trafficking in the region. This means such as the African States, American States, Arab States and European States. All these regions have, alongside other international documents in the field of international human rights law, adopted certain treaties, conventions, declarations or other legal documents which deal exclusively with the questions of human rights law in that particular region.

The aim of this section is to deal with the provisions of certain regional documents of human rights law in order to examine the limits of their application and enforceability and whether they are already consolidated in the system of national, regional and international human rights. The manner in which the relevant provisions are expressed may of course vary according to the needs of the region and cultural understandings or interpretations of human rights norms. But it must be asserted that there are indeed no essential differences between the relevant provisions of human rights in one region and another region or the world as a whole. The question is mostly a matter of cultural and social presentation of the norms and not of fundamental recognition of the law. Human rights norms are used to describe the legal protections which individuals have in general, in order to refer to their particular rights within their own or other territories. As a whole, the relevant provisions regarding the rights of women and children provide a useful indication and approach which are the subject of our examination below.

African States

The Contribution of the African Charter

Recognition of the principle of human rights came very late to the continent of Africa. This was for several reasons *inter alia* the colonialization of the African states by different politically stronger states, the exploitation of individuals on a vast scale for the purposes of the slave trade and not least the wholesale monopolization of African natural resources as well as the economy by whites and the non-existence of well-established government. Moreover, the African states could not achieve their complete independence even after the establishment of the United Nations Organization in 1945. Africa has therefore suffered from many political decisions including apartheid which was officially practiced in South Africa up until almost the end of the twentieth century. These and many other reasons explain why the principles of human rights have been slow to develop in Africa.

The first principles of human rights were formulated in Africa in 1981. This is known as the African [Banjul] Charter on Human and Peoples' Rights and came into force on 21 October 1986. The Charter has in principle recognized the collective rights of individuals. This means that the individual's and the people's rights are connected to one another and should not be treated in isolation. After many deliberations the Charter was finally ratified by the majority of African States.[1] The Charter does not deal directly with the question of trafficking and the term is not used. But it declares the inalienable rights of individuals and protects them from unlawful discrimination. The term "sex trafficking" may therefore be covered by the prohibition of "discrimination" across various categories and more importantly by the term "exploitation". This means that the Charter does not permit the sex trafficking of women; on the contrary, it has by all means prohibited its practice. It says that "Every individual shall have the right to the respect of the dignity inherent in a human being and to the recognition of his legal status. All forms of exploitation and degradation of man particularly slavery, slave trade, torture, cruel, inhuman or degrading punishment and treatment shall be prohibited."[2]As

[1] OAU Doc. CAB/LEG/67/3 rev. 5, 21 I.L.M. 58 (1982).
[2] Article 5 of the Charter.

is obvious, the word "man" is used with its traditional meaning in the above section and is equally applicable to women, men and children.

Similarly, the African Charter regards respect for family unity as a very important principle for the prevention of discrimination and equality. It specifically sets out that "The State shall ensure the elimination of every discrimination against women and also ensure the protection of the rights of the woman and the child as stipulated in international declarations and conventions."[3] Here the Charter concludes that it relies heavily on other international human rights conventions or declarations regarding the rights of women and children. By these provisions the African Charter enlarges the definition and scope of the applicability of the law to cases of discrimination, exploitation, slavery, and trafficking in women and children. This means also that it accepts the provisions of international instruments regarding the prohibition of trafficking, including sex trafficking of children. Interestingly, the relevant provision sets out that the protection of women and children is an obligation of states and it notably does not limit the application of international conventions or declarations. The states parties to the African Charter are therefore to ensure the implementation of all relevant international conventions or declarations which have been adopted before or after the entrance of the Charter into force.

Although the Charter has adopted a considerable number of rights and duties for individuals within its content, its provisions regarding the implementation of the Charter are not strong enough and therefore need modifications. The only contribution of the African Charter to the practical implementation of its provisions is entered into its Article 26. It reads that "States parties to the present Charter shall have the duty to guarantee the independence of the Courts and shall allow the establishment and improvement of appropriate national institutions entrusted with the promotion and protection of the rights and freedoms guaranteed by the present Charter." The above provisions are rather vague and create controversy concerning the application of the provisions of the Charter. This is because the states parties are, directly and indirectly, permitted to decide about its practical implementation. This means that they may have different levels and degrees of rights and duties for their citizens due to various interpretations. Consequently, discrimination will not be limited effectively and may be continued. As has been proved in the contemporary system of international criminal justice, since the adoption of the Charter, Africans have been among the main victims of sex trafficking and abuse of the rights

[3] Article 3 (3).

of women and children. This has been carried out during times of both peace and war. Africans have even sometimes been the target of sex trafficking by United Nations peacekeepers. These and many other issues, such as the use of children for sex trafficking during wartime and as a weapon of war, for example, during the Sierra Leone conflict or in Darfur in Sudan, have created a very urgent situation for the effective implementation of human rights and humanitarian law of armed conflicts in the African continent.

It was due to the shortcomings of the African Charter that the Protocol to the African Charter on Human and Peoples' Rights on the Establishment of an African Court on Human and Peoples' Rights was adopted in 1998.[4] The Protocol aims to bring into reality the implementation of the African Charter and its wider respect in the African region.[5]According to the Protocol, an African Court on Human and People's Rights has to investigate various complains which are bought before its jurisdiction concerning violations of human rights instruments.[6] One of the strong reasons for the creation of the statute of the Court was the report of the African Commission on Human and Peoples' Rights, which proved that full implementation of the provision of human rights under the Charter was impossible if there would not be established a body which could assist the victims of human rights violations.

Therefore, the Court may refer not only to violations of the African Charter when investigating a case, but also, to any other instruments of human rights ratified by the States concerned.[7] Some of the main provisions of the Court are the followings:

> *Article 1 Establishment of the Court*
> There shall be established within the Organization of African Unity an African Court Human and Peoples` Rights hereinafter referred to as "the Court", the organization, jurisdiction and functioning of which shall be governed by the present Protocol.
> *Article 2 Relationship between the Court and the Commission*
> The Court shall, bearing in mind the provisions of this Protocol, complement the protective mandate of the African Commission on Human

[4]OAU/LEG/MIN/AFCHPR/PROT.1 rev.2 (1997).

[5] The Protocol entered into force on 1 January 2004 by the ratification of fifteen states parties.

[6] One of the basic reasons for the creation of the Court was the progressive development of democracy in several African states including Namibia, Malawi, Benin, South Africa, Tanzania, Mali, and Nigeria. Another reason was that among the African populations there could be seen strong movements to create an effective independent human rights court.

[7] Article 7.

and Peoples` Rights hereinafter referred to as "the Commission", conferred upon it by the African Charter on Human and Peoples` Rights, hereinafter referred to as "the Charter".
Article 3 Jurisdiction
The jurisdiction of the Court shall extend to all cases and disputes submitted to it concerning the interpretation and application of the Charter, this Protocol and any other relevant Human Rights instrument ratified by the States concerned. In the event of a dispute as to whether the Court has jurisdiction, the Court shall decide.

One of the most problematic statements on the Protocol of the African Charter on Human and Peoples' Rights on the Establishment of an African Court of Human and Peoples' Rights is its Article 5 which limits access to the Court. For instance, complaints concerning exploitation of various forms including sex trafficking cannot directly be submitted by individuals who are the victims of sex trafficking. Those who are entitled to access the Court are *i)* the African Commission on Human Rights, *ii)* African Intergovernmental Organizations, *iii)* the State Party against which the complaint has been submitted at the Commission, *iv)* the State Party whose citizen is a victim of a human rights violation, *v)* the State Party, which had lodged a complaint to the Commission, *vi)* when a State Party has an interest in a case, it may submit a request to the Court to be permitted to join, *vii)* the Court may entitle relevant Non Governmental organizations (NGOs) with observer status before the Commission, and individuals to institute cases directly before it, in accordance with article 34 (6) of the Protocol. In other words Article 5 (3) of the Protocol outlines that "the Court may entitle relevant NGOs with Observer Status before the Commission and individuals to institute cases directly before it". This is however subject to the prior approval of the State which is accused of human rights violations. This means an individual or a non-governmental organization with observer status may submit a complaint to the Court only if the state has already authorized such a procedure according to a declaration under Article 34(6).[8] Therefore, individuals are not directly permitted to bring petition to the Court. This is one of the serious weaknesses of the Protocol. In practice, complaints may be ignored because of the non-existence of a declaration.

---

[8] Article 34 (6) of the Protocol has emphasized the necessity of the Declaration on two occasions. According to it "At the time of the ratification of this Protocol or any time thereafter, the State shall make a declaration accepting the competence of the Court to receive cases under article 5 (3) of this Protocol. The Court shall not receive any petition under article 5 (3) involving a State Party which has not made such a declaration."

The Court was basically established in 2006, its duties are the implementation of the rights of individuals as a whole, and the prevention of sex trafficking.[9] It should, however, be stated that its establishment alone cannot be expected to ensure the implementation of the principles and norms of international human rights law due to the fact that social, economic, cultural, and political development in Africa is very slow, for instance, concerning the equal rights of man, woman and child. One of the reasons for this is that the cultural attitudes of some of the African nations have not yet adapted to the changes of modern civilization concerning the full equality of women including in private and social life.[10] For instance, women are still victims of genital mutilation in some regions of Africa, and polygamy is permitted among a large number of African peoples. These and many other reasons, such as the international interests among various organized groups in sex trafficking in Africa, economic interests, natural resources, and the desire of individuals to have political authority over one another's nations, have created a large number of problems that widen the gap between the rights of men, women, and children.

Another problem of the Statute of the Court is that it lacks a section which deals exclusively with the rights of children who have been serious victims of sex trafficking. This is because a large number of those who are involved in the sex trade have great interests in sex trafficking based on children. According to a very simple calculation, there are over 38,000 children in Africa who are engaged in the sex trade serving tourists.[11]

The Protocol to Strengthen the African Charter

The rapid increase of sex trafficking in Africa, and the non-existence of proper provisions to protect the rights of women in the region, constitute two of the essential reasons for the adoption of the Protocol to the African

---

[9] The Court adopted its final Rules of Court in 2010.

[10] Cultural reasons were also stated in other human rights instruments relating to Africa. For instance, the Protocol on the protection of the rights of women has stated that "States Parties shall commit themselves to modify the social and cultural patterns of conduct of women and men through public education, information, education and communication strategies, with a view to achieving the elimination of harmful cultural and traditional practices and all other practices which are based on the idea of the inferiority or the superiority of either of the sexes, or on stereotyped roles for women and men." Protocol to the African Charter on Human and Peoples' Rights on the Rights of Women in Africa (2000).

[11] www.pmg.org.za/minutes/20050623-human-trafficking-molo-songololo-home-affairs-department- and-saps-briefings - 41k.

Charter on Human and Peoples' Rights on the Rights of Women in Africa.[12]The Protocol is one of the effective instruments of human rights law helping in the development of the rights of women on that continent.[13] The Protocol aims to guarantee many rights that have not been properly considered in other instruments of human rights in Africa. It enumerates a number of rights for women such as civil, political, economic, social and cultural rights. All these rights also attempt to protect the dignity and security of all women whether in times of peace or war. Outstanding as it is, like any other regional document its purposes have to be adapted to the situation of the countries in this part of the world.[14]The Protocol constitutes, therefore, the first African instrument which deals directly with the rights of women and their protection from various harmful activities including organized criminality.[15]

For the purposes of decreasing sex trafficking and other discrimination as well as any other serious violations of human rights principles against women and children, the Protocol has strongly requested the national governments to take appropriate legislative, institutional and other measures against trafficking. Parties should formulate elements which increase the principle of equality between women and men. In particular article 3 of the Protocol concerning the right to dignity recognizes that:

1. Every woman shall have the right to dignity inherent in a human being and to the recognition and protection of her human and legal rights;
2. Every woman shall have the right to respect as a person and to the free development of her personality;
3. States Parties shall adopt and implement appropriate measures to prohibit any exploitation or degradation of women;

---

[12] Adopted by the 2nd Ordinary Session of the Assembly of the Union, Maputo, CAB/LEG/66.6 (Sept. 13, 2000); reprinted in 1 Afr. Hum. Rts. L.J. 40, entered into force Nov. 25, 2005.

[13] It was adopted by the 2nd Ordinary Session of the Assembly of the African Union, Maputo, Mozambique on 11 July 2003.

[14] The ratification of the Protocol was not as easy as it had initially seemed it could be. It was finally ratified by the following states and came into force on 25 November 2005. These states were Benin, Cape Verde, Comoros, Djibouti, Gambia, Libya, Lesotho, Mali, Malawi, Namibia, Nigeria, Rwanda, South Africa, Senegal and Togo.

[15] In fact, the Assembly of Heads of State and Government of the Organization of African Unity meeting in its Thirty-first Ordinary Session in Addis Ababa, Ethiopia, in June 1995, endorsed by resolution AHG/Res.240 (XXXI) the recommendation of the African Commission on Human and Peoples' Rights to elaborate a Protocol on the Rights of Women in Africa.

4. States Parties shall adopt and implement appropriate measures to ensure the protection of every woman's right to respect for her dignity and protection of women from all forms of violence, particularly sexual and verbal violence.

The Protocol asks the states parties for the establishment of mechanisms and accessible services which may deal with the victims of crimes against women. According to it, these services should focus on effective rehabilitation and compensation for all those who have been subjected to violations. Therefore, the provisions of Article 3 particularly complement the provisions of Article 4.[16] It has a long list specifying violations against women and the duties of the parties to take effective measures for the prevention and elimination of these various violations. It reads that:

1. Every woman shall be entitled to respect for her life and the integrity and security of her person. All forms of exploitation, cruel, inhuman or degrading punishment and treatment shall be prohibited.
2. States Parties shall take appropriate and effective measures to:

a) enact and enforce laws to prohibit all forms of violence against women including unwanted or forced sex whether the violence takes place in private or public;
b) adopt such other legislative, administrative, social and economic measures as may be necessary to ensure the prevention, punishment and eradication of all forms of violence against women;
c) identify the causes and consequences of violence against women and take appropriate measures to prevent and eliminate such violence;
d) actively promote peace education through curricula and social communication in order to eradicate elements in traditional and cultural beliefs, practices and stereotypes which legitimise and exacerbate the persistence and tolerance of violence against women;
e) punish the perpetrators of violence against women and implement programmes for the rehabilitation of women victims;
f) establish mechanisms and accessible services for effective information, rehabilitation and reparation for victims of violence against women;
g) prevent and condemn trafficking in women, prosecute the perpetrators of such trafficking and protect those women most at risk;
h) prohibit all medical or scientific experiments on women without their informed consent;
i) provide adequate budgetary and other resources for the implementation and monitoring of actions aimed at preventing and eradicating violence against women;
j) ensure that, in those countries where the death penalty still exists, not to carry out death sentences on pregnant or nursing women.

---

[16] The article relates to The Rights to Life, Integrity and Security of the Person.

Within the provisions of another article, the Protocol goes even further and aims at the elimination of any harmful practices. The term "harmful practices" in the Protocol means any practices which negatively affect the human rights of women and which are against the recognized international standards of human rights. This means that the Protocol condemns any action which may, by one means or another, violate the human rights of women. For the eradication of such practices, which include categories of violations against women such as exploitation and sex trafficking, the states parties are requested to take the necessary legislative measures. States parties have also a recognized duty to protect women who are in a position to be subjected to any forms of violence or any other harmful practices.[17] The Protocol therefore encourages all parties to take the necessary measures in order that women can access justice for the re-establishment of their rights. They are asked to support a local, national, regional and continental initiative which campaigns for the legal rights of women.[18] These also include other rights such as economic and social welfare rights in order to prevent various forms of exploitation.[19]

One of the most impressive developments within the Protocol concerns the protection of women in armed conflict. The peculiarity of this development is that it recognizes violence against women in the time of armed conflict as equivalent to crimes against humanity, war crimes or genocide. This development may be regarded as one of the most valuable achievements in the system of human rights in general and in the system of international criminal law in particular. One reason for this promotion of the rights of women may be the effect of recent wars within the African continent and the other reason may be the systematic exploitation of women as a means of warfare. Thus, the Protocol strongly calls upon the responsibility of the parties to take the necessary measures for the prevention of these violations in armed conflict.[20] It reads that:

---

[17] Article 5.

[18] Article 8.

[19] Article 13 of the Protocol reads that states parties should "c) ensure transparency in recruitment, promotion and dismissal of women and combat and punish sexual harassment in the workplace; d) guarantee women the freedom to choose their occupation, and protect them from exploitation by their employers violating and exploiting their fundamental rights as recognised and guaranteed by conventions, laws and regulations in force; ... g) introduce a minimum age for work and prohibit the employment of children below that age, and prohibit, combat and punish all forms of exploitation of children, especially the girl-child; [...] m) take effective legislative and administrative measures to prevent the exploitation and abuse of women in advertising and pornography."

[20] Article 11.

1. States Parties undertake to respect and ensure respect for the rules of international humanitarian law applicable in armed conflict situations which affect the population, particularly women.
2. States Parties shall, in accordance with the obligations incumbent upon them under the international humanitarian law, protect civilians including women, irrespective of the population to which they belong, in the event of armed conflict.
3. States Parties undertake to protect asylum seeking women, refugees, returnees and internally displaced persons, against all forms of violence, rape and other forms of sexual exploitation, and to ensure that such acts are considered war crimes, genocide and/or crimes against humanity and that their perpetrators are brought to justice before a competent criminal jurisdiction.
4. States Parties shall take all necessary measures to ensure that no child, especially girls under 18 years of age, take a direct part in hostilities and that no child is recruited as a soldier.

The above provisions employ, among many other terms, the term "rape and other forms of sexual exploitation." The Protocol identifies exploitation which also covers trafficking as a form of rape. In particular, it emphasises that the commission of such acts falls into the category of several international crimes, i.e., war crimes, genocide and crimes against humanity. Consequently, the Protocol without doubt emphasises that the nature of an act which violates human rights law within the regional law of Africa does not preclude its recognition as a crime under international criminal law. This means that the perpetrators of acts against women in a time of armed conflict may be prosecuted and punished for crimes against humanity, war crimes or genocide regardless of the provisions of the relevant regional law, even though, they claim that they did not mean to violate the provisions of international criminal law. The significant value of this principle is that the perpetrators of violence against the rights of women cannot receive a lighter punishment under a national system because of the status of their actions under national legislation. The perpetrators may therefore be prosecuted and punished under the provisions of the ICC based on the fact that crimes against women also fall under the three categories of crimes within its Statute. In other words, with the above provisions, systematic and intensive violations against women, such as exploitation or sex trafficking, are made subject to the full legislative power of states parties and the ICC in the identification of the crimes.

In the last sub-paragraph (4) of Article 11, the Protocol focuses on the protection of minors who are under 18 years old. This provision has been entered into the Protocol in order to prevent various forms of exploitation of young girls including prostitution and rape. This has also been based on the fact that during the Rwanda and Sierra Leone wars, girls were exploited and raped by the conflicting parties.[21]

It is also the responsibility of the contracting parties to the Protocol to guarantee economic and social welfare rights for women and young girls and prevent any form of exploitation. The parties must thus guarantee women the freedom to choose their occupation and provide serious protection for them in order for them to be released from all forms of exploitation by their employers. They should also introduce a minimum age for work and seriously prohibit the employment of children. They should therefore combat and punish all forms of exploitation conflicting in one way or another with the rights of children, especially the girl-child.[22] Although the relevant provision of the article concerns the conditions of work, it obviously refers to the prohibition of prostitution by force or other methods of exploitation. This may particularly be seen from the next provision of the Protocol which reads that states parties should "take effective legislative and administrative measures to prevent the exploitation and abuse of women in advertising and pornography."[23]

Responsibility for the control of the implementation of the Protocol is given to the African Commission on Human and Peoples' Rights which was established to monitor the compliance of states parties to the African Charter. This means that the Commission will have the power to oversee and administer the purposes and provisions of the Protocol. However, it must unfortunately be asserted that the implementation of the provisions of the Protocol has not been sufficiently robust. Various forms of violation against women in Africa denote this miserable fact, for instance, every 26-36 seconds a woman and every 15 seconds a child is raped in South Africa alone.[24]

---

[21] The protocol protects also female minors in other situations. For instance it reads that states parties must "protect women, especially the girl-child from all forms of abuse, including sexual harassment in schools and other educational institutions and provide for sanctions against the perpetrators of such practices" Article 12 (c).

[22] Article 13 (d), (g).

[23] Article 13 (m).

[24] Itano, Nicole (24 02 2003). "South Africa Begins Getting Tough on Rape". Women's News. http://womensenews.org/story/rape/030224/south-africa-begins-getting-tough-rape.

American States

The states on the American continent have been increasingly active concerning the protection of the fundamental rights of humanity. They have therefore formulated several regional documents dealing in one way or another with the matter of the protection of human beings and prevention of unlawful and unjustified actions. The first instrument of human rights in the region goes back to the American Declaration of the Rights and Duties of Man which was adopted in 1948. Although, the Declaration has no conventional power, it is considered one of the most important instruments of human rights in the world. It constitutes the first international human rights instrument which was adopted at the same year of the Declaration of Human Rights by the General Assembly of the United Nations. The American Declaration on human rights governs a number of rights in the same way as the Universal Declaration of Human Rights. It sets out inalienable rights such as the civil, cultural and political rights of citizens of the states parties. It emphasises that the "fulfilment of duty by each individual is a prerequisite to the rights of all. Rights and duties are interrelated in every social and political activity of man. While rights exalt individual liberty, duties express the dignity of that liberty."

It was after the initiation of the above Declaration that the American Convention on Human Rights was twenty one years later adopted at the Inter-American Specialized Conference on Human Rights in San José, Costa Rica, on the 22nd of November in 1969. This was one of the major achievements in the protection of the rights of woman and man and a good step towards democratization of human rights norms and principles. It was also a great achievement to set up bodies for the implementation of those rights in the form of the Inter-American Commission on Human Rights and an Inter-American Court.[25] The American Convention on Human Rights came into force on 18 July 1978. The Inter-American Court of Human Rights was established in 3 September 1979. The Court is situated in San José, Costa Rica.[26]

The Convention does not necessarily deal with the problem of sex trafficking but it establishes rights to humane treatment including physical, mental and moral integrity.[27] It states the rights of women in several

---

[25] See Article 33.

[26] States which have accepted the compulsory jurisdiction of the Inter-American Court are Argentina, Barbados, Bolivia, Brazil, Chile, Colombia, Costa Rica, Dominican Republic, Ecuador, El Salvador, Guatemala, Haiti, Honduras, Mexico, Nicaragua, Panama, Paraguay, Peru, Suriname, Uruguay and Venezuela.

[27] Article 5.

propositions and calls for the prohibition of all forms of slavery. In this way it enters into the question of trafficking in women. Concerning freedom from slavery, it reads that:

1. No one shall be subject to slavery or to involuntary servitude, which are prohibited in all their forms, as are the slave trade and traffic in women.
2. No one shall be required to perform forced or compulsory labour. This provision shall not be interpreted to mean that, in those countries in which the penalty established for certain crimes is deprivation of liberty at forced labour, the carrying out of such a sentence imposed by a competent court is prohibited. Forced labour shall not adversely affect the dignity or the physical or intellectual capacity of the prisoner.
3. For the purposes of this article, the following do not constitute forced or compulsory labour:
    a. work or service normally required of a person imprisoned in execution of a sentence or formal decision passed by the competent judicial authority. Such work or service shall be carried out under the supervision and control of public authorities, and any persons performing such work or service shall not be placed at the disposal of any private party, company, or juridical person;
    b. military service and, in countries in which conscientious objectors are recognized, national service that the law may provide for in lieu of military service;
    c. service exacted in time of danger or calamity that threatens the existence or the well-being of the community; or
    d. work or service that forms part of normal civic obligations.

The above rights are also supported by the right to personal liberty[28] and non-discrimination.[29] In particular, the Convention establishes a duty of the state to protect the rights of children in various situations. According to it "Every minor child has the right to the measures of protection required by his condition as a minor on the part of his family, society, and the state."[30] A general interpretation of the above clause means that the rights of the child have to be protected in different social relations and that sex trafficking of children is against the rights of children and should be prohibited by all means available. The provisions above should also be read in conjunction with the provisions of the Additional Protocol to the American Convention on Human Rights in the

[28] Article 7.
[29] Article 24.
[30] Article 19.

Area of Economic, Social and Cultural Rights "Protocol of San Salvador" from 1988.[31]

Protection of the Victims of Trafficking

Due to the rapid development of the trafficking in persons, and especially the trafficking of minor children, for the purpose of sexual exploitation of various forms, the United States has actively engaged in its prevention. For these fundamental reasons, the United States government adopted the Victims Trafficking and Violence Protection Act in 2000.[32] The Act constitutes one of the legal instruments against trafficking, including sex trafficking in women and children.[33] It therefore aims, *inter alia*, at the elimination of the sex trade, involuntary servitude and slavery. Essentially the Act consists of three divisions. These are: 1) the Trafficking Victims Protection Act[34] 2), the Violence against Women Act[35] and 3) Miscellaneous Provisions.[36]

The Act sets forth a definition for severe forms of trafficking in persons. Accordingly, it means "(A) sex trafficking in which a commercial sex act is induced by force, fraud, or coercion, or in which the person

---

[31] Article 16.

[32] According to US Citizenship and Immigration Services, the Act provides "individuals who have been victimized in the most severe fashion with the ability to: remain in the US (temporarily and in some cases longer) and receive federal and state assistance; protections for certain crime victims including victims of crimes against women; and law enforcement agencies with a comprehensive law that will enable them to pursue the prosecution and conviction of traffickers." See www.uscis.gov/portal/site/uscis/menuitem.5af9bb95919f35e66f614176543f6d1a/?vgnextoid.

[33] The Victims of Trafficking and Violence Protection Act of 2000 (Public Law 106-386, 114 Stat. 1464-1548).

[34] The "Trafficking Victims Protection Act of 2000," consists of certain provisions concerning (1) purposes and findings of the Act; (2) definitions; (3) annual country reports on human rights practices; (4) an interagency task force to monitor and combat trafficking; (5) the prevention of trafficking; (6) protection and assistance for victims of trafficking; (7) minimum standards for the elimination of trafficking; (8) assistance to foreign countries to meet minimum standards; (9) actions against governments failing to meet minimum standards; (10) actions against significant traffickers in persons; (11) strengthening prosecution and punishment of traffickers; and (12) authorizations of appropriations.

[35] This concerns, *inter alia*, different domestic matters regarding women and migration.

[36] This has different aims concerning terrorism's victims. It is also connected with the political aims of the United States government.

induced to perform such act has not attained 18 years of age; or (B) the recruitment, harbouring, transportation, provision, or obtaining of a person for labour or services, through the use of force, fraud, or coercion for the purpose of subjection to involuntary servitude, peonage, debt bondage, or slavery." As it is demonstrated in the above, the Act considers sex trafficking as constituted by a commercial sex act in which some form of force is employed in order to exploit the victim. According to this Act, the term "sex trafficking" may be employed concerning a person who has not yet attained 18 years of age. Thus, the Act sets forth a definite age for sex trafficking.[37] According to the Act, almost all those who are the victims of sex trafficking are in dreadful social and financial conditions and cannot exercise their right of free decision.[38]

---

[37] A critical conclusion here is that the Act accepts that a person who is under the age of 18 years old constitutes juridically speaking a child who needs protection. Sex trafficking of such persons is considered a crime and violates the provisions of the Act. But at the same time, the United States government has not yet ratified the Convention on the Rights of the Child, and, according to federal law, persons who have not attained 18 years of age may actively participate in military activities. This is thus a double policy of application of law.

[38] According to the Act "(4) Traffickers primarily target women and girls, who are disproportionately affected by poverty, the lack of access to education, chronic unemployment, discrimination, and the lack of economic opportunities in countries of origin. Traffickers lure women and girls into their networks through false promises of decent working conditions at relatively good pay as nannies, maids, dancers, factory workers, restaurant workers, sales clerks, or models. Traffickers also buy children from poor families and sell them into prostitution or into various types of forced or bonded labour. (5) Traffickers often transport victims from their home communities to unfamiliar destinations, including foreign countries away from family and friends, religious institutions, and other sources of protection and support, leaving the victims defenceless and vulnerable. (6) Victims are often forced through physical violence to engage in sex acts or perform slavery-like labour. Such force includes rape and other forms of sexual abuse, torture, starvation, imprisonment, threats, psychological abuse, and coercion. (7) Traffickers often make representations to their victims that physical harm may occur to them or others should the victim escape or attempt to escape. Such representations can have the same coercive effects on victims as direct threats to inflict such harm. (8) Trafficking in persons is increasingly perpetrated by organized, sophisticated criminal enterprises. Such trafficking is the fastest growing source of profits for organized criminal enterprises worldwide. Profits from the trafficking industry contribute to the expansion of organized crime in the United States and worldwide. Trafficking in persons is often aided by official corruption in countries of origin, transit, and destination, thereby threatening the rule of law."

Within another paragraph the Act defines the term "sex trafficking". According to it, sex trafficking "means the recruitment, harbouring, transportation, provision, or obtaining of a person for the purpose of a commercial sex act." The act therefore aims in a considerable number of paragraphs to prevent violence against women and children and protect their legal status.[39] Of particular importance is the use here of the term "commercial sex act." The scope of this term and its definition is subject to various discussions. This is because the term "commercial sex act" may apply not only to forced prostitution and exploitation, but also to those acts which are not necessarily the results of force, but which encourage a person to engage in the sex trade. In other words, the term opens the possibility of recognising other forms of sexual exploitation that do not directly come under the term trafficking but may have the same character.

Arab States

The Concept of Prohibition in Islamic Law

The rapid development of the principles of international human rights law within different regions has also been featured in the legislation of Arab states. This may particularly be examined within the provisions of the Cairo Declaration of Human Rights in Islam. The Declaration is the product of the Organization of the Islamic Conference which was adopted by Arab states in 1990. The Declaration is based on the law of *Shari'a*, which means its provisions, rules and principles are essentially the extension and interpretation of Islamic law and its sources.[40] The

[39] The Victims of Trafficking and Violence Protection Act of 2000 (Public Law 106-386, 114 Stat. 1464-1548).

[40] For the examination of Islamic law from different points of views including its sources and its provisions concerning international relations see *inter alia* Haroon Khan Sharwani, *Studies in Muslim Political Thought and Administration* (1959); Majid Khadduri (ed)., *Law in the Middle East* (1955); Majid Khadduri., *War and Peace in the Law of Islam* (1955); Majid Khadduri, 'Islam and the Modern Law of Nations,' 50 *American Journal of International Law* (1956), pp.358-72. J. Harris Proctor (ed.), *Islam and International Relations* (1965); Lippman, Matthew, Sean McConville, and Mordechai Yerushalmi., *Islamic Criminal Law and Procedure: An Introduction* (1988); Majid, Khadduri, *The Islamic Theory of International Relations and Its Contemporary Relevance* in Proctor, 24-ff; *The Islamic Law of Nations*: Shaybani's Siyar (Majid, Khadduri, translator, 1966); M. Cherif Bassiouni (ed.), *The Islamic Criminal Justice System* (1982); R. Smith R. Bosworth., *Mohammed and Mohammedanism* (1889); Osman Abd-el-Malek al-Saleh, 'The Right of the Individual to Personal Security in Islam' in Bassiouni,

Declaration is thus based on the *Qur'an* and the *Sunnah* rather than on other secular sources of law.[41]

The Declaration has taken into consideration a number of rights that are significant for the recognition of the equality of women and men and the recognition of these rights by the legal authorities of relevant states. The words of the Declaration do not, however, encompass all the rights that have been entered into other international human rights instruments in the United Nations. This means that its scope of application compared with some other international instruments is rather limited.[42]

The Declaration has subjected all principles of human rights to the Islamic Sharia. For instance, it reads that "All the rights and freedoms stipulated in this Declaration are subject to the Islamic Sharia."[43] The Declaration also makes it clear that no concept of crime or punishment may be implemented except as provided for in the Sharia.[44] More clearly, the Declaration limits the right to freedom of religion.

The Declaration has recognized a considerable number of rights for the protection of women and children. It stresses that all types of discrimination are prohibited and there should not be any difference between women and men. For instance, like other documents of international human rights, it prohibits any discrimination which may arise on grounds of race, colour, language, belief, sex, religion, political affiliation or social status. According

---

pp.55-90; Ahmad, Muhammed Khalafalla, 'Islamic Law, Civilization and Human Rights,' 12 *Egyptian Review of International Law* (1956); Muhammad Salim, Al-'Awwa, 'The Basis of Islamic Penal Legislation' in Bassiouni, pp.127-47. Ibrahim Shihata, 'Islamic Law and the World Community,' I, No.4 *Harvard International Club Journal* (1962); Farhad Malekian., 'Islamic Criminal Justice Systems' in the Encyclopaedia of Criminology & Criminal Justice' (Jay S. Albanese, editor, 5 voles, 2013).

[41] For the consideration of these sources see Farhad Malekian, *Principles of Islamic International Criminal Law: A Comparative Search* (2011).

[42] "Although the declaration presents those most important fundamental principles of human rights in Islam and its purpose is to bring them into the attention of the Islamic states, the basic principles of the declaration have been very limited and could have been formulated in more radical way to achieve all aspects of human rights views proclaimed under the United Nations Charter. In any event, the principles of the Cairo Declaration of Human rights in Islam or the principles of Universal Declaration of Human Rights are repeatedly violated by certain states of the world without due regard to their declaratory principles or legislative and theological approaches." Farhad Malekian, *Documents on the Principles of International Human Rights* (2007), p. 2010.

[43] Article 24.

[44] Atyicle 19.

to the Declaration, all men are equal in terms of basic human dignity and no one has superiority over another. With this the Declaration emphasises that "woman is equal to man in human dignity" which means that her integrity should not, by one way or another, be violated, and this integrity should be respected during all stages of her life.[45]

Although the Declaration does not directly refer to the prohibition and eradication of the trafficking of women and children, it has clearly stated that "Human beings are born free, and no one has the right to enslave, humiliate, oppress or exploit them, and there can be no subjugation but to God the Most-High."[46] Here the Declaration uses three similar terms which have by one means or another been connected to the prohibition of different forms of trafficking, including sex trafficking. These terms are a) enslaving a person for various purposes, b) humiliating a person in various ways including by enslaving them and c) oppressing a person by means of insult, torture, buying, selling and prostitution, and d) exploiting a person by means of enslavement, forced labour, coercion, or sex trafficking. The Declaration aims without doubt at the prohibition of any institutional or organized criminality directed against the natural rights of others. In fact, the four terms "enslave", "humiliate", "oppress" and "exploit" are synonymous with the term "sex trafficking". This is because the last term consists, in a wider aspect, of all the four above-mentioned terms.

Suppression under the Arab Charter

The Arab Charter on Human Rights is also a regional instrument in the field of human rights which has exclusively come into force between the Arab States. This Charter is one of the significant achievements within the law of human rights which was adopted by the Arab League Council in 1994.[47] It aimed to list a number of rights for individuals and to announce the equality between both genders within the Arab nations. However, it soon emerged that the Charter was not going to be signed by the members of the League. It was upon this non-ratification of the Charter that the Arab League decided to bring a new revised addition of the Charter before the Arab states. This was finally adopted and signed without any amendment

---

[45] Article 6.

[46] Article 11 (a).

[47] The members of the Arab League Council are Algeria, Bahrain, the Comoros, Djibouti, Egypt, Iraq, Jordan, Kuwait, Lebanon, Libya, Mauritania, Morocco, Oman, Palestine, Qatar, Saudi Arabia, Somalia, Sudan, Syria, Tunisia, United Arab Emirates and Yemen.

by the Summit of Heads of Member States of League Council at Tunis on the 22nd of May in 2004.

The revised instrument focuses on a considerable number of rights which were not properly tackled by the Declaration of Human Rights in Islam. Another essential difference between the Declaration and the Charter is that the former is simply a declaration and has no binding force while the latter has treaty status based on the fact that it was officially signed by the member states of the League. This position of the Charter strengthens its provisions and their enforcement will possess juridical rather than just moral enforceability. The revised addition has confirmed several documents of the United Nations, such as the Universal Declaration of Human Rights, the International Covenant on Civil and Political Rights and the International Covenant on Economic, Social and Cultural Rights, and the Cairo Declaration on Human Rights in Islam. This means that the value of the Cairo document has greatly increased and may be interpreted also in the light of the above instruments.

The Charter lists a number of rights and duties of the state to guarantee certain rights. It has especially stated that the rights of women are equal to those of men. It provides that "Men and women are equal in respect of human dignity, rights and obligations within the framework of the positive discrimination established in favour of women by the Islamic Shariah, other divine laws and by applicable laws and legal instruments."[48] Consequently, "each State party pledges to take all the requisite measures to guarantee equal opportunities and effective equality between men and women in the enjoyment of all the rights set out in this Charter."[49] The Charter has by this introduction entered into other discussions concerning the rights of women and it defends through the whole of its content the principle of non-discrimination against women in various social stages. The Charter states also the principle of the prohibition and eradication of different forms of trafficking including sex trafficking of all types. This includes trafficking in human organs, all forms of slavery, servitude under any circumstances, as well as exploitation of children.[50] It reads that

1. All forms of slavery and trafficking in human beings are prohibited and are punishable by law. No one shall be held in slavery and servitude under any circumstances.
2. Forced labour, trafficking in human beings for the purposes of prostitution or sexual exploitation, the exploitation of the prostitution

[48] Article 3 (3).
[49] *Ibid.*
[50] Article 9 of the Charter.

> of others or any other form of exploitation or the exploitation of children in armed conflict are prohibited.[51]

In its consideration of trafficking, the conclusions of the Charter are not comprehensive, but they present nevertheless some of the most important factors regarding the progressive development of human rights law condemning violations of the rights of women and children as well as discrimination against them. Although the shortcomings of the Charter concerning certain rights of women have been criticised, its significant function governing the prevention of sex trafficking cannot be ignored.[52] The Arab Charter tries to establish certain rights for individuals and prevents violations against women and children.[53]

In order to implement the provisions of the Charter, it has also created an Arab Human Rights Committee. It consists of seven members coming from the states parties. Its function is, *inter alia*, to examine reports relating to the recognition of human rights and their development under the relevant legal authorities of the states parties to the Charter. But, the serious deficiency of the Charter is that it does not create a Human Rights Court or a regional court dealing with violations of the principles of international human rights law or the Charter itself. This is because the Arab Human Rights Committee is not by itself strong enough to investigate serious violations of the universal rights of man within the Arab states. Although trafficking may be prevented to some extent within the Arab states, violations of the Charter are very frequent and prevention depends also in accordance with what criteria the term "trafficking" is

---

[51] Article 10.

[52] "Over time the fundamental defects of the Charter must be addressed through revision and the addition of optional protocols. Urgent priorities include the need for provisions that guarantee rights which have the status of peremptory norms of customary international law. For example, provisions that allow States to arbitrarily deprive persons of their lives; to execute children; deny freedom of thought, conscience and religion; permit the advocacy of national, racial or religious hatred; deny persons of marriageable age the right to marry; or deny minorities the right to enjoy their own culture, profess their own religion, or use their own language must all be eradicated. The failure to address these omissions and inconsistencies will continue to perpetuate the perception that Arab States are not truly committed to universal human rights when, in reality, the Charter provides the best opportunity in a generation to advance protection and promotion in the region." Mervat Rishmawi, *The Revised Arab Charter on Human Rights: A Step Forward?* 5 (2) Human Rights Law Review (2005), pp.361-376. hrlr.oxfordjournals.org/cgi/content/full/5/2/361.

[53] See the Charter.

applied, and, specifically of how trafficking of a sexual character is defined in the territories of relevant states parties.

European States

Protection of Human Rights and Fundamental Freedoms

The European states' struggle towards the prohibition of sex trafficking has its own historical chapters. Since the end of World War II they have been engaged in the abolition of various aspects of trafficking including slavery, forced labour, exploitation, enforced servitude, prostitution and also organized criminality. But, it is also a fact that the some of the European states are notorious for having engaged in the slave trade and other forms of trafficking of human beings.[54] That is to say, there has often been a contrast and conflict between the authorities and those who were conducting the various forms of trafficking. Of particular importance is that some of the European states have chosen double policies concerning the prohibition of trafficking. This is the policy of prevention or legislation and the policy of permission. Clear examples are the authorities of Germany and Greece who have, by one means or another, permitted in certain situations the development of sex trafficking.[55] Consequently, European legislation dealing with the questions of sex trafficking should be examined from different aspects. In general, one should not put aside that all these actions have, more or less, been based on the economic interests of individuals, organized groups or states involved in the matter of sex trafficking.

The first cornerstone for the prevention of sex trafficking may be found within the provisions of the European Convention on human rights, signed in 1950, and coming into force in 1953. The Convention was formulated under the authority of the European Council which was established in 1949. The Convention is also the first international convention regarding the principles of international human rights law which was formulated after the adoption of the Declaration of Human Rights in 1948. It was

---

[54] European countries forced Africans onto slave ships for over 300 years. For example, in Britain and other parts of the British Empire, merchants despatched 11250 voyages to Africa for slaves. According to Professor of Economic history, David Richardson, ships carried at least 3.4 million enslaved Africans to Americas. http://abolition.e2bn.org/slavery_45.html. Visited on 11-04-2013.

[55] In connection with the summer Olympic Games in 2004 and the World Cup in football in 2006. www.uri.edu/artsci/wms/hughes/germany_world_cup.doc; www.voanews.com/english/ archive/2004-06/a-2004-06-25-17-1.cfm.

extremely valuable in the development of the basic principles of human rights law, and especially when in 1998 the Convention was amended by Protocol 11, it achieved some of the most progressive developments of the principles of human rights law. Protocol 14 of 2004 is a further improvement which came into force in 2010.

Among the most important principles of the Convention is the creation of the European Court of Human Rights. According to this new modification of the Convention, the Court is empowered to examine cases which are brought directly by individuals before its jurisdiction. This means that individuals may bring complaints before the Court for alleged violations of their rights in the Convention. Among these rights are prohibitions regarding situations of slavery, servitude and compulsory labour which are incompatible with the purposes of the Convention.[56] The Convention prohibits all practices of discrimination against women and men. In particular, it reads that "The enjoyment of the rights and freedoms set forth in this Convention shall be secured without discrimination on any ground such as sex, race, colour, language, religion, political or other opinion, national or social origin, association with a national minority, property, birth or other status."[57]

Although, the Convention does not refer to the prohibition of sex trafficking, the general provisions of the Convention regarding slavery apply to this violation of human rights.[58] But whether individuals may bring cases against their states before the European Court of Human Rights for violations of the relevant provisions of the Convention, such as those applying to slavery, in connection with sex trafficking according to the provisions of the Convention is rather doubtful. This is based on the fact that although both the German and Greek governments have indirectly engaged in or supported the practices of sex slavery in recent times, the involvement of the Court in these cases has not been reported. One reason for this may be the provisions of the national legislation of Germany which officially permits prostitution and requires women involved in this

---

[56] Article 4. Four cases dealing with this article have been tried by the Court of which one was found to be a violation of article 4. That was Siliadin (2005). A violation had not occurred in the following cases; De Wilde, Ooms and Versyp (1971), Van Droogenbroeck (1982) and Van der Mussele (1983).

[57] Article 14. The European Convention for the Protection of Human Rights (ECHR).

[58] The relevant provisions should also be read in conjunction with the provisions of Article 3 of the Convention regarding the institution of torture. It provides that "No one shall be subjected to torture or to inhuman or degrading treatment or punishment."

business to pay tax. This means in reality that the value of the principle of *erga omnes* is seriously reduced, especially when one realises that the function of the principle is *inter alia* to create rights and duties for other states in order to bring claims against a state which has violated the interests of the community of states. Thus, the laws of those member states of the European Union which permit any form of prostitution or internal trafficking go without doubt against the fundamental principles of *jus cogens* norms and therefore violate transnational or international criminal law principles as a whole.

In general, it must be stated that the provisions of the original Convention and the later Convention regarding the protection of human rights have been very weak and there have been complaints by states and individuals concerning their implementation by signatory governments. Moreover, the European Court of Human Rights has, for one reason or another, been unable to examine all relevant cases. It is for these reasons that to the provisions of the Convention have been added a number of other protocols which aim to strengthen the Convention wherever it falls short, such as in its prohibition of sex trafficking. However, it must not be forgotten that other human rights instruments which are ratified by the European states have strongly encouraged the development and practice of the Court regarding the prohibition of sex trafficking. One of the most recent developments is the Charter of Fundamental Rights of the European Union which was signed in 2000. It states that "trafficking in human beings is prohibited."[59] The legal effect of the Charter on the instruments of human rights law in Europe was minimal until the coming into force of the Treaty of Lisbon on 1 December 2009. The provisions governing various forms of trafficking are, however, developed in the Council of Europe Convention on Action against Trafficking in Human Beings. The new Convention has covered from different aspects the deficiencies which were seen in the provisions of the Charter and has created workable definitions governing the crime of sex trafficking in Europe.

The Council of Europe against Trafficking in Human Beings

The growing problem of human trafficking has become the main reason for the formulation and ratification of a number of instruments in human rights governing the prohibition of various forms of trafficking. Some of the notorious criminal organizations to which this branch of jurisprudence

---

[59] Article 5 (3).

has developed in response come from Colombia, Eastern Europe, Hong Kong, Japan and Russia. These criminal organizations control the biggest markets in the world, including Europe. This among many other reasons has created strong motivations among the European States to fight against trafficking. It was therefore for many reasons that the Council of Europe drafted a convention on action against trafficking in human beings.

The Council of Europe Convention on Action Against Trafficking in Human Beings was intended to be a landmark piece of legislation broad enough to cover all aspects of the crime of trafficking. The Convention came into force on 1 February, 2008.[60] It has created a two-pillar system for the application and implementation of its basic provisions. The first pillar of the Convention is the evaluation of states' compliance with the provisions of the Convention, which will be exercised by the Group of Experts on action against trafficking in human beings. The second pillar of the Convention contains an inter-governmental political body, the Committee of the states parties, which may take into consideration different recommendations for measures to be taken by a state party to implement the conclusions of the Group of Experts on action against trafficking in human beings.

Purposes

One of the main purposes of the Council of Europe Convention on Action Against Trafficking in Human Beings is the prevention of trafficking. For this purpose, the Convention requires the states parties to take necessary measures and actions against any form of trafficking. It also asks parties to ensure, in one way or another, the necessary protections for the victims. The Convention has therefore three main purposes which may be divided into the following sub-chapeaus. These are

a) to prevent trafficking,
b) to combat trafficking,
c) to protect the human rights of the victims of trafficking,
d) to design a comprehensive framework for the protection and assistance of victims,

[60] On 3 May 2005, the Committee of Ministers adopted *the Council of Europe Conventionon Action against Trafficking in Human Beings (CETS No. 197).* The Convention was opened for signature in Warsaw on 16 May 2005, on the occasion of the 3rd Summit of Heads of State and Government of the Council of Europe and entered into force on 1 February 2008. www.coe.int/t/dghl/monitoring/trafficking/Docs/Convntn/FSAction_en.asp#TopOfPage,07042008.

e) to provide protection for witnesses,
f) to ensure effective investigation,
g) to ensure effective prosecution,
h) to guarantee gender equality, and,
i) to promote international cooperation on action against trafficking in human beings.[61]

Consequently, as demonstrated above, the Convention has a considerable number of requirements that are important for the appropriate implementation of its policy. In other words, the Convention puts a heavy weight on matters such as the protection of victims and witnesses. In addition, the Convention considers the implementation of its provisions to be impossible without effective international cooperation between member states and other states of the world. This policy of the Convention has been seen as a necessary condition for the eradication of trafficking in persons by the contracting parties. Although the chief policy of the Convention is effective cooperation between the states parties, it has not clarified the degree or scope of interpretation of the word 'cooperation'. This means that the degree and level of cooperation between states parties depends on the different contributions by states parties and the methods by which the provisions of the Convention are discussed and implemented.

Scope of Application

The Council of Europe Convention on Action against Trafficking in Human Beings has been formulated in a manner that enables it to cover all types of trafficking. This policy of the Convention has several purposes. Firstly, it does not limit the scope of the application of the Convention to a specific form of trafficking. Secondly, it prevents, directly or indirectly, states, groups or individuals from engaging in acts of trafficking by reasoning that their acts do not come under the scope of the Convention. Thirdly, the Convention creates a self-conducting system, which means that its interpretation does not rest on its scope of definition alone, but also on the intention of the accused to engage in the unlawful trafficking of human beings. Consequently, its policy is very clear. It says that "this Convention shall apply to all forms of trafficking in human beings, whether national or transnational, whether or not connected with organised crime." These provisions apply to the trafficking in human beings not only within national territories, but also to its transnational forms.

[61] Article 1 (1).

Of particular importance is the fact that the provisions of the Convention are not only applicable to organised crime, but also apply to those actions that are not planned, conducted or committed in connection with organized criminality but by individual initiative. In other words, to apply the provisions of the Convention one does not need to prove that the relevant actions violating the preventive policy of the Convention were committed collectively.

Definitions

One of the greatest difficulties in the preparation of a new international convention is the definition of its objects and subjects. The reason is that the definition must not only be hard and decisive, but also, as much as possible, flexible for the purpose of recognition of the acts for which it is formulated. In addition, a definition should not, as much as possible, conflict with other definitions of a similar character. The Council of Europe Convention on Action Against Trafficking in Human Beings has hence tried to meet certain requirements for the definition of its object, i.e., trafficking in human beings.

According to the Convention, the definition of trafficking in human beings may be applied to acts such as *i)* recruitment, *ii)* transportation, *iii)* transfer, *iv)* harbouring, and *v)* receipt of persons for the purpose of exploitation. The relevant part of the Convention states that the above conducts must be "by means of the threat or use of force or other forms of coercion, of abduction, of fraud, of deception, of the abuse of power or of a position of vulnerability or of the giving or receiving of payments or benefits to achieve the consent of a person having control over another person, for the purpose of exploitation."[62] Thus, one of the significant elements required for a conduct to be recognized as falling under the provisions of the trafficking convention is that the act of recruitment, transportation, transfer, harbouring and receipt of persons has been committed in order to exploit a person. It means also that as long as the listed conducts are for any other purpose than exploitation, they fall under other legislation and the Convention on the trafficking of human beings cannot be applied.

Moreover, the provisions of the Convention on the trafficking of human beings may also not be applied if the recruitment, transportation, transfer, harbouring and receipt of persons is connected with smuggling of persons. This is because there are quite different purposes between the

---

[62] Article 4 (a).

trafficking of human beings and people smuggling. The latter is based on free consent since individuals have usually paid a certain amount of money to certain persons to assist them in illegally gaining entry into another country. The former is involuntary, since the person who is the victim of human trafficking has been denied legal rights and is subject to exploitation by another person or persons.[63] Moreover, the Convention clearly states that "The consent of a victim of 'trafficking in human beings' to the intended exploitation set forth in subparagraph (a) of this article shall be irrelevant where any of the means set forth in subparagraph (a) have been used."[64] The provisions presented here clarify that in order to recognise an act under the definition of trafficking in human beings, consent expressed by the victim has no relevance. There are several reasons for this *inter alia*:

- consent is very difficult to prove,
- consent may be expressed under threat,
- consent may have been given under coercion,
- consent given to forced labour is not valid,
- consent given to prostitution or other forms of sexual exploitation, forced labour or services, slavery or practices similar to slavery, servitude or the removal of organs may be for the purpose of self-defence of the victim when she has been threatened with death,
- consent of a person for her own trafficking is impossible to prove,
- consent to slavery has no legal value for the defence of the accused since the slave trade is already prohibited
- consent of a child has no juridical basis

Although the issue of consent should not be important in the implementation of the Convention, the national courts may interpret the scope and the degree of the term 'consent' differently.

In the first Finnish trafficking case, the provisions on trafficking were applied only in a very stereotypical case. The District Court and the Court of Appeal considered that the other plaintiffs were "only" procured as they had agreed to travel to Finland and to prostitute themselves. This interpretation emphasises the prior-consent of a victim. The court gives the impression that only physical force or deception can constitute trafficking. It fails to give sufficient weight to the conditions under which the plaintiffs

---

[63] According to the Convention "'Victim' shall mean any natural person who is subject to trafficking in human beings as defined in this article." Article 14 (e).
[64] Article 4 (b).

were kept in prostitution. This interpretation also fails to take adequately into account other individual or societal factors that produce and maintain trafficking. As a result of this limited interpretation, victims of trafficking might be left unidentified and therefore outside of the system of victim assistance.[65]

The Convention has further clarified the above position. It states further that trafficking in human beings may consist of one or several acts. These include *i)* prostitution, *ii)* sexual exploitation, *iii)* forced labour, *iv)* forced services, *v)* slavery, *vi)* practice of slavery, *vii)* servitude and, finally, *viii)* removal of organs. Obviously, all the listed acts between *i* to *viii* have to be conducted, in one way or another, with the purpose of exploiting the relevant person. Consequently, prostitution and sexual exploitation fall under the definition of trafficking in human beings. With the difference that one includes the actual act of sexual intercourse while the other may be confined to other acts such as the production of pornography.[66]

---

[65] Trafficked Women, Foreign Prostitutes and the Limits of Consent www.helsinki.fi/rpol/naisoikeus/Roth_linkit/Law%20and%20Anthropology.pdf.

[66] One of the significant developments of the issue of prohibition of pornography of children in Europe can be examined in the provisions of the Council of Europe's Convention on Cybercrime. The Convention was opened for signature in Budapest in 2001 and came into force in 2004. A considerable number of states such as the United States, Canada, Japan, and other countries were engaged in the formulation of the convention. Many states in the world have also signed and ratified it. The convention is the first international treaty on crimes relating to internet and computer networks. The basic purposes of the treaty are to create a common criminal policy, harmonise legislation and effective cooperation between the states parties against cybercrime. Article 9 of the Convention relates to offences concerning child pornography. It reads that "Each Party shall adopt such legislative and other measures as may be necessary to establish as criminal offences under its domestic law, when committed intentionally and without right, the following conduct: a) producing child pornography for the purpose of its distribution through a computer system; b) offering or making available child pornography through a computer system; c) distributing or transmitting child pornography through a computer system; d) procuring child pornography through a computer system for oneself or for another person; e) possessing child pornography in a computer system or on a computer-data storage medium. 2 For the purpose of paragraph 1 above, the term "child pornography" shall include pornographic material that visually depicts: a) a minor engaged in sexually explicit conduct; b) a person appearing to be a minor engaged in sexually explicit conduct; c) realistic images representing a minor engaged in sexually explicit conduct. 3. For the purpose of paragraph 2 above, the term "minor" shall include all persons under 18 years of age. A Party may, however, require a lower age-limit, which shall be not less than

In any event, as is discussed above, trafficking in human beings takes different forms and does not necessarily apply to acts of sex trafficking. But this does not necessarily mean that trafficking in human beings which falls under forced labour and forced services or slavery and servitude cannot also be identified under the term 'sex trafficking'. This is because trafficking of a woman or a child may simultaneously fall under the definition of sexual exploitation and slavery and forced labour. This depends on the circumstances of the case and the conditions under which the victim is exploited by an individual or an organized group. All these vary from case to case depending also on the historical development of events around the victim and the way in which the fee was paid. Thus, an act of sexual exploitation may fall into several categories, the separation of which may be very difficult and sometimes unnecessary.

More important is the fact that the Council of Europe Convention on Action against Trafficking in Human Beings has taken a much harder line concerning the cases in which children are the victims. The word 'child' here applies to a person who is under eighteen years of age.[67] The Convention then goes further and states that "The recruitment, transportation, transfer, harbouring or receipt of a child for the purpose of exploitation shall be considered 'trafficking in human beings' even if this does not involve any of the means set forth in subparagraph (a) of this article."[68] Here, the policy of the Convention is surely to protect the rights of children from any interference which may prejudice their situation. The Convention has not therefore seen any need to take into account other arguments concerning the position of a child who has been the victim of trafficking in human beings. With this policy the Convention aims to ensure that the rights of children are protected and that their age as minors does not hinder their legal defence before criminal courts in Europe.

---

16 years. 4. Each Party may reserve the right not to apply, in whole or in part, paragraphs 1, sub-paragraphs d. and e, and 2, sub-paragraphs b. and c."

[67] Article 4 (d).

[68] Article 4 (c). The subparagraph (a) of the article provides that "'Trafficking in human beings' shall mean the recruitment, transportation, transfer, harbouring or receipt of persons, by means of the threat or use of force or other forms of coercion, of abduction, of fraud, of deception, of the abuse of power or of a position of vulnerability or of the giving or receiving of payments or benefits to achieve the consent of a person having control over another person, for the purpose of exploitation. Exploitation shall include, at a minimum, the exploitation of the prostitution of others or other forms of sexual exploitation, forced labour or services, slavery or practices similar to slavery, servitude or the removal of organs."

Prevention of Trafficking

One of the serious problems with the system of international criminal law, including criminal human rights law, is the problem of the implementation of their provisions and also their policies of prevention. The Council of Europe Convention on Action against Trafficking in Human Beings has listed several techniques which states are asked to use to fight against trafficking in persons. For this reason, the Convention employs six techniques for the prevention of trafficking in human beings. These are co-ordination, development of education, promotion of human rights norms, integration of migrants, integration of children, and non-governmental engagement.

According to the first policy of prevention, states parties are under certain Conventional obligations to take the necessary measures to strengthen the provisions of national law. This is in order to create more effective co-ordination between different internal bodies which are responsible for the prevention and combating of trafficking from various points of view. This may be called the policy of *co-ordination*.[69]

According to the second policy, it is the duty of states parties to take effective and essential measures for encouraging and increasing the development of research programmes which are helpful for the prevention of trafficking in human beings.[70] These programmes may include information, social and economic initiatives and training programmes, education campaigns, awareness raising, in particular for persons who may be in a position to be likely victims of trafficking, and for professionals concerned with trafficking in human beings. This policy may be described as a policy based on the *development of education*.[71]

---

[69] Article 5 (1).

[70] Article 6 of the Convention has strengthened these provisions. It says that "To discourage the demand that fosters all forms of exploitation of persons, especially women and children, that leads to trafficking, each Party shall adopt or strengthen legislative, administrative, educational, social, cultural or other measures including: a. research on best practices, methods and strategies; b. raising awareness of the responsibility and important role of media and civil society in identifying the demand as one of the root causes of trafficking in human beings; c. target information campaigns involving, as appropriate, inter alia, public authorities and policy makers; d. preventive measures, including educational programmes for boys and girls during their schooling, which stress the unacceptable nature of discrimination based on sex, and its disastrous consequences, the importance of gender equality and the dignity and integrity of every human being."

[71] Article 5 (2).

The third preventive policy of the Convention may be characterised as the *promotion of human rights norms*. According to this policy, the states parties to the Convention should promote human rights principles and access to its purposes. Accordingly, states parties should employ gender mainstreaming and a child-sensitive approach in the implementation, development and assessment of all the policies and programmes that have been mentioned in its second policy of prevention.[72]

The fourth policy of prevention is based on the *integration of migrants* in order for them to be granted residency status. Accordingly, each party is responsible for taking appropriate and effective measures, as may be necessary, to create the possibility for migration to take place legally through dissemination of accurate information by relevant authorities within the state. This should create the possibility for entry into and remaining in a state's territory.[73]

According to the fifth preventive measure, states parties should take specific measures to reduce children's vulnerability to trafficking. This should be facilitated by creating a protective environment for children. This policy may be called the *integration of children*.[74] The policy is one of the significant instruments within the Convention for the protection of the rights of the child and prevention of the development of sex trafficking or sexual exploitation of children.

The sixth policy is addressed to encourage non-governmental bodies. Accordingly, measures should be taken where appropriate to enable non-governmental organisations or relevant institutions to engage in the prevention of trafficking in human beings and victim protection or assistance. This policy may be called *non-governmental engagement*.[75]

All the policies in the above should be read both separately and in conjunction with one another. This is because co-operation between the different organs of states is a necessary condition for the prevention of trafficking in human beings.[76] The co-operation may also be carried out between institutions of one state with another. However, one problem with these six different types of co-operation is that the degree and the level of their application are not clear. This is because they may be interpreted differently according to the circumstances of the time and the economic

---

[72] Article 5 (3).
[73] Article 5 (4).
[74] Article 5 (5).
[75] Article 5 (6).
[76] This is especially important in the case of control of trafficking using border control measures, security and control of documents and legitimacy and validity of documents. See Articles 7, 8 and 9.

condition of the relevant state. Moreover, a state may not be able to apply the relevant provisions due to the specifications of its immigration policy.

Another serious problem is that the State authorities may not in practice put a heavy emphasis on the protection of foreign victims of prostitution. This means that the language of the Convention which encourages the states parties to take measures for the prevention of sex trafficking in human beings without discrimination on any ground such as sex, race, colour, language, religion, political or other opinion, national or social origin, association with a national minority, property, birth or other status effective, may not always be possible to implement.[77] Although one cannot deny that the provisions of the Convention insist on the employment of measures to protect and promote the rights of victims by the states parties, they may be interpreted differently in practice.[78]

Substantive Criminal Law

One of the valuable contributions of the Council of Europe Convention on Action Against Trafficking in Human Beings is the criminalization of all acts which come under the definition of trafficking in human beings. The Convention thus aims to underline that trafficking in human beings is a crime and this has to be formulated into the legislation of states parties. Article 18 of the Convention speaks about this matter. The article obliges all states parties to take such necessary legislative measures as may be necessary to formulate provisions that recognize certain conducts, which are listed in Article 4, as criminal offences.

However, Article 18 specifies a condition, the existence of which is recognized necessary for the purpose of the criminalization of certain acts, namely, the presence of intention. Consequently, due to the provisions of the article, an act which appears to constitute the trafficking of human beings, but has not occurred with the intention of the perpetrator, cannot be recognized as criminal conduct. In other words, all acts that are

---

[77] Article 3.

[78] "It has been rather difficult to acknowledge human rights violations involved in foreign prostitution as attitudes towards prostitutes have been rather negative.... Since 1999, an alien may be refused to enter the country if there are reasonable grounds to suspect that he or she may sell sexual services. In 2001, both selling and purchasing of sexual services in public places were criminalised. The amendments have argued to marginalise foreign prostitutes and to make them more vulnerable to exploitation and violence both from the side of sex-buyers and procurers." Trafficked Women, Foreign Prostitutes and the Limits of Consent. www.helsinki.fi/rpol/naisoikeus/ Roth_linkit /Law%20and%20Anthropology.pdf.

enumerated in the definition of trafficking in human beings must, by one means or another, be committed with the intention of the participant.

The legislator does not however clarify what are the criteria of intention. This is because the word 'intention' has been always a subject of debate in jurisprudence. The controversy is over its real definition, how to actually prove when a conduct may be identified as involving clear intention. One of the reasons why the legislator has required the existence of intention as a necessary condition for the recognition of criminality may be the traditional concept of crime and criminality within criminal systems which requires intention as a necessary element for the recognition of the criminality of the accused person. According to this classical theory, before an accused person could be proven guilty of a wrongful act, the existence of a guilty mind was required; this was called 'intention'. However, it may not be necessary in all situations to prove the existence of intention. Intention may not absolve the perpetrator from the consequences of wrongful conduct. A person who engages in the recruitment, transportation, transfer, harbouring and receipt of persons may hardly claim that it was not his/her intention to engage in the sex trafficking of human beings. Even negligence in the preparation of and participation in a conduct may rest on some kinds of intention that may not need to be proved. According to the general principles of law, a person is responsible for her/his conduct and the person who is carrying out an act cannot escape from her/his responsibility. The question as to whether the accused had the intention of committing the crime of trafficking in human beings may not be necessary as long as the perpetrator knew that she/he was carrying out an act that required such actions for its accomplishment. A clear example of this is defamation. This is when a person makes a statement that seriously offends another person. She/he may later on claim that there was no intention to defame. But, the complainant may claim to have been defamed based on the fact that the statement against the complainant has been published.

Similarly, the transportation of a group of women and girls in a vessel under particular conditions does not necessarily need proof of intention for its prosecution. The circumstances of the case allow for indirect intention and even indifferent intention, if not direct. In any case, the provisions of Article 18 have some difficulty in the identification of criminal conduct based on the fact that a criminal court will always face the situation in which the accused may escape from prosecution by resorting to the claim that there was no intention to commit the act. The legislator should have been more careful about the use of the term "intention" within the article.

The term is particularly susceptible to misuse in the case of sexual abuse, exploitation and trafficking of children.[79]

The existence of intention is also considered a necessary condition in the other stages of trafficking in human beings. For instance, states parties should adopt legislative and other measures as may be necessary to establish as criminal offences the following acts. These are *a)* forging a travel or identity document; *b)* procuring or providing such a document; *c)* retaining, removing, concealing, damaging or destroying a travel or identity document of another person. But, the acts *a* to *c* must be committed intentionally and for the purpose of enabling the trafficking of human beings.[80]

The Convention also asks the states parties to criminalize the use of the services of a victim since this is necessary for the prevention of trafficking in human beings. Accordingly, the parties should, if they find it necessary, adopt legislative provisions or other measures to establish as criminal offences under their national law, the exploitative use of services as stated within the provisions of Article 4, when the accused is aware that a person is a victim of trafficking.[81]

Attempt and Other Acts

The Convention on trafficking in human beings has taken the general policy of other international conventions concerning the attempt to commit and the aiding or abetting in the preparation of criminal conduct. Each state party should therefore adopt legislative measures, as may be seen necessary to establish as criminal offences, when committed intentionally, the aiding or abetting of the commission of any of the offences listed within the provisions of relevant articles.[82] In addition to this, each state party should also adopt legislative and other measures as may be necessary to establish as criminal offences when committed intentionally, any attempt to commit the offences detailed in the provisions of the Convention.[83]

---

[79]For a close examination of the issue see Kerstin Nordlöf, 'Economic Raison d'être of Trafficking in Children' in Rätteni den Ekonomiska Krisen (2012), pp.191-214.

[80] Article 20.

[81] Article 19.

[82] See Article 21 (1) including Articles 18-20.

[83] Article 21 (2).

Joint Criminal Responsibility

Some of the valuable provisions of the Council of Europe Convention on Action Against Trafficking in Human Beings are contained in Article 22 concerning corporate liability. This is divided into three categories: criminal, civil and administrative.[84] According to this article, the criminal responsibility of a legal person is taken into serious consideration. Although, the article does not speak about the concept of collective responsibility, it makes it clear that a legal person which has been engaged in the trafficking of human may be found criminally responsible. The Convention has therefore underlined that the prosecution and punishment of offenders does not necessary release a corporate body from its legal liability before the process of criminal justice. Consequently, states parties have agreed to adopt certain legislative measures for this purpose. According to Article 22, parties should adopt such legislative and any other measures as may be necessary to guarantee that a legal person may be criminally responsible for criminal offences enumerated in the Convention. These acts should, however, have been committed for the benefit of the corporate body by any natural person who has carried out the act individually or as part of an organ of the legal person. She/he should have a leading position within the machinery of the legal person as based on: A) "a power of representation of the legal person;" B). "an authority to take decisions on behalf of the legal person;" C) "an authority to exercise control within the legal person."[85] Yet, apart from the provisions in the above, each state party "shall take the measures necessary to ensure that a legal person can be held liable where the lack of supervision or control by a natural person referred to in paragraph 1 has made possible the commission of a criminal offence established in accordance with this Convention for the benefit of that legal person by a natural person acting under its authority."[86] Accordingly, the provisions in the above aim, in one way or another, to underline that when the legal characterization or the legal personality of a corporate body has been employed to carry out the criminal conduct, that engagement should not be ignored by the legislator. In particular, when one looks at different stages of trafficking in human beings, one may easily see that the commission of a criminal offence, as established with due regard to the provisions of the Convention, cannot be carried out without the legal personality of an organized institution or body. Still, in certain cases it will be very difficult

[84] Article 22 (3).
[85] Article 22 (1).
[86] Article 22 (2).

to prove that the acts have not been carried out for the benefit of that legal person by a natural person who was acting under its authority. In any event, the legislator of the Convention has divided the liability of the corporate body into criminal, civil and administrative. But this does not preclude the criminal responsibility of natural persons.[87]

The parties are also responsible for taking the necessary measures, including enacting legislation, to ensure that the criminal offences within the Convention are punishable offences due to the existence of certain necessary sanctions. They should be sure that neither natural persons nor legal persons can escape from the prosecution of criminally wrongful conduct committed in connection with trafficking in human beings.[88] States parties should also consider aggravating circumstances in the determination of the penalty for offences, with due regard to the provisions of Article 18 when "a. the offence deliberately or by gross negligence endangered the life of the victim; b. the offence was committed against a child; c. the offence was committed by a public official in the performance of her/his duties; d. the offence was committed within the framework of a criminal organisation."

In any event, each party with due regard to its legal system, should provide conditions under which the penalty will not be imposed on victims for their involvement in unlawful activities. This will be based on the fact that they have been forced or compelled to carry out certain acts. Moreover, the Convention also considers previous convictions when determining the penalty. This is dealt with in the Convention under the title of non-punishment.[89]

Principles of Jurisdiction

The Council of Europe Convention on Action against Trafficking in Human Beings has also put forward certain measures for the prosecution of those who have committed the crime of trafficking in human beings. This section of the Convention was seen as necessary in order to implement its legal requirements. The Convention permits all states parties to exercise their jurisdiction over national persons or legal persons. There are, however, certain conditions under which a state party may exercise its jurisdictions over the offender. These are:

---

[87] Article 22 (4).
[88] Article 23.
[89] Article 26.

1. The offence is committed within the territory of the relevant state. This is based on the principle of territoriality.[90]
2. The offence is committed on board a ship flying the flag of that Party. This condition is based on the principle of flag.[91]
3. When the crime is committed on board an aircraft registered under the laws of that Party. This is also based on the application of the principle of flag.[92]
4. The offence is committed by one of the nationals of the state or by a stateless person who has his or her habitual residence in the territory of that state, if the offence is punishable under criminal law where it was committed, or if the offence is committed outside the territorial jurisdiction of any State. This is the application of the principles of territoriality or passive personality.[93]
5. The offence is committed against one of its nationals. This is based on the principle of protection.[94]

6. When more than one state party claims jurisdiction over an alleged offence, the states parties involved should, where appropriate, consult to determine the most reasonable jurisdiction for prosecution. This is the application of the principle of cooperation.[95]

One of the serious problems with the above list concerning the exercise of jurisdiction by a state party over the accused, is that the relevant provisions do not take into consideration the principle of universality. This principle creates a wider possibility for all states to punish the offenders and does not permit the accused to escape from prosecution and punishment. Another problem is that the Convention also does not take into consideration the principle of complementarity. This principle would permit any of the other contracting states to exercise jurisdiction over the accused if, for one reason or another, the state in question could not punish the perpetrator or failed to do so. Although the Convention requests the exercise of jurisdiction in cases where an alleged offender is found in the territory of a state but that state does not extradite him/her to another state party after having received a request for extradition solely on the basis of his/her nationality, this provision does not ensure the application of the two aforementioned principles.[96]

---

[90] Article 31 (1, a).
[91] Article 31 (1, b).
[92] Article 31 (1, c).
[93] Article 31 (1, d).
[94] Article 31 (1, e).
[95] Article 31 (4).
[96] Article 31 (3).

Prosecution and its Subjects

The Council of Europe Convention on Action against Trafficking in Human Beings also contains articles concerning prosecution and proceedings. The states parties should ensure that investigation into and prosecution of offences listed in the Convention are carried out in the best manner and are not only based on the report of accusation submitted by the victims. This may only be a reason for investigation if the offence has, in whole or in part, been committed within the territory of the relevant state party.[97] Other avenues should however be available for the victims in order to submit their complaint. The complaint may be dealt with in due regard to the provisions of internal law of the state party in which the offence was committed.[98] Furthermore, a state party to the Convention may facilitate the role of non-governmental organizations when supporting the victims.[99]

The Convention also contains certain provisions governing the protection of victims, witnesses and collaborators. According to it, parties should adopt legislative or other measures where necessary to provide effective and appropriate protection from potential retaliation or intimidation, in particular during and after the investigation and prosecution of perpetrators, for:

- a Victims;
- b As appropriate, those who report the criminal offences established in accordance with Article 18 of this Convention or otherwise co-operate with the investigating or prosecuting authorities;
- c Witnesses who give testimony concerning criminal offences established in accordance with Article 18 of this Convention;
- d When necessary, members of the family of persons referred to in subparagraphs a and c.[100]

Parties should also adopt legislative measures which may provide various types of protection for the victims, witnesses and informants. This may include relocation, identity change, physical protection, and social assistance in order to obtain jobs.[101] Special protection should also be provided for a child based on the best interests of the child.[102] Each state

---

[97] Article 27 (1).
[98] Article 27 (2).
[99] Article 27 (3).
[100] Article 28 (1).
[101] Article 28 (2).
[102] Article 28 (3).

party should also pass "such legislative or other measures as may be necessary to provide, when necessary, appropriate protection from potential retaliation or intimidation in particular during and after investigation and prosecution of perpetrators, for members of groups, foundations, associations or non-governmental organisations which carry out the activities set out in Article 27, paragraph 3."

As is demonstrated in the above, the Convention aims to provide protection to victims, witnesses and informants. One weakness of all these protections is that the Convention in the relevant parts uses the term "when necessary". Since the term is not defined, it means the scope of the definition and applicability of the term "when necessary" depends on the interpretation of the legal authorities of the relevant state. This may vary from case to case depending on the circumstances and whether the authorities consider that it is appropriate to make more sufficient and workable regulations. It would have been more logical for the article to have been clear about this matter, and to have avoided such a vague term concerning the protection of victims, witnesses and collaborators. This is in particular important when one considers that clarity is fundamentally essential for the protection of victims of sex trafficking who have been the subjects of various accusations.[103] This is also significant when a victim is the subject of an organized crime or transnational crime and has been transported from one country to another by kidnapping or other measures. Her family may be in danger during the course of the investigation, prosecution and judgement. Although the positive impact of the Convention is very welcome,[104] a minor weakness of the Convention may cause great danger for the victims and they may not therefore be willing to

[103] Article 30 of the Convention also tries to provide sufficient guarantee for the victims during court proceedings. It reads that "In accordance with the Convention for the Protection of Human Rights and Fundamental Freedoms, in particular Article 6, each Party shall adopt such legislative or other measures as may be necessary to ensure in the course of judicial proceedings: a. the protection of victims' private life and, where appropriate, identity; a. victims' safety and protection from intimidation, in accordance with the conditions under its internal law and, in the case of child victims, by taking special care of children's needs and ensuring their right to special protection measures."

[104] For instance, Article 29 (1) provides that "Each Party shall adopt such measures as may be necessary to ensure that persons or entities are specialised in the fight against trafficking and the protection of victims. Such persons or entities shall have the necessary independence in accordance with the fundamental principles of the legal system of the Party, in order for them to be able to carry out their functions effectively and free from any undue pressure. Such persons or the staffs of such entities shall have adequate training and financial resources for their tasks."

communicate with the judicial authorities. The danger may even be more hazardous when the victims are children.[105]

Remarks

The Council of Europe Convention on Action against Trafficking in Human Beings has indeed set out certain important principles for the prevention of trafficking in human beings, the value of which cannot be denied.[106] Obviously, for our purposes, it has focused on the prevention and elimination of sex trafficking, including that of women and children. The policy for its application is, however, within most of its articles, dependent on the interpretation of the states parties. It is up to the states to take the necessary legislative or other measures regarding the prevention of trafficking.

According to the Convention, sex trafficking in human beings constitutes a serious crime. This clear criminalization makes the position of the Convention very important and creates a clear policy for the implementation of the Convention on a regional level. In particular, this will help with the identification of criminal activities against children.

Various types of cooperation under the Convention strengthen its legal and moral approach to the protection of victims. The Group of Experts on Action against Trafficking in Human Beings (GRETA) is also one of the key players in the implementation of the provisions of the Convention by the contracting parties. The intention of all these measures and policies of the Convention is clearly the orientation and centralization of jurisdiction and prosecution over the accused persons, as well as the regional protection of victims. The aim is to synchronize the relevant legislative measures governing the trafficking of human beings. This is with the full

---

[105] Even the provisions of Article 33 governing measures relating to endangered or missing persons may not be sufficient as long as all the terms in the Convention are not clear. The relevant article reads that "1 When a Party, on the basis of the information at its disposal has reasonable grounds to believe that the life, the freedom or the physical integrity of a person referred to in Article 28, paragraph 1, is in immediate danger on the territory of another Party, the Party that has the information shall, in such a case of emergency, transmit it without delay to the latter so as to take the appropriate protection measures. 2 The Parties to this Convention may consider reinforcing their co-operation in the search for missing people, in particular for missing children, if the information available leads them to believe that she/he is a victim of trafficking in human beings. To this end, the Parties may conclude bilateral or multilateral treaties with each other."

[106] Conny Rijken, Trafficking in Persons: A Prosecution from a European Perspective (2003).

ambition of hindering the development of the crime within the member states of the Council of Europe.[107]

[107] See *also* Farhad Malekian., 'The Law Governing Crimes against Women Constituting *Obligatio Erga Omnes' in Crimes Against Women* (David Pike, 2010), pp.3-22.

CHAPTER SIX

ABOLITION OF SLAVERY AND SUPPRESSION OF THE WHITE SLAVE TRADE IN CHILDREN

Introduction

The sex trafficking and sexual exploitation of women and children have long been treated as illegal and involvement in them has been criminalized by many international conventions dealing implicitly or explicitly with the question of the prevention and elimination of trafficking. In fact, within the system of international law, sex trafficking or sexual exploitation has been historically assimilated to "white slave traffic." The term was especially commonly used in the context of the sexual exploitation of young girls. This was based on the fact that children or young girls in such circumstances were not asked to express their consent.[1]This term has been employed within a number of relevant international conventions in order to speak about the illegal nature of the trade. Interestingly, the relevant conventions concerning the suppression of the white slave traffic were adopted in the period of formulation and ratification of the instruments applicable to slavery. Thus, there existed a uniform movement regarding the question of the abolition of slavery and acts constituting slavery after the end of World War I. This is based on the fact that an examination of both terms, i.e., "abolition of slavery" and suppression of "white slave traffic" demonstrates that both areas have similar aims and ambitions. The abolition of slavery puts an end to the trade in human beings and the suppression of white slave traffic aims to prevent and eliminate the concept by all means. Both terms also denote unjustified and illegal forced labour imposed by those who exercise some sort of ownership over a person.

There are a considerable number of international instruments dealing with slavery and sex trafficking. Instruments dealing with slavery and institutions similar to slavery are the 1926 Slavery Convention and 1956

---

[1] en.wikipedia.org/wiki/Sexual_slavery, visited on 22-10-2012.

Supplementary Convention on the Abolition of Slavery, the Slave Trade, and Institutions and Practices Similar to Slavery. Instruments applicable to sex trafficking are the 1904 International Agreement for the Suppression of the White Slave Traffic, the 1910 International Convention for the Suppression of the White Slave Traffic, the 1921 International Convention for the Suppression of the Traffic in Women and Children, the 1933 International Convention for the Suppression of the Traffic in Women of Full Age, and the 1949 Convention for the Suppression of the Traffic in Persons and the Exploitation or the Prostitution of Others.

The purposes of the conventions relating to the abolition of slavery and suppression of sex trafficking are *inter alia* to protect and secure the position of women or minors and to prevent and criminalize all acts of slavery or practices similar to slavery. These purposes of the conventions have been emphasized within their provisions and are today considered as an important part of customary international criminal law. This section examines the relevant provisions of these important instruments and their present situation within different rules of contemporary international law. Our purpose is to see whether the instruments are an integral part of the international law of *jus cogens* and create *erga omnes* obligations upon all states of the world to eradicate the sexual slavery of women and children.

Universal Declaration of Human Rights

One of the most relevant instruments in the area of sex trafficking, sexual exploitation and slavery or institutions similar to slavery is the Universal Declaration of Human Rights which was adopted by the UN General Assembly in 1948.[2] Thereafter the provisions of the Declaration were adopted by a large number of states. Although the Declaration is not an international convention, its provisions constitute the first and the most recognized norms of customary international law and it is also an integral part of *jus cogens* norms because of its very important and determinative functions. The norms of the Declaration are binding upon all states of the world without regard to their acceptance of its provisions. The chief reason for this is that the principles or norms of the Declaration constitute the most highly recognized values of the international community as a whole.

The Declaration clearly states many principles regarding the abolition of slavery, the slave trade as well as the sex trafficking and the exploitation of children. According to its first relevant principle "All human beings are born free and equal in dignity and rights. They are

[2] See also chapter III section on The Value of Human Rights Declaration.

endowed with reason and conscience and should act towards one another in a spirit of brotherhood."[3] The above principle should also be read in conjunction with its principle "Everyone is entitled to all the rights and freedoms set forth in this Declaration, without distinction of any kind, such as race, colour, sex, language, religion, political or other opinion, national or social origin, property, birth or other status. Furthermore, no distinction shall be made on the basis of the political, jurisdictional or international status of the country or territory to which a person belongs, whether it is independent, trust, non-self-governing or under any other limitation of sovereignty."[4]

According to the third principle of the Declaration, which is also one of the most violated principles, regarding the sex trafficking and exploitation of children, "Everyone has the right to life, liberty and security of person."[5] This principle is completed by principle four which requires the abolition of all forms of slavery and similar institutions which may be practiced by organized groups. The principle reads that "No one shall be held in slavery or servitude; slavery and the slave trade shall be prohibited in all their forms."[6]

Principle five of the Declaration obliges all states to take the necessary measures for the prohibition of all practices which may result in torture or may be considered to constitute cruel, inhuman or degrading treatment or punishment.[7] According to principle six, everyone has the right to be respected and acknowledged as a person before the law.[8] Principle six has been strengthened with principle seven which condemns all forms of discrimination. It reads that "All are equal before the law and are entitled without any discrimination to equal protection of the law. All are entitled to equal protection against any discrimination in violation of this Declaration and against any incitement to such discrimination."[9]

Finally, the provisions of principle eight are very relevant for the victims of slavery, the slave trade, sex trafficking and sexual exploitation, including of children. It creates rights for every victim "the right to an effective remedy by the competent national tribunals for acts violating the fundamental rights granted him by the constitution or by law."[10] This

---

[3] Article 1.
[4] Article 2.
[5] Article 3.
[6] Article 4.
[7] Article 5.
[8] Article 6.
[9] Article 7.
[10] Article 8.

means that all victims of sex trafficking have an internationally recognized legal right to ask for compensation wherever their cases are under investigation. Principle eight is also applicable in the case of regional and international courts/tribunals. This is because when the Declaration of Human Rights was adopted there was not yet any regional or international court which could investigate and prosecute the given case. This problem has largely been solved by the creation of a number of regional courts. Thus, the victims of trafficking may, as with any other citizen, ask for compensation.

Abolition of Institutions of Slavery

Development

The term "slavery" constitutes one of the most recognized terms of international law which has always been used in connection with different international instruments. The term implies the position of a person who has been denied any rights of her/his own and who is taken by force by another person or organization in order to be sold, exploited and used in whatever manner may be deemed necessary for the benefit of the owner. The practice of slavery has existed since the beginning of civilization and governments have directly or indirectly permitted its practice. The majority of practices of slavery may be categorized in three ways. The first is when a person is sold within a nation for the purpose of slavery or heavy servitude without appropriate compensation. The second is when states in wartime, due to the provisions of the state of war, could take their enemies for the purpose of slavery. The third occurred in peacetime, when the most powerful European nations engaged in the practice of slavery and hunted the population of most of their colonies, especially in the African continent, in order to sell them in the slave trade markets.[11] With the development of international communications and transport facilities on the sea, they could transport millions of people from one part of the world to another and sell them as human chattels for any purpose. That is why slavery means the total exploitation of a person by another person. The important aspect of this trade was that the taking of slaves was most often practiced under the supervision of organized governmental or non-governmental groups – all of which effectively had permission from their own state. It was almost like a competition between the European states to introduce their slaves into different countries and markets. Among these

[11] Jean Allain, Slavery in International Law (2012).

slaves were also women and children who were sold and exploited by their owners, not only for work in their farms and homes, but also for sexual purposes. Thus, female children had several functions and purposes. They could be exploited for sex and work and were convenient for different purposes because of their young age and immaturity.

Efforts

There have been many efforts to suppress slavery and the slave trade. The first efforts may be traced back to the beginning of the nineteenth century and the Paris Peace Conference of 1814-1815. This was later continued at the Congress of Vienna in 1915. After this time several treaties were signed in which the question of the abolition of slavery and the slave trade were taken into serious consideration. These were the 1841 Treaty of London, the 1862 Treaty of Washington, the General Act of the Brussels Conference of 1889-90 and the 1919 St. Germain-en Laye Convention. Due to the establishment of the League of Nations, a Slavery Convention was adopted in 1926. This was the first international convention which dealt directly with the question of slavery and its abolition. The second official and important instrument was formulated under the United Nations' authority in 1956. This is the Supplementary Convention on the Abolition of Slavery, the Slave Trade, and Institutions and Practices Similar to Slavery.

Abolition within the First Slavery Convention

The first official effort for the abolition of slavery and the slave trade and institutions similar to slavery was made under the auspices of the League of Nations. In fact, because of the requirements of the earlier conferences and meetings, the 1926 Slavery Convention was adopted and came into force in 1927. The chief policy of the Convention is to abolish slavery. According to the Convention, slavery is "the status or condition of a person over whom any or all of the powers attaching to the right of ownership are exercised." It further defines the slave trade as "all acts involved in the capture, acquisition or disposal of a person with intent to reduce him to slavery; all acts involved in the acquisition of a slave with a view to selling or exchanging him; all acts of disposal by sale or exchange of a slave acquired with a view to being sold or exchanged, and, in general, every act of trade or transport in slaves."[12] It is with the above

[12] Article 1.

definition that trafficking in persons or sex trafficking and sexual exploitation of children are assimilated to the condition of slavery. This is because the victim has no right of her/his own, and all powers of ownership are exercised over the victim's body and personality by another.

The Convention has also recognized the duty of the contracting parties to "adopt all appropriate measures with a view to preventing and suppressing the embarkation, disembarkation and transport of slaves in their territorial waters and upon all vessels flying their respective flags."[13] These provisions of the Convention are also among those important provisions that bind the states parties to react against trafficking in persons in whatever form, including sex trafficking or the sexual exploitation of children.

Other provisions of the 1926 Convention call upon the states parties to take all necessary measures for the suppression of slavery within their own territories or territories under their control. They are also asked to give the necessary assistance to one another in order to fulfil the purposes of the Convention. The Convention also aims to put an end to forced labour and asks the contracting parties to "recognise that recourse to compulsory or forced labour may have grave consequences and undertake, each in respect of the territories placed under its sovereignty, jurisdiction, protection, suzerainty or tutelage, to take all necessary measures to prevent compulsory or forced labour from developing into conditions analogous to slavery."[14]

According to the provisions of the Convention, states parties also agreed to impose severe penalties for infractions of the provisions of the Convention.[15] However, the provisions of this Convention were not yet effective enough to put an end to the institution of slavery. The words of the Convention were not given the necessary recognition within the national legislation of different states. The Convention had in fact no practical effect in the prevention of slavery. It aspired for international justice but without any decisive empowerment policy. The time had come to make the provisions of the Convention much more practical and workable.

---

[13] Article 3.

[14] Article 5.

[15] Article 6.

Supplementary Convention on the Abolition of Slavery, the Slave Trade, and Institutions and Practices Similar to Slavery

A New Convention

The need for the creation of a new instrument for the abolition of slavery and institutions similar to slavery was one of the serious questions in the international legal and political community before the Second World War. The outbreak of the war and the establishment of the United Nations made it more urgent. In particular, the question needed more consideration since the Charter of the United Nations stands for the implementation of human rights and the abolition of various forms of slavery. This became more of a reality with the acceptance of the Universal Declaration of Human Rights in 1948. Thus the United Nations, in order to put an end to various forms of slavery, adopted in 1956 the Supplementary Convention on the Abolition of Slavery, the Slave Trade, and Institutions and Practices Similar to Slavery of 1926.[16] The Convention came into force precisely one year after its adoption on 30 April 1957.

Descriptions

The Convention has modified a number of the provisions of the 1926 Convention. The provisions of the 1956 Convention are without doubt important for the abolition, prevention, elimination, prosecution and punishment of all forms of slavery, including sexual exploitation, sex trafficking, slavery, forced labour and also all selling of children, including those who are sold for the welfare of the child. Article 1 of the Convention constitutes a landmark for the abolition of slavery and practices similar to slavery. It provides a number of definitions for a number of positions that are assimilated to slavery and are prohibited. According to it slavery "means, as defined in the Slavery Convention of 1926, the status or condition of a person over whom any or all of the powers attaching to the right of ownership are exercised, and "slave" means a person in such condition or status."[17]

---

[16] It was adopted by a Conference of Plenipotentiaries convened by an Economic and Social Council resolution 608(XXI) of 30 April 1956 and enacted at Geneva on 7 September 1956.

[17] Article 7.

Parties to the Convention should take all practicable and necessary legislative and other measures in order to bring about progressively the complete abolition or abandonment of debt bondage, serfdom and the labour of children less than 18 years of age according to certain conditions. According to it, all these acts should as soon as possible be prohibited regardless of the provisions of the 1926 Convention regarding the definition of slavery. Interesting portions of the definition relate to debt bondage and exploitation of children. It reads that:

> (a) Debt bondage, that is to say, the status or condition arising from a pledge by a debtor of his personal services or of those of a person under his control as security for a debt, if the value of those services as reasonably assessed is not applied towards the liquidation of the debt or the length and nature of those services are not respectively limited and defined;
>
> (d) Any institution or practice whereby a child or young person under the age of 18 years, is delivered by either or both of his natural parents or by his guardian to another person, whether for reward or not, with a view to the exploitation of the child or young person or of his labour.[18]

The descriptions or definitions which are given in the above constitute some of the important principles for the recognition of acts falling under the convention on slavery. They may also apply to the conditions of the victims of sex trafficking or sexual exploitation. This is because many of the victims of sex trafficking may be taken into trafficking based on debt bondage and be forced into prostitution and to provide other sexual services. The sexual exploitation of children may also be assimilated to slavery because they are kept by force and are exploited through acts which are neither permitted by law nor by customary law. The Convention has therefore foreseen the situation of a child who is under 18 and has been placed in a position of exploitation by his/her biological parents or guardians. It makes this action illegal as it constitutes an engagement in the act of slavery.

Slave Trade

The 1956 Convention on slavery gives a clear definition of the slave trade. This definition was not given under the provisions of the 1926 Slavery Convention. The definition has broadened the concept of the slave trade in order to cover all acts falling in one way or another into the provisions of

[18] Article 1.

the convention. The slave trade "means and includes all acts involved in the capture, acquisition or disposal of a person with intent to reduce him to slavery; all acts involved in the acquisition of a slave with a view to selling or exchanging him; all acts of disposal by sale or exchange of a person acquired with a view to being sold or exchanged; and, in general, every act of trade or transport in slaves by whatever means of conveyance."[19]

This definition may also be employed in the case of sex trafficking when traffickers transport the victims of trafficking from one country to another. The Convention criminalizes the slave trade or acts the intention of which is to reduce persons to the status of slavery through transporting them in various forms.[20] In addition to the definition of the slave trade in the above paragraph, the Convention also clarifies that the slave trade is the "act of conveying or attempting to convey slaves from one country to another by whatever means of transport, or of being accessory thereto."[21] The convention also recognizes the duty of the contracting parties to take the necessary measures for the application of severe penalties to persons convicted for having engaged in the slave trade. It also states that the contracting parties should "take all effective measures to prevent ships and aircraft authorized to fly their flags from conveying slaves and to punish persons guilty of such acts or of using national flags for that purpose." States should also "take all effective measures to ensure that their ports, airfields and coasts are not used for the conveyance of slaves."[22]

One of the relevant principles of the 1956 Convention for sex trafficking and sexual exploitation is the principle of the freedom of the victims from all contracts or agreements which may have been obtained by the traffickers. According to it, "Any slave who takes refuge on board any vessel of a State Party to this Convention shall *ipso facto* be free."[23] This means that since the victims of trafficking are under conditions of slavery, they should not be denied help by the states parties to the slavery conventions or instruments applicable to sex trafficking or sexual exploitation of women and children.

For the implementation of the above provisions, the parties are responsible for working with one another through various forms of cooperation and exchange of information which may be seen as necessary for the prevention of slavery and the slave trade.[24]

---

[19] Article 7.
[20] See the above paragraph.
[21] Article 3 (1).
[22] Article 3 (2).
[23] Article 4.
[24] Article 3.

Attempt

The 1956 Convention on slavery like other international legal instruments applicable within international criminal law has also, within its provisions, criminalized attempts or conspiracies to commit the act in question. Consequently, those who commit acts which constitute attempted slavery, according to the provisions of the Convention, may be brought before the criminal jurisdiction of the contracting parties and be punished for those criminal acts. Concerning this matter, the convention states that: "The act of enslaving another person or of inducing another person to give himself or a person dependent upon him into slavery, or of attempting these acts, or being accessory thereto, or being a party to a conspiracy to accomplish any such acts, shall be a criminal offence under the laws of the States Parties to this Convention and persons convicted thereof shall be liable to punishment."[25]

The above provisions without doubt represent the effective criminalization of "slavery, the slave trade and institutions and practices similar to slavery". Consequently, the provisions of the Convention are also helpful in the criminalization of sex trafficking and sexual exploitation of children and in the identification of criminals. This also means that the perpetrators of the exploitation of children cannot flee their criminal responsibility and punishment by resorting to the plea that their criminal conduct was merely an attempt or conspiracy to commit such crimes. Both are recognized as criminal offences and are punishable by states because of the special international character of the crimes and their *jus cogens* nature.

The First International Agreement for the Suppression of "the White Slave Traffic"

The beginning of the twentieth century was marked by the suppression of slavery in general and the suppression of sex trafficking and the sexual exploitation of women and young girls in particular. However, it must be noted that while the most significant international conventions for the abolition of slavery were formulated after the end of the First World War, the conventions against "white slave traffic" were initiated at the beginning of the twentieth century. This means that the prevention of sex trafficking was not recognized by the contracting parties as part of the prevention of all types of institutions of slavery, since the criminal acts

[25] Article 6 (1).

relating to white slave traffic were seen as offences against the interests of the states of Europe and their own populations. In other words, when the first instruments governing the prohibition of "white slave traffic" were ratified, the trafficking of slaves was still permitted within the laws of most European states. Ironically, the first application of the principles of human rights law were therefore seen as necessary in connection with the prevention and elimination of "white slave traffic" since it was seen as harmful to the social structure of European states.

It is for the above reason that some of the European states gathered[26] and discussed the provisions of the International Agreement for the Suppression of the "White Slave Traffic" and finally adopted it in 1904.[27] The agreement clearly aimed at the abolition of "white slave traffic" and not the slave trade as a whole, but it was probably also a move towards the abolition of the slave trade and sex trafficking in black persons, in particular women and girl children.

Criminalization

One of the great achievements within the provisions of the International Agreement for the Suppression of the White Slave Traffic was the criminalization of "the white slave traffic". The contracting parties unanimously recognized that "being desirous of securing to women of full age who have suffered abuse or compulsion, as also to women and girls under age, effective protection against the criminal traffic known as the White Slave Traffic". With this principal recognition, the contracting parties formulated several important articles focusing on the prevention of "white slave traffic". For this purpose they undertook to establish legal authorities who could work for the aims of the agreement and charged them with the coordination of all necessary information concerning the procuring of women or girls for immoral purposes abroad.[28]

---

[26] These include His Majesty the King of the United Kingdom of Great Britain and Ireland and of the British Dominions beyond the Seas, Emperor of India, His Majesty the German Emperor, King of Prussia, in the name of the German Empire, His Majesty the King of the Belgians, His Majesty the King of Denmark, His Majesty the King of Spain, the President of the French Republic, His Majesty the King of Italy, Her Majesty the Queen of the Netherlands, His Majesty the King of Portugal and of the Algarve, His Majesty the Emperor of all the Russians, His Majesty the King of Sweden and Norway as well as the Swiss Federal Council.

[27] International Agreement for the Suppression of the "White Slave Traffic," 18 May 1904, 35 Stat. 1979, 1 L.N.T.S. 83, *entered into force* 18 July 1905.

[28] Article 1.

The agreement put a heavy weight on the prevention of "the white slave traffic" in the border territories of states and required the contracting parties to place controls on systems of transportation. It recognized the duty of each government to undertake "to have a watch kept, especially in railway stations, ports of embarkation, and en route, for persons in charge of women and girls destined for an immoral life. With this object instructions shall be given to the officials, and all other qualified persons, to obtain, within legal limits, all information likely to lead to the detection of criminal traffic."[29] It further asked the contracting parties to provide all information about the principals, accomplices and victims of the traffic, whenever they saw it as necessary, to the diplomatic services, consular agents or any other competent authorities.[30] This meant, *inter alia*, that the sexual exploitation of children could, for the purpose of prevention, also be reported to consular or diplomatic agents of state parties.

Repatriation

Repatriation constitutes one of the important provisions of the International Agreement for the Suppression of the White Slave Traffic. The policy is based on the theory that the victims should be returned to their country of origin. According to other provisions of the agreement, the contracting parties have undertaken to "when the case arises, and within legal limits, to have the declarations taken of women or girls of foreign nationality who are prostitutes, in order to establish their identity and civil status, and to discover who has caused them to leave their country. The information obtained shall be communicated to the authorities of the country of origin of the said women and girls, with a view to their eventual repatriation."[31] According to the agreement, "the Repatriation shall only take place after agreement as to identity and nationality, as well as place and date of arrival at the frontiers."

Throughout the agreement the prevention of the extension of the traffic is seen as one of its necessary conditions by the contracting parties. They also undertake to assist the victims, as much as possible, to return to their countries. The agreement encourages the states parties to assist the victim to return to her country of origin or in the direction of her country of origin, if the woman or girl does not have the possibility of paying the cost of transfer, and neither do her husband, relations or guardian.[32] In practice,

[29] Article 2.
[30] Article 2.
[31] Article 3.
[32] Article 4.

this meant any assistance to the victim in returning to her own country of origin depended on the generosity of the country in which she was discovered to be the victim of the criminal offence by the relevant authorities of the host state. The policy of the agreement regarding repatriation is rather weak and does not sufficiently protect the rights of the victim, especially when the victim is a minor and may easily be mistreated.

Women of Colonies

One of the important policies of the agreement related to the respective colonies of the contracting states. This was because the agreement did not automatically apply to colonial territories. It treated this question in a separate declaration annexed to the International Agreement for the Suppression of the White Slave Traffic. According to the provisions of the declaration, the contracting states had adopted different policies towards the application or non-application of the agreement concerning their colonies. This meant that the key purpose of the agreement, which was to protect women and girl children from unlawful trafficking, was only applied to those women or girls who had the nationality of states with full sovereign power and jurisdiction over their territories. The women and girls of the colonies who were victims of prostitution, unlawful exploitation or sex trafficking were openly discriminated against and their integrity would not be seen as equal to the integrity of European women.[33] The agreement is therefore a clear mark of unequal and discriminatory treatment between the women of the world. This is particularly obvious concerning white and black females. The provisions of the agreement make it clear that the political, cultural and religious powers of Europe did not put any effort into the prevention of the exploitation of the women and children of Africa.

---

[33] For instance, according to Article 2 of the Declaration "The Government of His Britannic Majesty declare that they reserve the right to accede to the Agreement, and to denounce it for each of the British Colonies or possessions." Of more or less similar line "The German Government declare that they reserve their decisions on the subject of their Colonies." Similar views were also expressed by the Danish and Spanish governments. But, the French, Italian and the Netherlands declared that the agreement was applicable to their colonies. The Portuguese government reserved "the right to decide subsequently whether the Agreement shall be put into force in any of the Portuguese Colonies." And the "Russian Government declare that the Agreement shall be applicable in its integrity to all the territory of the Empire in Europe and in Asia."

The Second International Convention for the Suppression of the White Slave Traffic

Modification

Due to the changing requirements of the time and the unsuccessful consequences of the first international agreement for the suppression of "white slave traffic", some governments of the world engaged in the formulation and adoption of a second international instrument with the intention of criminalizing the traffic. This was the International Convention for the Suppression of the White Slave Traffic adopted in 1910. Although the provisions of the Convention were intended to put an end to the sex trafficking or prostitution of women and female children, they were not as effective as had been expected during its formulation and it did not take a long time before the need for the adoption of a new instrument was felt among states. It is on the basis of these inadequacies of the Convention that the addition of much-needed amendments was begun. Thus, it was amended by the Protocol Amending the International Agreement for the Suppression of the White Slave Traffic, and Amending the International Convention for the Suppression of the White Slave Traffic in 1949.[34] The purpose of this modification was to bring the provisions of the instrument into line with the needs of the time and to be sure that all dimensions of the traffic came under its remit.

Criminalization

The 1910 Convention for the Suppression of the White Slave Traffic openly criminalized sex trafficking of women and young children. It stated that "Whoever, in order to gratify the passions of another person, has procured, enticed, or led away, even with her consent, a woman or girl under age, for immoral purposes, shall be punished, notwithstanding that the various acts constituting the offence may have been committed in different countries."[35] The statement of the Convention clearly focuses on the international criminal character of the act of sex trafficking and

---

[34] International Convention for the Suppression of the "White Slave Traffic," May 4, 1910, 211 Consol. T.S. 45, 1912 GR. Brit. T.S. No. 20, *as amended by* Protocol Amending the International Agreement for the Suppression of the White Slave Traffic, and Amending the International Convention for the Suppression of the White Slave Traffic, May 4, 1949, 2 U.S.T. 1999, 30 U.N.T.S. 23, *entered into force* June 21, 1951.

[35] Article 1.

prostitution. In particular, the Convention attempted to criminalize all acts which were committed against children. The provisions of the Convention criminalize acts of white slave traffic, even if they are committed in or take place in different countries.

Complicity

Complicity is generally recognized as a crime in criminal law and it is therefore prosecutable by law. According to the relevant provisions of the Convention for the Suppression of the White Slave Traffic, any complicity by a person in the traffic is prohibited and should also be considered a punishable offence. The Convention clearly states that any person "in order to gratify the passions of another person, has, by fraud, or by means of violence, threats, abuse of authority, or any other method of compulsion, procured, enticed, or led away a woman or girl over age, for immoral purposes, shall also be punished, notwithstanding that the various acts constituting the offence may have been committed in different countries."[36] These provisions have obviously recognized the criminal liability of the person who has by one means or another facilitated the commission of the wrongful conduct.

The Convention employs the term "immoral purposes" with the aim of criminalizing white slavery. The Convention does not however clarify the definition of the term and its legal applicability. It seems that the term "immoral purposes" is a general term for the identification of the crime and therefore many acts may come under the provisions of the Convention. This means that the Convention may not only be applicable to the sexual exploitation of women and children but also to acts that affect indirectly the victims of the crime, such as pornography, sexual activities of all types which do not involve actual sexual penetration, and employing women and especially children in bars, cabarets, clubs and similar establishments where there is an expectation of sexual interaction with customers. These considerations aside, the term "immoral purposes" may be objected to on the basis that the term may be sufficiently vague to allow perpetrators to escape from appropriate prosecution.

Other provisions of the Convention request the parties to take the necessary legislative measures for the application and implementation of the provisions of the Convention. To this end, they should cooperate with one another in order to provide the necessary information and assistance to suppress white slave trafficking.

---

[36] Article 2.

International Convention for the Suppression of the Traffic in Women and Children

Creation

The shortcomings of states parties in the implementation of the provisions of the earlier instruments of 1904 and 1910 for the prevention of white slave traffic led to the creation of a third major international legal instrument for the prevention of sex trafficking in women and children. This instrument is the International Convention for the Suppression of the Traffic in Women and Children which was adopted in 1921 and came into force on 1922. The preamble of the Convention illustrates that the purpose of the Convention is to "secure more completely the suppression of the Traffic in Women and Children." This means that the Convention in its preamble accepts the insufficiency of the earlier instruments and tries to improve upon them with new provisions. It is also significant to mention here that the convention omits the term "white slave trafficking" and opens the window for the criminalization of the sexual exploitation of women and children. This change of policy might have depended on the effect of the establishment of the League of Nations and represents a very narrow move towards the internationalization of humanity.

Key policy

The key policy of the International Convention for the Suppression of the Traffic in Women and Children is to prevent trafficking in females, with a particular emphasis on the protection of children. The states parties have agreed "to take all measures to discover and prosecute persons who are engaged in the traffic in children of both sexes and who commit offences within the meaning of Article 1 of the Convention of 4 May 1910."[37] However, the 1921 Convention aims to avoid the problem of interpretation which had been raised with regard to the ambiguous provision of one of the articles of the 1910 Convention. This was because the 1910 Convention used the term "led away a woman or girl over age" within its Article 2. This was later clarified in its Final Protocol by the following words "As regards the suppression of the offences provided for in Articles 1 and 2, it is fully understood that the words 'woman or girl under age, woman or girl over age' refer to women or girls under or over twenty completed years of age. A law may, nevertheless, fix a more advanced age

[37] Article 2. For Article 1 of the 1910 Convention see the above section.

for protection, on condition that it is the same for women or girls of every nationality."[38] It was due to the above situation that the 1921 Convention also modified the limit of age and added a new age. According to the 1921 Convention, in the final Protocol of the Convention of 1910, the phrase "twenty completed years of age" shall be amended by the phrase "twenty-one completed years of age".[39]

Assistance

The International Convention for the Suppression of the Traffic in Women and Children aims to encourage cooperation between the states parties and requires all states to take the necessary legislative measures for the prevention of trafficking in women and children. States parties are also, according to the provisions of the existing treaties, required to extradite criminals. In cases where there is no extradition treaty between the parties, they will seek to reach an agreement in order to prosecute those who have violated the provisions of the 1921 Convention.[40] The Convention also emphasises the importance of the punishment of all those who engage in the criminal conducts as described in the provisions of Articles 1 and 2 of the 1910 Convention.[41]

Lost policy

In general, it must be asserted that these three instruments governing the prevention of acts of trafficking in women and children or "white slave traffic" were not successful in the application and implementation of their provisions. One problem was that they came into force in a period dominated by the First and Second World Wars and a very heavy economic depression in the world, which caused the contrary effect to that intended by the Conventions. Although we do not deny that the provisions

[38] No B of the Final Protocol.

[39] Article 5 of the 1921 Convention.

[40] States parties have also undertaken "in connection with immigration and emigration to adopt such administrative and legislative measures as are required to check the traffic in women and children. In particular, they undertake to make such regulations as are required for the protection of women and children travelling on emigrant ships, not only at the points of departure and arrival, but also during the journey, and to arrange for the exhibition, in railway stations and in ports, of notices warning women and children of the danger of the traffic and indicating the places where they can obtain accommodation and assistance." Article 7.

[41] Article 3.

of the relevant instruments helped in the development of the criminalization of all types of trafficking, especially that of children, the economic circumstances in the world meant that they failed to fulfil their real intentions.

Another problem was that the League of Nations was not sufficiently strong and the will of the states parties in the League were divided by conflicting interests. The Report to the Council of the League of Nations by the Traffic in Women and Children Committee on the work of its twelfth session implied the growing development of the white slave traffic and prostitution. The energies of the stronger members of the League were, however, directed towards the preparation of agreements regarding questions of the aggression of their opponents. The serious problem of the sexual exploitation of women and children thus became a matter of only minor interest to the states of the world. This theory is supported by the fact that the outbreak of the two world wars led to the sexual exploitation of women and children during the wars. Among the most egregious examples was the opening of official prostitution houses for soldiers, such as the Japanese Comfort Women services during the Second World War. It is estimated that over 100,000 women across Asia were victims of enforced prostitution by the Japanese Imperial Forces. Officially sanctioned brothels were also established to serve the armies fighting in Europe. Clear examples of these are the German camp brothels in World War I, and the German military brothels in World War II. It is calculated that at least 34, 140 females were forced to serve as prostitutes in these brothels. All of these violations highlighted the fact that sexual slavery or situations equivalent to slavery were officially permitted, even though they were prohibited within the provisions of international criminal conventions.

It must nevertheless be asserted that the instruments from 1904, 1910 and 1921 are today regarded as an integral part of customary international law, since it is now a generally accepted rule of international law that trafficking has to be prevented and if possible eliminated using all available means. A close examination of a considerable number of international instruments in human rights law also implies that the relevant instruments have an important function in the consolidation of the principles of human rights law governing women and children.[42]

[42] For instance see the Convention on the Rights of the Child.

International Convention for the Suppression of the Traffic in Women of Full Age

Criminalization

The chief aim of the 1933 International Convention for the Suppression of the Traffic in Women of Full Age was to complete the provisions of the 1904, 1910, 1921 instruments relating to the prevention of the white slave traffic in women and children. With this intention, the Convention aimed to criminalize acts against women. A glance at the provisions of the earlier instruments and the Convention proves that it makes, more or less, similar provisions for the criminalization of trafficking against women who are the victims of sexual exploitation. Article 1 of the Convention reads that: "Whoever, in order to gratify the passions of another person, has procured, enticed or led away even with her consent, a woman or girl of full age for immoral purposes to be carried out in another country, shall be punished, notwithstanding that the various acts constituting the offence may have been committed in different countries. Attempted offences, and, within the legal limits, acts preparatory to the offences in question, shall also be punishable."

One problem of the above formulation is that the Convention does not give a precise definition of full age, only using the phrase "a woman or girl of full age". The Convention also does not provide a clear boundary between the term "women" and the term "girl of full age". Although, these are some of the problems of the Convention, they may be solved with reference to the provisions of the 1910 and 1921 Conventions governing white slave traffic.[43] Nevertheless, the Convention makes much more radical provisions compared with the earlier instruments with regard to the matter of criminalizing the trafficking of women brought from colonies. For instance, the 1904 agreement was very conservative concerning this matter and the states parties to that agreement reserved certain rights concerning their colonies, but this attitude was changed within the new document. According to it "For the purposes of the present Article, the term "country" includes the colonies and protectorates of the High Contracting Party concerned, as well as territories under his suzerainty and territories for which a mandate has been entrusted to him."[44] Although this change of attitude was merely stated and had no real practical impact, it helped in the creation of rules that could apply to all women and girls

---

[43] See the preceding sections.
[44] Article 1.

without any regard to the international legal personality of their states. It was with these types of developments that the international legal community was preparing itself to create rulings that could treat all women and girl children equally.

Legislation

Parties to the International Convention for the Suppression of the Traffic in Women of Full Age undertook to take the necessary measures within their national laws for the prevention of trafficking. They were required to ensure that the offences stated in the convention were punished in accordance with their gravity.[45] The Convention strove also for an effective policy of cooperation in order to fulfil its intentions. According to this policy:

> The High Contracting Parties undertake to communicate to each other in regard to any person of either sex who has committed or attempted to commit any of the offences referred to in the present Convention or in the Conventions of 1910 or 1921 on the Suppression of the Traffic in Women and Children, the various constituent acts of which were, or were to have been, accomplished in different countries, the following information (or similar information which it may be possible to supply under the laws and regulations of the country concerned):
> (a) Records of convictions, together with any useful and available information with regard to the offender, such as his civil status, description, finger-prints, photograph and police record, his methods of operation, etc.
> (b) Particulars of any measures of refusal of admission or of expulsion which may have been applied to him. These documents and information shall be sent direct and without delay to the authorities of the countries concerned in each particular case by the authorities named in Article 1 of the Agreement concluded in Paris on 18 May 1904 and, if possible, in all cases when the offence, conviction, refusal of admission or expulsion has been duly established.[46]

Thus, the Convention pulls together all of the information regarding a person who has, by one means or another, been convicted of the preparation or commission of the relevant acts of trafficking. These may also include measures of refusal of admission or of expulsion which may have been applied. With all these measures the Convention aims to

[45] Article 2.
[46] Article 3.

compile a proper record of those who have been engaged in the commission of the relevant offences. The Convention has therefore a policy of the internationalization of the registration of criminals with the sole purpose of creating effective control over offenders convicted for trafficking in women and children.

Disputes

The Convention listed the ways in which the contracting parties should resolve any dispute arising in the interpretation or application of its provisions. This policy of the Convention is based on any applicable treaties between the parties, diplomatic solutions, arbitral or judicial settlements, reference to the Permanent Court of International Justice and the pacific settlement of international disputes.[47] Several methods for resolving international disputes concerning the proper understanding of the language of the Convention imply the difficulties which arose in the practical implementation of its provisions.

Convention for the Suppression of the Traffic in Persons and of the Exploitation of the Prostitution of Others

Intention

The establishment of the United Nations Organization has opened a new chapter in the prevention and prohibition of the sex trafficking and prostitution of women and young girls. Since the earlier instruments criminalizing various forms of sexual exploitation of women and children were not effective, the United Nations took responsibility for the preparation of an international instrument which could cover all forms of sex trafficking. This is known as the Convention for the Suppression of the Traffic in Persons and of the Exploitation of the Prostitution of Others which was adopted by the General Assembly resolution 317(IV) in 1949. The Convention is in fact the development of the provisions of a 1937 draft proposal of the League of Nations relating to sex trafficking and its intention is also to "make feasible the conclusion of a convention consolidating" the position of the earlier instruments in the field. These are the International Agreement of 18 May 1904 for the Suppression of the White Slave Traffic, as amended by the Protocol approved by the General

[47] Article 4.

Assembly of the United Nations on 3 December 1948, International Convention of 4 May 1910 for the Suppression of the White Slave Traffic, as amended by the above-mentioned Protocol, International Convention of 30 September 1921 for the Suppression of the Traffic in Women and Children, as amended by the Protocol and approved by the General Assembly of the United Nations on 20 October 1947 and the International Convention of 11 October 1933 for the Suppression of the Traffic in Women of Full Age, as amended by the aforementioned Protocol. The Convention for the Suppression of the Traffic in Persons and of the Exploitation of the Prostitution of Others entered into force in 1951 and with its entrance has introduced many new rulings concerning the prohibition of sex trafficking in women and children.

Punishment

One of the most significant intentions of the Convention for the Suppression of the Traffic in Persons and of the Exploitation of the Prostitution of Others is to make the acts of sex trafficking in women punishable. For this reason it has taken the relevant words of the earlier international instruments into recognition while simplifying them into two divisions. It reads that the contracting parties "agree to punish any person who, to gratify the passions of another: (1) Procures, entices or leads away, for purposes of prostitution, another person, even with the consent of that person; (2) Exploits the prostitution of another person, even with the consent of that person."[48]

A comparative examination with the relevant provisions of the previous instruments as listed above implies the fact that the Convention does not, by contrast with the policy of those other instruments, put any weight on the consent of the victims. In fact, the Convention demonstrates that the term "consent" loses its legal validity when it comes to the question of sex trafficking and prostitution. Consequently, leading away a person, in one way or another, with the purpose of sexually exploiting or using that person for prostitution is by itself sufficient reason to be found criminally liable under the provisions of the Convention. This means that under criminal procedures for the prosecution of the accused, the claim that the victim had given consent to be employed by another person may be rejected entirely by the criminal court according to the circumstances of the case and the seriousness and gravity of the criminalization of sexual exploitation or prostitution.

---

[48] Article 1.

Knowledge

Knowledge appears to have a definite effect on the attribution of criminal responsibility to the accused. This can be seen from the examination of the relevant provisions of the Convention for the Suppression of the Traffic in Persons and of the Exploitation of the Prostitution of Others. States parties may thus punish a person who had knowledge of their involvement in criminal conduct. The punishment can therefore be applied to any person who "1) Keeps or manages, or knowingly finances or takes part in the financing of a brothel; (2) Knowingly lets or rents a building or other place or any part thereof for the purpose of the prostitution of others."[49] Accordingly, there are two main targets within the above provisions: these are the financing of a brothel, or permitting the use of a building for the purposes of prostitution. Both these acts denote the participation of the accused if it has been carried out with their prior knowledge. It is on this account that the Convention also makes clear that any attempt to commit or participate in committing the above mentioned crimes is also punishable.[50] But according to the Convention, participation should be limited to intentional participation in the commission of acts stated within its provisions, and also "to the extent permitted by domestic law, acts of participation shall be treated as separate offences whenever this is necessary to prevent impunity."[51] The term "impunity" was not entered into other instruments. This is the first time that the Convention has aimed to make clear that the policies of the preceding international instruments and its own do not permit any form of impunity from prosecution and punishment. Although, the Convention refers to intentional rather than unintentional participation, this does not mean that those who have been engaged in preparations for the offences by different means are practically permitted to escape prosecution by claiming that they had no intention of committing the crime.

Abolition and Disqualification

Parties to the Convention for the Suppression of the Traffic in Persons and of the Exploitation of the Prostitution of Others are also invited to take necessary measures for the abolition of any rule or provision which may permit the development of sex trafficking or sexual exploitation. According to the Convention, parties have agreed to "take all the

[49] Article 2.
[50] Article 3.
[51] Article 4.

necessary measures to repeal or abolish any existing law, regulation or administrative provision by virtue of which persons who engage in or are suspected of engaging in prostitution are subject either to special registration or to the possession of a special document or to any exceptional requirements for supervision or notification."[52] This aim of the legislator is also strengthened by other provisions which try to erect a boundary between those who have been convicted and other ordinary citizens. Consequently, a person who lives within the territory of one state and has previously been convicted in another state in connection with sex exploitation or sex trafficking as stated in the Convention, may have his earlier conviction taken into consideration for the purpose of a) "establishing recidivism" or b) "disqualifying the offender from the exercise of civil rights."[53] Although these two principles which are entered into the Convention are very significant for the possible commission of sex offences, they are rather controversial when it comes to questions of international human rights law. "Disqualifying the offender from the exercise of civil rights" may drive such persons towards the commission of further crimes and may consequently aid the development of criminality.

Extradition

The Convention for the Suppression of the Traffic in Persons and of the Exploitation of the Prostitution of Others, like the previous instruments applicable to the prostitution of women, attempts to punish all offenders and therefore puts a heavy weight on the institution of extradition. For this reason, the Convention chooses several policies of extradition. First of all, the Convention makes it clear that the offences listed in the provisions of the Convention should be regarded as extraditable offences within the provisions of any extradition treaty which has been signed between two or more states parties. It also makes it a conventional duty of states to include the relevant offences within the provisions of any future agreements as extraditable offences.[54] In cases where states parties do not make extradition conditional on the basis of the existence of an extradition treaty, they should make the offences within the Convention extraditable between themselves. In this case extradition should be granted with due regard to the legislation of the state requesting it.[55] The Convention further

[52]Article 6.
[53] Article 7.
[54] Article 8.
[55] Article 8.

reads that "where the extradition of nationals is not permitted by law, nationals who have returned to their own State after the commission abroad of any of the offences … shall be prosecuted in and punished by the courts of their own State."[56]

The Convention also clarifies that the above provisions should "not apply when the person charged with the offence has been tried in a foreign State and, if convicted, has served his sentence or had it remitted or reduced in conformity with the laws of that foreign State." Here the Convention focuses on the principle of *ne bis in idem* which constitutes one of the important principles of law and international criminal law. The intention of the principle is to prohibit double jeopardy.[57]

---

[56] Article 9.

[57] For the principle of *ne bis in idem* see J. Vervaele, "The Transnational *ne bis in idem* Principle in the EU: Mutual Recognition and Equivalent Protection of Human Rights", 1 *Utrecht Law Review* (2005), p.100. See also Chapter I.

CHAPTER SEVEN

STRENGTHENING THE PROHIBITION OF SEX TRAFFICKING IN CHILDREN

Introduction

The various international conventions for the protection of children have generally failed up until recent times. This failure is most tangible concerning sexual and labour exploitation of children.[1] Among the most grave and disturbing aspects of sex trafficking is its impact on children. As a matter of fact, children have always been one of the groups most vulnerable to exploitation in the world. Children have not only been used for various forms of sexual exploitation but also as a flexible source of forced labour including slavery. They are the only subjects of sex trafficking that cannot in any way express even insignificant forms of legal consent. In particular, this is of considerable importance in the case of children of a very young age, e.g., 5, who are sold for sexual exploitation and are abused by the owners or customers in any manner that fits their sexual interests. This means that the capacity for avoiding dangerous sexual encounters is very limited for a child victim of sexual exploitation compared with that of an adult woman who is also exploited. Therefore, the analysis of the sexual exploitation of children is much more difficult than it is in the case of women.

The systems of international criminal law and human rights law have for a long period of time been active in putting an end to the sexual exploitation of children. This may be examined within the provisions of a number of international documents which fall within both branches of law. The aim of most of these instruments has been to describe the position of children and their need for society's protection at different stages. Although in other sections of this book, the position of children has been dealt with in conjunction with other relevant matters, this chapter is

---

[1] Farhad Malekian, Kerstin Nordlöf, *Confessing the International Rights of Children* (2012). See also Farhad Malekian, Kerstin Nordlöf (eds),The Sovereignty of Children in Law (2012).

exclusively focused on the examination of the sex trafficking in children and its consideration within different international human rights instruments. Our purpose is to examine to what degree and level the provisions of international human rights law, humanitarian law or international criminal law consider the integrity of children and their age relating to the questions of various forms of sex trafficking or exploitation.

Geneva Declaration of the Rights of the Child

One of the earliest important instruments dealing with the position of children is the Geneva Declaration of the Rights of the Child of 1924. The Declaration was formulated in order to protect the inalienable rights of children from various forms of violation during times of peace or war. The declaration was adopted by the International Save the Children Union at Geneva on 23 February 1923 and was also later adopted by the League of Nations on 26 September 1924. The same Declaration was later re-approved in 1934. The Declaration recognized that "mankind owes to the Child the best that it has to give, declare and accept it as their duty that, beyond and above all considerations of race, nationality." It further set out five important principles regarding the position of children. These were:

> 1. The child must be given the means requisite for its normal development, both materially and spiritually.
> 2. The child that is hungry must be fed, the child that is sick must be helped, the child that is backward must be helped, the delinquent child must be reclaimed, and the orphan and the waif must be sheltered and succoured.
> 3. The child must be the first to receive relief in times of distress.
> 4. The child must be put in a position to earn a livelihood, and must be protected against every form of exploitation.
> 5. The child must be brought up in the consciousness that its talents must be devoted to the service of its fellow men.

These five principles of the Declaration all aim at the protection of the rights of children, not only on a national, but also on an international basis. In particular, section four of the Declaration emphasises that children "must be protected against every form of exploitation." The word "every form" refers not only to slavery, forced labour and forced displacement, but also to sex trafficking and sexual exploitation. Without doubt the aim of the declaration was to promote the position of children in an official document in order to protect them from any unlawful and unjustified conduct. However, one cannot deny the fact that the aims of the Declaration were very limited and did not take into consideration many rights for the protection of children. This weakness of the Declaration can be seen in the criminal activities Germany committed against children during the Second World. In any event the Declaration was an important initiative in the development of the rights of children concerning sexual exploitation and trafficking. The fulfilment of the idea of the protection of children became more possible with the creation of the United Nations Organization.

Declaration of the Rights of the Child

The establishment of the United Nations proved that some of the principles of international human rights law which were formulated into the Charter of the organization cannot be protected without their effective protection within different international instruments dealing directly with the matter of states' interests. Thus, the Declaration of the Rights of the Child was adopted by the United Nations General Assembly in 1959. The purpose was to remedy those shortcomings of the Declaration of Human Rights including the United Nations Charter. The Declaration was also adopted in order to improve upon the limited approach which was expressed by the Geneva Declaration of the Rights of Child in 1934. Although, both declarations from 1934 and 1959 have similar names, their principles, provisions and aims cannot at all be compared with one another. The former Declaration has very restricted and vaguely defined provisions while the latter is comparatively very broad and detailed in its provisions.

The General Assembly Declaration of the Rights of the Child was originally adopted by the Assembly in Resolution 1389 (XIV). As a whole, the Declaration consists of ten principles dealing with different aspects relevant for the protection of the rights of the child in different social contexts. One of the most important principles of the Declaration is the first one which aims to integrate, very briefly, the provisions of the 1948 Universal Declaration of Human Rights into this new Declaration. It provides that each child has a right to enjoy all the rights set forth within the Declaration of 1948. It further states that "Every child, without any exception whatsoever, shall be entitled to these rights, without distinction or discrimination on account of race, colour, sex, language, religion, political or other opinion, national or social origin, property, birth or other status, whether of himself or of his family." Similarly, the Declaration has in principle eight tried to secure the rights of children in peace and wartime. It states that "The child shall in all circumstances be among the first to receive protection and relief."

The most important part of the Declaration for the prohibition of various forms of exploitation of children is principle nine. It reads that "The child shall be protected against all forms of neglect, cruelty and exploitation. He shall not be the subject of traffic, in any form."[2] Principle nine consolidates some of the terms of general principles of law and customary law concerning the position of children. These are *a*) protection, *b*) neglect, *c)* cruelty, *d)* exploitation and *e)* trafficking. All these terms can be found within the provisions of many laws and even within the general principles of law that are generally accepted by almost all nations of the world. For instance, the word "cruelty" is used in the case of torture. The word "protection" is a generally accepted and recognized term for children within family relations. More crucially, several words such as "neglect" and "cruelty" are used in connection with the words "exploitation" and "trafficking". Principle nine has in fact taken into consideration both aspects of sex trafficking, which means that sex trafficking and exploitation for various purposes including sexual slavery are all equivalent to violations of the "protection" of the child.

The provisions of principle nine should also be read in conjunction with the provisions of principle eight. This is because principle eight clearly states that children should "in all circumstances" be among the first to receive various forms of protection. This may be interpreted as implying that when the legal authorities are in a position to help the victims of sex trafficking, priority should be given to children.[3] It may also be understood that when the legal authorities are formulating national legislative measures for the protection of victims and prohibition of sex trafficking, they should give first consideration to the protection of children.

One very serious problem regarding the ten principles within the Declaration is that they do not have the legal effect of law-making treaties and therefore do not create binding obligations on the members of the

[2] Furthermore, the Declaration within the same principle (9) read that "The child shall not be admitted to employment before an appropriate minimum age; he shall in no case be caused or permitted to engage in any occupation or employment which would prejudice his health or education, or interfere with his physical, mental or moral development."

[3] Principle 10 reads that "The child shall be protected from practices which may foster racial, religious and any other form of discrimination. He shall be brought up in a spirit of understanding, tolerance, friendship among peoples, peace and universal brotherhood, and in full consciousness that his energy and talents should be devoted to the service of his fellow men."

United Nations. Although it would have been much more practical to formulate the provisions of the Declaration into an international convention, this would have been impossible in 1959 when the world had to deal with many other matters during the Cold War. In any event, one cannot deny that the Declaration is one of the most important instruments governing the protection of children and prevention of the sexual exploitation of children or their trafficking. Moreover, one should not ignore the fact that the important functions and purposes of the Declaration increase its very legal validity within customary international human rights law and its application at an international level. Therefore, the Declaration must be seen as one of the significant instruments of *jus cogens* law and as consequently applicable to all states as part of peremptory norms that cannot be denied by any state. A major reason for the classification of the Declaration within *jus cogens* law is that respect for its ten principles is vital for the international community as a whole and the Declaration has the potential to assist in the maintenance of international justice and peace. For instance, one of the strong objections of the opponents of the Gaza war in 2008 was that the Israeli armed forces had violated these fundamental principles of humanity governing the protection of children during war and peace time.[4]

Convention on the Rights of the Child

Overview

The shortcomings of the various international human rights instruments relating to the consideration of the rights of children and the need for their consolidation into a single international legal instrument which could deal solely with questions of children and their protection have been tangible since the establishment of the United Nations. In fact, the international legal and political community were unable to deal adequately with the questions of the protection of children up until recent times. This was for several reasons such as: *a)* the unwillingness of the great political powers in the world, *b)* the military need of many nations to use children in times of war, *c)* the interests of most states in giving priority to other serious questions of discrimination such as apartheid in South Africa and *d)* the vulnerable position of females in peace and wartime. The formulation of the Convention on the Rights of the Child became much more pressing

[4] See Farhad Malekian, 'Judging International Criminal Justice in the Occupied Territories',12 *International Criminal Law Review* (2012) 827–869.

when the European states became aware that sex trafficking in children was rapidly increasing in Europe and their jurisdictions were becoming some of the biggest markets in the world. In particular, the use of children in wartime for several purposes including sexual exploitation, and infringement of the rights of children by the conflicting parties, finally came together as central reasons for the creation of the Convention on the Rights of the Child in 1989.

It must be asserted that the Convention is one of the most important legal documents applicable to the rights of children in the world. It aims at the protection of the rights of children from various forms of harm including sexual abuse, slavery, trafficking, exploitation, forced labour, violations of integrity and any other social, economic and juridical or political violence.[5] It came into force in order to gain the consent of the majority of states of the world for a single convention. This was because many states did not participate in the provisions of other international conventions governing human rights law and had either not signed or ratified conventions which in one way or another limited their sovereign independence. Consequently, the Convention came into force to create unanimity and a common understanding of certain national and international matters within the provisions of a single instrument. The Convention also has two protocols. One of the significant works of the Convention is the establishment of the Committee on the Rights of the Child with the purpose of examining and investigating matters relevant to the position of children. The number of experts in the Committee has been increased from ten to eighteen. This was due to an amendment which came into force on 18 November 2002.

Characterization

The Convention on the Rights of the Child has formulated a number of useful principles or provisions within its content. These principles or provisions are taken from many sources of the system of international law and have long been accepted within that system. Some of these principles or provisions can also be found within the content of the civil legislation of states parties or as general principles of law. Furthermore, the origins for some provisions of the Convention may be seen within the provisions of the international humanitarian law of armed conflict such as the

---

[5] The convention was adopted and opened for signature, ratification and accession by General Assembly Resolution 44/25 of 20 November 1989. It entered into force on 2 September 1990.

provisions of the Geneva Conventions of 1949 or its additional Protocol of 1977. Yet many of these provisions or principles have been dealt with within certain declarations of the Red Cross governing the protection of civilians. Similarly, the provisions of the Universal Declaration of Human Rights, many of the conventions applicable to the abolition of slavery, prostitution and sex trafficking as well as conventions of the International Labour Organization have protected the rights of children in certain situations. At a similar level are the conventions and resolutions dealing with apartheid, racial discrimination and torture.[6]

Whilst we do not deny that many of the provisions of the Convention on the Rights of the Child are new, many of its principles and provisions merely reflect and restate the earlier provisions of the system of international law. These and many other reasons that have been discussed in other sections prove that the principles of the Convention can be considered as an integral part of the international law of *jus cogens*, and as consequently having the character of obligation *erga omnes*. In other words, because of their important function and value for the protection of fundamental principles of the international community as a whole, they are to be implemented by all states regardless of their signature or ratification.

Definition

The earlier instruments have almost no provisions regarding the criteria for being recognized as a child. They have mostly taken a general policy regarding the protection of the child. This has made the policy of the earlier instruments very difficult to apply. In particular, this problem was tangible when under certain circumstances the child came under civil or criminal procedures or was forced to witness in certain cases. Most seriously, states could employ children for various purposes and claim that they were no longer children under their legislation. This means that a legal age was not clearly set out within international conventions and children could be used for prostitution, slavery, forced labour, and also in the course of armed conflicts.

From the beginning, the Convention on the Rights of the Child has aimed to solve this problem by setting an age limit for the legal definition of childhood. For this reason it says that for the aims of the provisions of the Convention, "a child means every human being below the age of eighteen years unless under the law applicable to the child, majority is

---

[6] See Farhad Malekian, *Documents on the Principles of International Human Rights* (2007).

attained earlier."[7] Consequently, the legal age of adulthood is set at eighteen and anyone younger is considered to enjoy the statutes applicable to the protection of children. However, one problem of the definition of a child within the Convention on the Rights of the Child is that it permits the contracting parties to have different age limits for the recognition of child status. In other words, the provision stating "unless under the law applicable to the child, majority is attained earlier" is rather broad and opens a window for the parties to escape from many of their obligations under the provisions of the Convention. The relevant provision is much more problematic when it comes to the identification of the position of children concerning sexual exploitation. A party to the Convention on the Rights of the Child may have different domestic provisions compared with the provisions of the instruments applicable to trafficking. This means that sexual exploitation of a child or sex trafficking of persons under the age of eighteen may be allowed within the legislation of the relevant party while not permitted by that of another party. Their respective laws may simply adopt different ages of majority which is permissible according to the provisions of the Convention.

Protection

The Convention on the Rights of the Child has provided a range of provisions protecting the rights of children in the world. They are applicable to any child and there is no difference in their applicability between one child and another child. It is in fact one of the basic duties of the parties to recognize the principle of equality between children. States parties are thus responsible for ensuring that within their jurisdiction equality is established for children "without discrimination of any kind, irrespective of the child's or his or her parent's or legal guardian's race, colour, sex, language, religion, political or other opinion, national, ethnic or social origin, property, disability, birth or other status."[8] These provisions of the Convention are strengthened by other provisions in order that the rights of the child are not prejudiced.[9]

With due regard to the above fundamental provisions, the Convention aims at the consolidation of the rights of the child in different social relations. These are rights such as rights to life, public or private social services, and protection in civil or criminal courts. Parties to the

---

[7] Article 1.
[8] Article 2 (1).
[9] Article 2 (2).

Convention have also ensured that a child shall not be separated from his or her parents against their will. This is however with the reservation that the separation may be possible only if it is in the best interests of the child. The development of the child from various points of view is also one of the most important aims of the Convention. In any event, parties have guaranteed that no child shall be subjected to arbitrary or unlawful interference with his or her privacy. This includes also her or his family and other important social matters.

Due to the provisions of the Convention, the whole integrity of the child is one of the central questions of her/his protection. It is for this reason that the Convention aims at the prevention and elimination of all activities which are against the rights of the child, such as the illicit transfer of children from one place to another and all types of mistreatment of children. The protections which are provided under the Convention may therefore be categorized under juridical, social, cultural, educational, and economic factors.

Exploitation

The subject of the exploitation of children has received most serious consideration in the Convention on the Rights of the Child. The subject became one of the important issues of the meetings of the representatives of states. It opened various discussions and became a strong reason for the formulation of a number of useful provisions for the prevention and, if possible, for the elimination of different forms of exploitation. One of the great achievements of the Convention is its provision to protect children from any unlawful transportation, which is against the basic rights of the child. For this reason, the contracting parties to the Convention are under a conventional duty to promote bilateral or multilateral treaties in order to have the necessary tools to combat the illicit transfer and non-return of children abroad.

According to the Convention any maltreatment of the child should be taken seriously into consideration by the legal authorities of states. The parties are under conventional obligation to take certain measures for the protection of children from any form of exploitation including negligence. According to the relevant provisions, states should take and apply "appropriate legislative, administrative, social and educational measures to protect the child from all forms of physical or mental violence, injury or abuse, neglect or negligent treatment, maltreatment or exploitation, including sexual abuse, while in the care of parent(s), legal guardian(s) or any other person who has the care of the child."[10] The foregoing provisions identify several general principles of law prevailing within the legislation of most states of the world. In fact, the legislators of the Convention have taken certain common provisions of criminal law which are applicable when the rights of adults have been violated. Their purpose is to emphasise the high value of the integrity of children and their protection within the legislation of states. That is why the legislator recognises certain conducts as violations of the rights of the child and as infractions of her/his integrity according to the general inspiration and motivation of the Convention. The legislator sets out the duties of states to take different appropriate measures including legislative provisions. Thus, it has clearly seen maltreatment or exploitation, including sexual abuse of a child, as serious infringements of her/his rights. Comparatively, all the above three terms are recognized as serious violations if they are committed against persons other than children.[11] That is why the Convention has taken the opportunity to bring to the recognition of the public that the child is entitled to enjoy equivalent protection to that enjoyed by adults.

The Convention has also foreseen the exploitation of the child, not only for sexual reasons, but also, through forced labour or any other maltreatment. According to it:

> 1. States Parties recognize the right of the child to be protected from economic exploitation and from performing any work that is likely to be hazardous or to interfere with the child's education, or to be harmful to the child's health or physical, mental, spiritual, moral or social development.
> 2. States Parties shall take legislative, administrative, social and educational measures to ensure the implementation of the present article. To this end, and having regard to the relevant provisions of other international instruments, States Parties shall in particular: (a) Provide for a minimum age or minimum ages for admission to employment;

[10] Article 19 (1).

[11] The Convention has further stated that "Such protective measures should, as appropriate, include effective procedures for the establishment of social programmes to provide necessary support for the child and for those who have the care of the child, as well as for other forms of prevention and for identification, reporting, referral, investigation, treatment and follow-up of instances of child maltreatment described heretofore, and, as appropriate, for judicial involvement."[11] Article 19 (2).

> (b) Provide for appropriate regulation of the hours and conditions of employment;
> (c) Provide for appropriate penalties or other sanctions to ensure the effective enforcement of the present article.[12]

Due to the above provisions, parties should prevent economic exploitation of the child and also any form of engagement in any work which may, by one means or another, prejudice the position of the child. The provisions in the above strongly emphasise the importance of the protection of the integrity of the child and the prevention of children from performing sexual services as these constitute violations of their physical and psychological well being.[13]

The most significant section of the Convention relating to the prohibition of sexual exploitation, sex trafficking, sexual abuse and sex slavery of the child is formulated in Article 34. It reads that:

> States Parties undertake to protect the child from all forms of sexual exploitation and sexual abuse. For these purposes, States Parties shall in particular take all appropriate national, bilateral and multilateral measures to prevent:
> (a) The inducement or coercion of a child to engage in any unlawful sexual activity;
> (b) The exploitative use of children in prostitution or other unlawful sexual practices;
> (c) The exploitative use of children in pornographic performances and materials.

The content of the article demonstrates several factors concerning the prevention and elimination of the sex trafficking of children. In fact, it focuses on different concepts of sexual abuse of the child. These include any form of sexual activity, sexual exploitation for prostitution and exploitation for pornography. All these categories denote without doubt the immorality and illegality of the abuse of children through sexual

[12] Article 32.

[13] The Convention even protects children from other forms of trafficking, for example, it reads that "States Parties shall take all appropriate measures, including legislative, administrative, social and educational measures, to protect children from the illicit use of narcotic drugs and psychotropic substances as defined in the relevant international treaties, and to prevent the use of children in the illicit production and trafficking of such substances." Article 33.

acts.[14]The Convention makes it also clear that the exploitative use of children for the purposes of pornography or prostitution is paradigmatic of the abuse of children. That is why the Convention refers to "other unlawful sexual practices" with the purpose of ensuring its scope of applicability stretches to the identification of criminal conducts against the child victim. In fact, the Convention with the words "other unlawful sexual practices" opens the door for the criminalization of any act which by one means or another aims at the sexual exploitation of children, such as child pornography on the internet, sexual performance by a child, or obscene or any other sexual images of children. But what constitutes pornographic performances and materials is obviously based upon sufficient evidence.

Interchangeable Terms

The Convention on the Rights of the Child seems to use certain terms concerning the sexual protection of children interchangeably with one another. This can be seen from the terms "exploitation", "traffic", "sexual abuse" and not least "maltreatment". All of these terms focus on the protection of children and without doubt on the prevention of certain conducts. Thus, the term "traffic in children" may fall within all of these terminological divisions and, according to the circumstances of the case and its level of development, may be employed where the terms "sexual abuse" or "sexual exploitation" are also used. This means that the use of a term within one article may not preclude its existence in another article if it has not been used. For instance, Article 35 of the Convention reads that "States Parties shall take all appropriate national, bilateral and multilateral measures to prevent the abduction of, the sale of or traffic in children for any purpose or in any form." Here the provisions of the article with the use of the phrase "the sale of or traffic in children for any purpose or in any form," apply to the unlawful exploitation of children and equally to their unlawful sexual abuse, including through sexual exploitation, sex trafficking and sex slavery.

On the one hand, the above interpretation can be supported by the examination of the provisions of Article 36. It reads that the contracting parties "shall protect the child against all other forms of exploitation prejudicial to any aspects of the child's welfare." Similarly, the provisions

---

[14] These three basic categories of the sexual abuse of children have been entered more forcibly and in greater detail into the provisions of a protocol which was some years later added to the body of the original Convention.

of Article 39 of the Convention emphasise the phrase “any form of … exploitation, or abuse.” This means that the conclusion of the article is that the terms “sexual abuse”, “sexual exploitation” or “traffic in children”, for example, are all of similar nature. On the other hand, the content of the Convention does not give a clear definition of the above terms. It seems that the Convention leaves the hands of the administrators of justice and the court authorities rather free concerning the use of different terminologies and their exchangeability. Consequently, a considerable degree of caution must be exercised in the case of the identification of sexual offences. Naturally, the states parties are obliged not to use certain legal terminologies which may prejudice the scope and applicability of the provisions of the Convention. In addition, they must not set aside that the whole purpose of the Convention is to guarantee the basic rights of children with an equitable and reasonable form of understanding of the exploitation issues affecting children.

Problematic Reservations

The Convention on the Rights of the Child which is considered to be one of the most significant conventions governing the rights of children and their protection from various forms of sexual exploitation has been undermined because of the reservations made to its basic principles. This can particularly be examined in the reservations and interpretative declarations made at the time of ratification. Reservations to the convention may be divided into three categories. These are those which are made by the Holy See, Islamic cultures, and other states.

Reservations made by the first two categories are very controversial. They may seriously affect the object and purpose of the Convention on the Rights of the Child. This does not necessarily mean that reservations or declarations made by other states parties upon signature or ratification do not reduce the legal validity of the provisions of the convention and its purposes.

The reservation made by the Holy See ensures that the provisions of the Church should not be ignored. In other words, it gives priority to the Catholic Church’s Canon Law which is in origin incomputable with the original purposes of the Convention. The reservation made by the Holy See clarifies that:

a) [The Holy See] interprets the phrase "Family planning education and services" in article 24.2, to mean only those methods of family planning which it considers morally acceptable, that is, the natural methods of family planning.

b) [The Holy See] interprets the articles of the Convention in a way which safeguards the primary and inalienable rights of parents, in particular insofar as these rights concern education (articles 13 and 28), religion (article 14), association with others (article 15) and privacy (article 16).
c) [The Holy See declares] that the application of the Convention be compatible in practice with the particular nature of the Vatican City State and of the sources of its objective law (art. 1, Law of 7 June 1929, nr. 11) and, in consideration of its limited extent, with its legislation in the matters of citizenship, access and residence.[15]

Similar views to the above have been expressed by Islamic states. According to the reservations made upon ratification, Islamic law has priority over the provisions of the Convention on the Rights of the Child. This means that Islamic provisions will be enforced by the Islamic authorities wherever they seem absolutely necessary. For instance, the government of Afghanistan "reserves the right to express, upon ratifying the Convention, reservations on all provisions of the Convention that are incompatible with the laws of Islamic *Shari'a* and the local legislation in effect." Similarly, the Algerian government stated that children's rights are based originally on Islamic religion and morality. According to the government of Pakistan, the elements of the Convention should be "interpreted in the light of the principles of Islamic laws and values." Along the same lines but more specific are the reservations made by the governments of Indonesia and Iran. According to the former:

> The 1945 Constitution of the Republic of Indonesia guarantees the fundamental rights of the child irrespective of their sex, ethnicity or race. The Constitution prescribes those rights to be implemented by national laws and regulations. The ratification of the Convention on the Rights of the Child by the Republic of Indonesia does not imply the acceptance of obligations going beyond the Constitutional limits nor the acceptance of any obligation to introduce any right beyond those prescribed under the Constitution.

According to the latter:

> The Islamic Republic of Iran is making reservation to the articles and provisions which may be contrary to the Islamic *Shariah*, and preserves the right to make such particular declaration, upon its ratification. The Government of the Islamic Republic of Iran reserves the right not to apply

[15] Multilateral Treaties deposited with the Secretary-General, Status as at 31 December 1991, United Nations, New York, 1992, pp.200-201.

any provisions or articles of the Convention that are incompatible with Islamic Laws and the international legislation in effect."

The reservation by the government of the Maldives made it clear that the list of the rights of children in the Convention on the Rights of the Child has to follow the provisions of Islamic law and custom. According to the reservation:

1) Since the Islamic *Shariah* is one of the fundamental sources of Maldivian Law and since Islamic *Shariah* does not include the system of adoption among the ways and means for the protection and care of children contained in *Shariah*, the Government of the Republic of Maldives expresses its reservation with respect to all the clauses and provisions relating to adoption in the said Convention on the Rights of the Child.
2) The Government of the Republic of Maldives expresses its reservation to paragraph 1 of article 14 of the said Convention on the Rights of the Child, since the Constitution and the Laws of the Republic of Maldives stipulate that all Maldivians should be Muslims.

Other Islamic states made serious limitations to the purposes of the Convention on the Rights of the Child. These included Iraq, Indonesia, Jordan, Kuwait, Malaysia, Mauritania, Morocco, Qatar, Oman, Saudi Arabia, Syria, and United Arab Emirates.

However most of the reservations were objected to by other countries. The reservation made by Iran was, for instance, objected to by the government of Ireland. It says that the "reservation poses difficulties for the States Parties to the Convention in identifying the provisions of the Convention which the Islamic Government of Iran does not intend to apply and consequently makes it difficult for States Parties to the Convention to determine the extent of their treaty relations with the reserving State." With regard to the reservations or declarations made by other states upon signature or ratification, the government of Norway made it clear that many of the states parties had already undermined the basis of international treaty law and the aims and purposes of the Convention on the Rights of the Child. With regard to the declaration made by Qatar upon ratification, the Norwegian government was of the view that the reservation "due to its unlimited scope and undefined character, is inadmissible under international law." According to Norway, similar problems undermining the provisions of the Convention existed in the Malaysian's reservation. The objection considered that the very broad scope of the reservation was incompatible with the object and purpose of the Convention, and that the monitoring system created under it was not optional. Therefore, it went further and clarified that the reservations to articles 44 and 45 were not permissible.

Alongside all this, the Vienna Declaration and Programme of Action in a section concerning Increased Coordination on Human Rights within the United Nations System calls upon states to withdraw their reservations to human rights conventions. It specifically asks that:

> 5. The World Conference on Human Rights encourages States to consider limiting the extent of any reservations they lodge to international human rights instruments, formulate any reservations as precisely and narrowly as possible, ensure that none is incompatible with the object and purpose of the relevant treaty and regularly review any reservations with a view to withdrawing them.[16]

The Vienna Declaration goes further and, with reference to the significant value of the Convention on the Rights of the Child and the duties of states not to reduce the function of the convention, emphasises that:

> 26. The World Conference on Human Rights welcomes the progress made in the codification of human rights instruments, which is a dynamic and evolving process, and urges the universal ratification of human rights treaties. All States are encouraged to accede to these international instruments; all States are encouraged to avoid, as far as possible, the resort to reservations.[17]

Despite the many discussions and statements by the United Nations bodies for the proper implementation of the Convention on the Rights of the Child, the provisions of the convention are not respected or are violated by many of the states parties.[18] This means different forms of abuse and exploitation of children are carried out and the merit of the convention for the sexual protection of children has been reduced effectively.

Inadequacy

The provisions of the Convention on the Rights of the Child are without doubt the integration of the provisions of a number of international

---

[16] Vienna Declaration and Programme of Action, U.N. Doc. A/CONF.157/24 ch. III (1993), Pt. I, (1994), *reprinted in* 14 Human Rights Law Journal,. 352, 357.

[17] Ibid., p. 356.

[18] William A. Schabas., 'Reservations to the Convention on the Rights of the Child', *Human Rights Quarterly* 18.2 (1996), pp. 472-491.

documents which have by one means or another developed the concept of the protection of children. They are also the development of general principles of law, customary rules and the basic requirements of the contemporary situation. Although, the Convention has great ambitions concerning the protection of children, the contemporary position of many children in the world as the victims of sex trafficking, diminishes its enforcement value. This shortcoming of the Convention and the need for sanctions to enforce its content are developed within other international documents of a similar type. Clear examples of documents in the same category are the Optional Protocol to the Convention on the Rights of the Child on the Sale of Children, Child Prostitution and Child Pornography, 2000, the Protocol to Prevent, Suppress and Punish Trafficking in Persons, Especially Women and Children, Supplementing the United Nations Convention Against Transnational Organized Crime, 2001 and the Optional Protocol to the Convention on the Rights of the Child on Communications Procedure, 2011.[19]

Optional Protocol to the Convention on the Rights of the Child on the Sale of Children, Child Prostitution and Child Pornography

Overview

Since the provisions of the Convention on the Rights of the Child were not specific concerning sex trafficking in children, the Optional Protocol to the Convention on the Rights of the Child on the Sale of Children, Child Prostitution and Child Pornography was adopted in 2000.[20] The Optional Protocol is also the product of the International Conference on Combating Child Pornography on the Internet, held in Vienna in 1999. In the opinion of the participants of the Conference, there was a desperate need for the criminalization of child pornography. Therefore, the Optional Protocol has promoted many of the provisions of the Convention on the Rights of the Child and created many rules for the enforcement of the provisions of international conventions applicable to the prohibition of child trafficking

[19] G.A. res. 55/25, annex II, 55 U.N. GAOR Supp. (No. 49) at 60, U.N. Doc. A/45/49 (Vol. I) (2001). See also General Assembly Resolution 66/138 of 19 December 2011.

[20] General Assembly Resolution A/RES/54/263 of 25 May 2000. It entered into force on 18 January 2002.

or sexual exploitation of children. The optional protocol has promoted certain provisions for the enforcement of international law through different channels such as jurisdictional factors and assistance in the extradition of perpetrators of acts against children including all types of sexual exploitation.

The Optional Protocol increases also the level of mutual assistance in the investigation of criminals, and in the seizure and confiscation of assets. The three international instruments, namely, the Optional Protocol, Convention on the Rights of the Child and the Optional Protocol on the Involvement of Children in Armed Conflict are integrally related to one another and present similar provisions on different aspects of the protection of children. The provisions of these three agreements must also be given priority in all relevant situations when dealing with the questions of the basic rights of children whether in war or peacetime.

Criminalization

The Optional Protocol to the Convention on the Rights of the Child on the Sale of Children, Child Prostitution and Child Pornography has clearly criminalized a considerable number of acts which violate the rights of children and their legal status. Thus, the criminalization of certain acts constitutes one of the great achievements in the provisions of the Optional Protocol. The Protocol focuses on the rapid development of child pornography on the internet and its danger for the integrity of children. Thus, it has a policy of criminalization of the production, intentional possession, transmission, importation, distribution, exportation and advertising of child pornography. According to Article 1 of the Optional Protocol, "States Parties shall prohibit the sale of children, child prostitution and child pornography as provided for by the present Protocol." For this purpose it defines three important terms within the provisions of its content. These are "sale of children", "child prostitution" and "child pornography". They are defined with the following words:

(a) Sale of children means any act or transaction whereby a child is transferred by any person or group of persons to another for remuneration or any other consideration;
(b) Child prostitution means the use of a child in sexual activities for remuneration or any other form of consideration;
(c) Child pornography means any representation, by whatever means, of a child engaged in real or simulated explicit sexual activities or any

representation of the sexual parts of a child for primarily sexual purposes.[21]

It is in fact the first time that these three terms have been defined within an international criminal agreement. All three terms, "sale of children", "child prostitution" and "child pornography" denote, by one means or another, the exploitation of children for sexual purposes. All three terms are interrelated and have similar aims with the difference that they apply to special circumstances regarding the violations of national and international laws for the protection of children.

Punishment

One of the truly significant principles of the Optional Protocol to the Convention on the Rights of the Child on the Sale of Children, Child Prostitution and Child Pornography is its strong insistence on the punishment of those who have committed the said crimes within its provisions. This aim of the Optional Protocol also helps in the enforcement of the other provisions of other international conventions such as the Convention on the Rights of the Child.

The Optional Protocol obliges all parties to criminalize and take penal measures against the "sale of children", "child prostitution" and "child pornography". The Optional Protocol clearly states that it is the duty of the states parties to ensure that as a minimum, certain acts are entered into their penal legislations. The obligations of the states parties apply regardless of whether such offences are committed in domestic relations, transnational actions, with individual initiation or on an organized basis. The parties should therefore react:

(a) In the context of sale of children as defined in article 2:
(i) Offering, delivering or accepting, by whatever means, a child for the purpose of:
a. Sexual exploitation of the child;
b. Transfer of organs of the child for profit;
c. Engagement of the child in forced labour;
(ii) Improperly inducing consent, as an intermediary, for the adoption of a child in violation of applicable international legal instruments on adoption;
(b) Offering, obtaining, procuring or providing a child for child prostitution, as defined in article 2;

[21] Article 2.

(c) Producing, distributing, disseminating, importing, exporting, offering, selling or possessing for the above purposes child pornography as defined in article 2.[22]

The Protocol has also criminalized other acts which have been committed in connection with the sale of children, child prostitution and child pornography or other acts as listed in the above. For this reason, subject to the provisions of the domestic legislation of states, similar provisions should be applied to any attempt to commit any of the said acts and to complicity or participation in these offences. Consequently, the Optional Protocol recognizes that a) attempt to commit; b) complicity in and c) participation in the above acts cannot be a reason to escape from criminal jurisdiction. Thus, the conditions for the prosecution and punishment of the criminals are not just the completion of the abovementioned offences. Any person may be found criminally responsible, even though the acts of sale or prostitution were not accomplished or were not successful for one reason or another. States parties are under an obligation to ensure that all such acts are punishable under their laws.[23] To this end the Optional Protocol states that all offences within its provisions shall be punishable by appropriate penalties that take into account the degree and level of the criminal conduct.[24]

Other important provisions of the Optional Protocol relate to the punishment of legal persons. Consequently, the criminal justice and punishment system used in the Optional Protocol has two purposes. One concerns the punishment of physical persons and the other concerns the punishment of legal persons.[25] Through this policy the Optional Protocol makes clear that all entities, institutions, organizations or any other collective body may also be brought under the jurisdiction of the relevant state party for prosecution and punishment. Therefore, depending on "the provisions of its national law, each State Party shall take measures, where appropriate, to establish the liability of legal persons for offences established in paragraph 1 of the present article. Subject to the legal principles of the State Party, such liability of legal persons may be

---

[22] Article 3 (1).
[23] Article 3 (2).
[24] Article 3 (3).
[25] The protocol has even stated that state parties "shall take all appropriate legal and administrative measures to ensure that all persons involved in the adoption of a child act in conformity with applicable international legal instruments." Article 3 (5).

criminal, civil or administrative."[26] This provision of the Optional Protocol is very important based on the fact that most activities concerning sex trafficking, particularly of children, are carried out under the supervision of legal persons. Of course, the liability of legal persons may vary due to the degree and level of its participation in the preparation and commission of the criminal acts. Thus, the liability of the legal person as it is stated in the above may be of different degrees.[27]

Jurisdiction

It has been one of the aims of the international conventions relating to the protection of children to establish effective jurisdiction over the perpetrators of sex trafficking or sexual exploitation of children. But other earlier international instruments are very cautious about this matter and have not substantively dealt with the question. This question was taken up in the international conference concerning the formulation of the Optional Protocol and finally entered into its provisions.

According to the Optional Protocol, states parties are under an obligation to establish their jurisdiction over the offences with consideration of its provisions.[28] Thus, a party may establish its jurisdiction when the offences are committed a) in its territory, b) on board a ship or c) an aircraft registered within its laws. Each state party can therefore create its jurisdiction over the offences mentioned in Article 3 (1) according to one of the following principles: *i)* when the alleged offender is a national of the relevant state or a person who has his habitual residence in its territory, or *ii)* when the victim is a national of that State.[29] This means that jurisdiction is essentially based on the two well-known traditional principles of territoriality and protection.

It is also the responsibility of the state party to establish its jurisdiction over offences when the offender is in its territory and it does not for one reason or another intend to extradite the alleged offender to another party based on the fact that she/he is one of its nationals.[30] Moreover, the Optional Protocol makes clear that without prejudice to its provisions governing the exercise of the jurisdiction of the state over alleged

[26] Article 3.
[27] Article 3 (4).
[28] Article 4 (1).
[29] Article 4 (2).
[30] Article 4 (3).

offenders, the state can exercise any criminal jurisdiction in accordance with its national criminal provisions.[31]

Extradition

One of the most important questions in the field of criminal law is the question of the extradition of criminals. This question has been developed within the framework of international criminal law and has become one of the most significant subjects of the law. The term "extradition" means in general to return criminals to the state which has asked for their extradition. The purpose of extradition is not necessarily to punish the extradited persons but to examine the whole case under the judicial machinery of the requesting state. This is in order to find out whether she/he has, by one means or another, participated in, committed, attempted, planned, guided or assisted in the commission of the crime. The extradited person may be cleared of all accusations or may be found guilty of the commission of the crime and therefore as bearing criminal responsibility for the criminal conduct.

Although the question of extradition constitutes one of the essential questions of criminal jurisdiction and justice, a state may not, in certain circumstances, wish to return the criminals to the requesting state and this may create a serious jurisdictional conflict between both sides. Yet the question may be even more complex when there are a number of states which assume, due to the provisions of their internal criminal legislations, the right of exercising jurisdiction over the accused. Thus, the host state may have to examine the application of several requesting states for the prosecution and punishment of the alleged offender. Thus the chief purpose of the extraction of accused persons should be the exercise of justice.[32]

The question of extradition is in particular very important in the case of sex trafficking and much more essential when we are dealing with cases

---

[31] Article 4 (4).

[32] However, it must be stated that there are other reasons for the extradition of accused persons. For instance, a state may ask for the extradition of certain persons, not necessarily for the purpose of prosecution and punishment, but in order to put a stop to the prosecution and punishment of relevant persons. This is when the requesting states do not wish their nationals to be prosecuted in another state. It may also be based on the fact that certain persons have a very important function within the political system of the state and that is why the state wishes to prevent any form of external jurisdiction over them. Thus, an application for the extradition of accused persons may have legal or political purposes.

relating to sex trafficking of children and their sexual exploitation. This serious question has also been taken into consideration within the provisions of the Optional Protocol to the Convention on the Rights of the Child on the Sale of Children, Child Prostitution and Child Pornography. According to it, all the crimes listed in its Article 3 are extraditable. This means that states may not adopt other measures which may make the extradition of criminals impossible. Thus, the crimes listed in the Optional Protocol are extraditable offences in any extradition treaty existing between the contracting parties. They should also be extraditable offences in every extradition agreement which may subsequently be ratified between the states parties to the protocol.[33] The remaining conditions of the Optional Protocol try to secure the principle of the prosecution and punishment of sex trafficking in children in situations in which the extradition of the accused person may face some difficulties. According to it:

2. If a State Party that makes extradition conditional on the existence of a treaty receives a request for extradition from another State Party with which it has no extradition treaty, it may consider the present Protocol to be a legal basis for extradition in respect of such offences. Extradition shall be subject to the conditions provided by the law of the requested State.
3. States Parties that do not make extradition conditional on the existence of a treaty shall recognize such offences as extraditable offences between themselves subject to the conditions provided by the law of the requested State.
4. Such offences shall be treated, for the purpose of extradition between States Parties, as if they had been committed not only in the place in which they occurred but also in the territories of the States required to establish their jurisdiction in accordance with article 4.
5. If an extradition request is made with respect to an offence described in article 3, paragraph 1, and the requested State Party does not or will not extradite on the basis of the nationality of the offender, that State shall take suitable measures to submit the case to its competent authorities for the purpose of prosecution.[34]

The Optional Protocol thus provides different alternatives for the extradition of criminals. This may depend on the circumstances of the case and the conditions of the law of the state in which the criminal is arrested. In any event, in order to punish the perpetrators of the sexual exploitation

---

[33] Article 5 (1).
[34] Article 5.

of children, such as their sale, prostitution or pornography, the Optional Protocol has insisted that its provisions should be regarded by the parties as grounds for extradition even if such provisions do not exist between the contracting parties. The purpose is here to secure the trial of the accused in situations in which the contracting states do not have a treaty of extradition.

Prevention of Impunity

Criminal cases can get very complicated when there is no treaty of extradition between the contracting parties. In particular, this question is very serious in the case of sex trafficking in children. This is because the crime is more often organized across several states and this makes the extradition of the accused persons very difficult and problematic. A fundamental problem is that several states may have different laws according to their national interests and these interests may not always overlap with the interests of other states. Furthermore, the provisions of some laws may in certain situations permit impunity and thus the accused may not be brought before an appropriate criminal jurisdiction. While these conflicts of legislation may not be tangible between most European states, they may be more substantial between the provisions of other states of the world.

The central aim of the Optional Protocol to the Convention on the Rights of the Child on the Sale of Children, Child Prostitution and Child Pornography is to bring the accused under criminal jurisdiction in order to prevent impunity, whether due to the provisions of the legislation of the host state or due to the weakness of the criminal justice system or its corruption. For this reason, the policy of the Optional Protocol is to encourage the contracting parties to assist one another in the matter of prosecution, jurisdiction and punishment of the accused whenever there is no treaty of extradition or there are some problems in the application of the law governing sex trafficking in children due to the legislation of one of the conflicting states.

The Optional Protocol therefore has various suggestions concerning the proper application of its provisions and the confiscation of the proceeds of crime.[35] The contracting parties are thus obliged to cooperate in the following matters.[36] These are

---

[35] Article 7 of the Optional Protocol has focused on the confiscation of all forms of material which have been relevant in the course of the commission of the crime. It reads that "States Parties shall, subject to the provisions of their national law: (a) Take measures to provide for the seizure and confiscation, as appropriate, of: (i)

a) Assistance in connection with investigations necessary for the establishment of the truth.

b) Assistance in the case of criminal proceedings constitutes one of the significant aims of the Optional Protocol when the case is already under practical development in their courts.

c) Assistance in the case of extradition proceedings is also considered an important element for the matter of prosecution.

d) The contracting parties should also give assistance to one another in order to obtain evidence at their disposal which is essential for the proceedings of the case.

e) Assistance between the contracting parties should be based on conformity with any relevant treaty in force.

f) The principle of mutual assistance in the implementation of the arrangements between parties is also one of the significant aims of the Protocol in order to bring the accused person under criminal jurisdiction.

g) Parties should also give assistance in accordance with their domestic law.[37]

Goods, such as materials, assets and other instrumentalities used to commit or facilitate offences under the present protocol; (ii) Proceeds derived from such offences; (b) Execute requests from another State Party for seizure or confiscation of goods or proceeds referred to in subparagraph (a) (i) and (ii); (c) Take measures aimed at closing, on a temporary or definitive basis, premises used to commit such offences."

[36] Article 6.

[37] All the above provisions are strengthened by the provisions of Article 10 of the Optional Protocol. According to this article: "1. States Parties shall take all necessary steps to strengthen international cooperation by multilateral, regional and bilateral arrangements for the prevention, detection, investigation, prosecution and punishment of those responsible for acts involving the sale of children, child prostitution, child pornography and child sex tourism. States Parties shall also promote international cooperation and coordination between their authorities, national and international non-governmental organizations and international organizations. 2. States Parties shall promote international cooperation to assist child victims in their physical and psychological recovery, social reintegration and repatriation. 3. States Parties shall promote the strengthening of international cooperation in order to address the root causes, such as poverty and underdevelopment, contributing to the vulnerability of children to the sale of children, child prostitution, child pornography and child sex tourism. 4. States Parties in a position to do so shall provide financial, technical or other assistance through existing multilateral, regional, bilateral or other programmes."

Protection of Child Victims

The question of justice is always interwoven with the questions surrounding the victims. In fact, the primary objective of national or international criminal justice is to resolve the consequences of criminally wrongful conduct which has been perpetrated against the victim. Even where this objective of justice is acknowledged, the exercise of justice may not always bring consolation and reparation to the victim and may even, on the contrary, seriously harm the victim and lead to feelings of confusion and regret after the conclusion of the judicial proceedings. This may especially be seen in the case of victims who have not yet attained the age of majority, or if their guardians are the offenders. This situation is much more acute in the case of the sexual exploitation of children in war or peacetime. Due to the sensitive position of the victims of child trafficking, sexual exploitation and sex slavery, the legislators of international conventions have formulated certain measures into their provisions in order to protect the victims of these crimes. Thus, the provisions of the Optional Protocol have also taken broadly similar measures to those of other international conventions regarding the protection of victims.[38]

Consequently, victims of crimes listed within the provisions of the Optional protocol who have come under different stages of the criminal justice process of the contracting parties should be protected against all actions which may jeopardise their position. In particular, parties should enact appropriate measures to protect the fundamental rights and interests of child victims by:

1. (a) Recognizing the vulnerability of child victims and adapting procedures to recognize their special needs, including their special needs as witnesses;
(b) Informing child victims of their rights, their role and the scope, timing and progress of the proceedings and of the disposition of their cases;
(c) Allowing the views, needs and concerns of child victims to be presented and considered in proceedings where their personal interests are affected, in a manner consistent with the procedural rules of national law;
(d) Providing appropriate support services to child victims throughout the legal process;
(e) Protecting, as appropriate, the privacy and identity of child victims and taking measures in accordance with national law to avoid the

[38] For instance, consult the Statutes of ICC, ICTR, ICTR and Sierra Leone.

inappropriate dissemination of information that could lead to the identification of child victims;

(f) Providing, in appropriate cases, for the safety of child victims, as well as that of their families and witnesses on their behalf, from intimidation and retaliation;

(g) Avoiding unnecessary delay in the disposition of cases and the execution of orders or decrees granting compensation to child victims.[39]

In the above provisions the legislators have anticipated many situations which may arise during the process of criminal jurisdiction. They have therefore tried to guarantee the rights of child victims under the legislation of different states parties. Although the above provisions try to evaluate and strengthen the position of the victim of sexual exploitation or other crimes listed in the Optional Protocol, these provisions are strengthened with further provisions.

Contracting parties must ensure that uncertainty as to the actual age of the victim is not considered a reason to prevent the initiation of criminal investigations, including investigations examining the age of the victim.[40] They should also ensure that the best interests of the child shall be the most important consideration during the proceedings. The best interests of children should also not be ignored by the system of criminal justice when they are victims of the offences.[41] Needless to say, the application of the provisions of the Optional Protocol should not in any way discriminate against the accused.[42]

The Advantages of the Optional Protocol

The Optional Protocol to the Convention on the Rights of the Child on the Sale of Children, Child Prostitution and Child Pornography is one of the most valuable instruments of international criminal law as it prohibits all forms of the sex trade affecting children. It is a milestone in the protection of the rights of children. The most important principles of the instrument are the following:

---

[39] Article 8 (1).

[40] Article 8 (2).

[41] Article 8 (6).

[42] According to other provisions of the protocol, those who work with victims of child exploitation should receive legal and psychological training, and their integrity should be protected. Article 8 (4) and (5).

a) Child pornography is prohibited by international instruments and is considered a serious crime against their integrity.

b) The sale of children is not permitted and is also considered a serious violation of the provisions of the protocol.

c) Child prostitution is a crime and must be prohibited using all means available.

d) All three categories of crimes, namely, child pornography, the sale of children and prostitution are an integral part of national, transnational and international criminal law.

e) The crimes can be committed on the basis of individual or collective action.

f) It is a duty of the contracting parties to cooperate with one another in the prevention and elimination of the above crimes.

g) In principle, crimes against children are extraditable and parties should do their best to ensure the extradition of the accused persons under the provisions of the Optional Protocol or their bilateral or multilateral conventions.

h) The states parties should take legislative and jurisdictional measures for the prosecution and punishment of perpetrators.

i) The victims of the crimes are to be protected by all states in all circumstances with consideration for their position and that of their families.

A general examination of the provisions of the Optional Protocol demonstrates its important function in the prevention and elimination of sexual crimes against children. Without doubt the existence of the provisions is vital for the protection of the principles of the United Nations and the development of its principles concerning the maintenance of peace, justice, equality and human rights law. They are to be respected by all states regardless of their signature or ratification of relevant international conventions, because of their very significant function in the protection of the fundamental values of the international community as a whole. By the phrase, "fundamental values of the international community", we mean those values which are basically essential for the protection of humankind from certain behaviours which violate the common sources of natural or positive law and their essences which are shared by all societies. Many of these values can be found within the scope of general principles of law that are common to almost all nations of the world, such as the protection of family unity, protection of children, prohibition of sexual exploitation of children and condemnation of sexual abuse of minors.

Problematic Reservations

The question of reservation in the system of the international law of treaties and in particular in the system of international human rights law has been one of the essential reasons for different forms of application, implementation and interpretation of the provisions of an international treaty. Most often, a reservation or declaration made at the time of signature or ratification of a treaty aims to minimise the scope and power of the treaty. It is on this basis that reservations to international human rights treaties are not often welcome. Although the drafters of a multilateral treaty may formulate specific provisions on reservations, this should not be interpreted as permission to reduce the effect of the treaty by states parties.

The provisions of the Optional Protocol to the Convention on the Rights of the Child on the Sale of Children, Child Prostitution and Child Pornography have also allowed for states parties to make reservations to the treaty. Therefore, reservations have been made in different ways. One of the most serious objections was that expressed against the reservation made by the government of Qatar. According to this reservation, Islamic law, rules or obligations have been given serious priority over the provisions of the Optional Protocol. Many states parties have therefore submitted objections to the reservation made by the government of Qatar; including Austria, Finland, the Netherlands, Ireland, Sweden, and the United Kingdom.

According to the objection submitted by the government of Ireland:

> The Government of Ireland have examined the reservation to the Optional Protocol to the Convention on the Rights of the Child on the Sale of Children, Child Prostitution and Child Pornography made by the Government of Qatar at the time of its accession to the Optional Protocol. The Government of Ireland are of the view that this reservation refers in a general manner to Islamic law without précising its content and therefore leaves other states parties in doubt as to the real extent of the state of Qatar's commitment to the Optional Protocol. It is in the common interest of States that treaties to which they have chosen to become parties are respected as to their object and purpose, by all parties, and that States are prepared to undertake any legislative changes necessary to comply with their obligations under the treaties.[43]

The Swedish government also submitted a strong objection to the reservation made by the government of Qatar to the Optional Protocol to

[43] http://treaties.un.org/Pages/Treaties.aspx?id=4&subid=A&lang=en.

the Convention on the Rights of the Child on the Sale of Children, Child Prostitution and Child Pornography. According to it the relevant reservation makes the Protocol subject to the provisions of the Islamic *shariah* and creates therefore a serious problem for the application of the provisions of the Protocol. The Swedish objection goes further and declares that the:

> ... reservation which does not clearly specify the provisions of the Convention to which it applies, and the extent of the derogation there from, raises serious doubts as to the commitment of Qatar to the object and purpose of the Protocol. The Government of Sweden would like to recall that, according to customary international law as codified in the Vienna Convention on the Law of Treaties, a reservation incompatible with the object and purpose of a treaty shall not be permitted.
>
> It is in the common interest of States that treaties to which they have chosen to become parties are respected as to their object and purpose, by all parties, and that States are prepared to undertake any legislative changes necessary to comply with their obligations under the treaties.[44]

Obviously, those reservations made by different states parties in order to minimise the effect of the Optional Protocol to the Convention on the Rights of the Child on the Sale of Children, Child Prostitution and Child Pornography are in conflict with the provisions of the law of treaties in international law. This is particularly serious in the case of reservations made to the treaties which basically deal with the areas of international human rights law. As is rightly stated it "is in the common interest of States that treaties to which they have chosen to become party are respected, as to their object and purpose, by all parties and that States are prepared to undertake any legislative changes necessary to comply with their obligations under the treaties."[45] Without any hesitation, all states have recognized international duties to respect international human rights law and these duties are particularly a part of obligation *erga omens*. It was probably based upon these obligations that the government of Qatar on 18 June 2008 informed the Secretary General that it had withdrawn its reservation made upon accession: "subject to a general reservation regarding any provisions in the protocol that are in conflict with the Islamic *Shariah*."

---

[44] Ibid.

[45] Objection made by the government of the Netherlands. http://treaties.un.org/Pages/Treaties.aspx?id=4&subid=A&lang=en.

Elimination of the Worst Forms of Child Labour

The International Labour Organization (ILO) has a considerable number of instruments for the protection of all workers in the world. Its rules and principles are applicable to almost every human being. One of the great achievements of the ILO is its provisions within the Convention concerning the Prohibition and Immediate Action for the Elimination of the Worst Forms of Child Labour.[46] The Convention is known among international lawyers as the Worst Forms of Child Labour.

The purpose of the Convention is to prohibit various forms of exploitative child labour. It takes into consideration many rules that are essentially important for the protection of children in work. The Convention prohibits the use of child labour, and demands the elimination of debt bondage, prostitution and pornography. The Convention has in particular prohibited the prostitution of children and makes it a legal duty of the contracting parties to take effective measures for the elimination of employment which constitutes the sexual abuse of children. For the purpose of the Convention, the term "the worst forms of child labour" comprises:

> (a) all forms of slavery or practices similar to slavery, such as the sale and trafficking of children, debt bondage and serfdom and forced or compulsory labour, including forced or compulsory recruitment of children for use in armed conflict;
> (b) the use, procuring or offering of a child for prostitution, for the production of pornography or for pornographic performances;
> (c) the use, procuring or offering of a child for illicit activities, in particular for the production and trafficking of drugs as defined in the relevant international treaties;
> (d) work which, by its nature or the circumstances in which it is carried out, is likely to harm the health, safety or morals of children.[47]

Whilst each sub-paragraph in the above is independent of the other sub-paragraphs, its strong connection with them should not be ignored. The reason is that the sale, trafficking, prostitution and enslavement of children, as well as many other forms of illicit activity are the result of the same actions and cannot be treated in isolation. A child may at the same time be the victim of slavery, prostitution, forced labour, trafficking, pornography and pornographic performance. It is for this basic reason that

---

[46] The Convention was adopted by the ILO on 7 June 1999 and entered into force on 19 November 2000.

[47] Article 3.

the identification of any act in the above may overlap with another act and denote a more serious violation of the child victim. All of the acts are also serious offences against the health, safety and morals of the child as a victim of the crime.

In order to prevent criminal acts against children, the Convention emphasises the duties of the members of the ILO. It states that "Each Member shall take all necessary measures to ensure the effective implementation and enforcement of the provisions giving effect to this Convention including the provision and application of penal sanctions or, as appropriate, other sanctions."[48] It further clarifies that "Each Member shall designate the competent authority responsible for the implementation of the provisions giving effect to this Convention."[49] These provisions obviously call upon the national and international responsibilities of the member states of the ILO to take certain necessary legislative measures for the penalization of acts against children and their prevention as well as their elimination.

The purposes of the Convention are developed by the provisions of the Worst Forms of Child Labour Recommendation in 1990.[50] In particular, the provisions of this recommendation have strengthened the criminal provisions of the Convention. It emphasises that:

> 11. Members should, in so far as it is compatible with national law, cooperate with international efforts aimed at the prohibition and elimination of the worst forms of child labour as a matter of urgency by:
>   (a) gathering and exchanging information concerning criminal offences, including those involving international networks;
>   (b) detecting and prosecuting those involved in the sale and trafficking of children, or in the use, procuring or offering of children for illicit activities, for prostitution, for the production of pornography or for pornographic performances;
>   (c) registering perpetrators of such offences.
> 12. Members should provide that the following worst forms of child labour are criminal offences:
>   (a) all forms of slavery or practices similar to slavery, such as the sale and trafficking of children, debt bondage and serfdom and forced or compulsory labour, including forced or compulsory recruitment of children for use in armed conflict;

[48] Article 7 (1).
[49] Article 7 (3).
[50] No. 190.

(b) the use, procuring or offering of a child for prostitution, for the production of pornography or for pornographic performances; and
(c) the use, procuring or offering of a child for illicit activities, in particular for the production and trafficking of drugs as defined in the relevant international treaties, or for activities which involve the unlawful carrying or use of firearms or other weapons.

One can conclude that the Convention and Worst Forms of Child Labour Recommendations have a very important function in the prevention of individual and organized acts against children and in the protection of the status of children. The criminalization of the offences has been seen by both instruments as a necessary corollary for the protection of the rights of children from the unlawful acts of individuals, organizations, and companies. Similar to other international conventions in the field, the relevant instruments reflect some of the most fundamental values of the international community as a whole. These values are also some of the most substantial parts of the principles of human rights law and without doubt have to be protected by any state. Both instruments may therefore also be considered as an integral part of customary international law for the purpose of the prevention of the exploitation of children.

Rights and Welfare of the Child in Africa

Overview

Due to several factors, African states have often had great difficulties in the protection of their children. This has partly arisen from the fact that their legislative systems have not been properly developed and partly because of the conditions of slavery as well as colonial rule imposed by European states upon the continent's population. The latter cause has also had a decisive impact on the first cause. The question of the protection of children has also been paid no attention in the development of policies for dealing with cultural, social, and economic issues. In short, African states have fought to achieve their independence and to regulate rules for various circumstances. For instance, since the establishment of the League of Nations and especially with the creation of the United Nations, the aim has been to protect the human rights of the population of African nations. The 1996 African Charter on the Rights and Welfare of the Child is a part of this struggle to protect the best interests of the child in all national, regional and international contexts.[51] The Charter is in fact based on the development of the Declaration on the Rights and Welfare of the African Child adopted by the Assembly of Heads of State and Government of the Organization of African Unity in 1979.[52] The Declaration calls on African States to take the necessary measures to protect and promote the rights and welfare of the African Child. But the words of the Declaration were not given any particular weight until 1990.

The African Charter focuses on many significant questions relating to the protection of children. In order to guarantee all forms of rights which have been recognized under its provisions, it places obligations on states parties to the Charter to take certain necessary measures within their laws for the formulation and implementation of those rights. It has also created an African Committee of Experts on the Rights and Welfare of the Child within the Organization of African Unity. The task of the Committee is to promote and protect the rights and welfare of the child which are stated within the African Charter.[53] The Committee consists of eleven members of high moral standing, integrity, impartiality and having sufficient competence and knowledge concerning the welfare of the child.

A significant feature of the African Charter is that its principles relating to the prohibition of the sexual exploitation of children, trafficking and abduction of children, trade in children and apartheid, as well as its principles on the humanitarian law of armed conflicts, are also similar to the provisions of international law. This means that the provisions of the Charter acknowledge the transnational character of certain acts which have already been recognized within the system of international criminal law. In other words, it opens the door for close cooperation between the two different systems and may be considered extremely useful in the protection of children in general and the prevention of the sexual exploitation, sale, prostitution, pornographic representation, and trafficking of children in particular.

---

[51] The African Charter was basically adopted and opened for signature by the Organization of African Unity (OAU) at the Twenty-Sixth Session of the Assembly of Heads of State and Government in Addis Ababa, Ethiopia on 11 July 1990. It entered into force on 29 November 1999. (OAU Doc. CAB/LEG/24.9/49).

[52] This was at its Sixteenth Ordinary Session in Monrovia, Liberia from 17 to 20 July 1979. (AHG/ST.4 Rev.l).

[53] Article 32.

Criminalization

The African Charter emphasises that, for its purposes, every human being who is below the age of eighteen is a child. It is with this clear definition that the rights which are formulated into the African Charter can protect a child from different forms of unlawful conduct. This definition also falls into line with the definition of a child in the Convention on the Rights of the Child adopted by the United Nations. The importance of this clear definition is that it prevents any conduct which goes against the rights of the child in war or peacetime. The definition also signals that the age of eighteen is a fitting criterion for the recognition of an adult person according to certain values of the international community as a whole.

The method of criminalization of the African Charter may generally be divided into two categories. One is based upon the prior criminalization of certain acts in other sources of law and the other is the criminalization of certain acts under its own provisions. The African Charter lists, for instance, the crime of apartheid and violations of international humanitarian law of armed conflict.[54] Certain other crimes that are listed in the Charter are derived from a considerable number of earlier international human rights instruments; such as the slave trade, trafficking and abduction, as well as sexual exploitation in various forms. Thus, one of the strongest points of the African Charter is the way in which it makes positive use of the legacy of the criminal activities of the European states against the African population and the commonly recognized conventions of international law. It is in this way that the Charter adopts the criminal definitions of other relevant instruments into its framework.

Sexual Exploitation

The sexual exploitation of children in Africa through various organized criminal activities has unfortunately been practiced for a long period of time. Therefore, African children have suffered from various criminal acts committed against them by individuals in accordance with their own decisions or individuals acting in organized groups. The African Charter on the Rights and Welfare of the Child, in order to put an end to these unlawful activities, has formulated a separate article dealing exclusively with this problem. To this end, it calls upon the responsibility of the states parties to take the necessary measures for the prevention of all types of

[54] See Articles 22 and 26 of the African Charter.

sexual exploitation or sexual abuse of children.[55] Thus, the states parties are asked to prevent and eliminate the following actions:

a) The inducement of a child to engage in any sexual activity.
b) Any situation which implies coercion and forces a child to engage in any sexual activity.
c) Any encouragement of a child to engage in any sexual activity.
d) The use or employment of children in prostitution or any other sexual practice or activity.
e) The employment or use of children in any pornographic activity.
f) The use of a child for the purpose of pornographic performance.
g) The use or employment of a child in any pornographic material.

The above list has a significant function in the identification of criminal activities which violate the rights, integrity and protection of children. Although each term, such as "inducement", "coercion" or "encouragement", may be the subject of various definitions in a criminal court, the scope of their definitions do not mitigate their legal applicability in the procedure of justice. This is so even in certain situations where two terms may have almost the same definition depending on the circumstances of each case. This is because the definition of the terms "inducement" or "encouragement may overlap with one another and denote similar acts. It seems that the purpose of legislators in the use of different terms has been to ensure that the criminal legislation of the states parties do not permit impunity and can be applied in all circumstances dealing, in one way or another, with the sexual exploitation of children.[56] Thus, sub-paragraphs (a) to (g) limit the offender's ability to flee from criminal prosecution by resorting to different allegations. The purpose of the legislation is to ensure that the criminalization of the sexual exploitation of children is not mitigated by various interpretations and that the provisions of the Charter are sufficient to convict perpetrators of sexual misconduct.

---

[55] Article 27.

[56] Furthermore, the provisions of Article 15 of the African Charter concerning prohibition of exploitation of children provides that "Every child shall be protected from all forms of economic exploitation and from performing any work that is likely to be hazardous or to interfere with the child's physical, mental, spiritual, moral, or social development."

Sale of Children

The African Charter on the Rights and Welfare of the Child, like other international instruments applicable to any form of sexual abuse of children, has taken certain measures for the prevention of trade in children. Therefore, it emphasizes the conventional obligation of states to take the necessary measures under their respective national legislation for the prevention of the sale, trafficking and abduction of children. According to the relevant provisions, the parties should ensure that their legislation includes the provisions concerning the following matters: *a)* the abduction of children should effectively be prevented by the parties, *b)* the sale of children should not be permitted and *c)* trafficking in children should be prohibited. According to the Charter, all the above acts, including the abduction, sale and trafficking of children should be prevented and eliminated regardless of the interests of the perpetrators. They should also be prevented even if they are carried out by parents or legal guardians of the child. Consequently, the Charter prohibits the sale of children in any form by any means, even though the sale is intended for the welfare of children.[57]

Begging

The involvement of children in begging has become a serious problem in the world. This problem has particularly occurred in countries in which the social services are very poor or corrupted. The problem of children begging in public places in certain regions is much more controversial and identifiable when one realises that most of these children are forced to engage in begging and their vulnerable position leads them towards their sexual exploitation or involvement in committing crimes. An interesting and significant provision of the African Charter concerns children who are forced or coerced to engage in begging.[58] The parties to it should therefore take effective measures for the prevention of the use of children in all forms of begging.

This provision of the African Charter also prevents the relevant children from falling prey to sexual exploitation, sale, trafficking and abduction. Although the relevant provision of the Charter is to be very much appreciated and welcomed for its prevention of various forms of exploitation of children, the Charter is silent concerning the children who

---

[57] Article 29 (a).
[58] Article 29 (b).

beg with other members of their family or collectively. Whether the provisions of the Charter can apply to this matter is very doubtful, although the children of these families may be more vulnerable and at risk of trafficking or sexual exploitation because of their poor circumstances. The seriousness of the question is much more obvious when one considers the present economic depression in the world.

Suppressing and Punishing Trafficking in Persons

Overview

Whilst the United Nations Convention against Transnational Organized Crime is the key legal document in the fight against organized crime, the Convention has solely the function of criminalizing certain acts and does not offer the necessary definition and consideration of the specifics of trafficking. It is for this reason that two other instruments were adopted by the United Nations in order to deal in detail with specific acts. One of these instruments deals with trafficking in persons and the other with the smuggling of persons. The first instrument is entitled the Protocol to Prevent, Suppress and Punish Trafficking in Persons, Especially Women and Children, Supplementing the United Nations Convention against Transnational Organized Crime and the second the Protocol against the Smuggling of Migrants by Land, Sea and Air. Both instruments have focused on various forms of trafficking, although their purposes vary from one another and they have different functions.

The Protocol to Prevent, Suppress and Punish Trafficking in Persons is a landmark in the criminalization of acts against women and children.[59] With its provisions, it has opened a window for the possible implementation of the instruments relating to the protection of women and children in the world. The Protocol is also the first international instrument which defines trafficking in persons. The preamble of the Protocol states clearly that the aim is to create a "universal instrument that addresses all aspects of trafficking in persons." Among a considerable number of important principles of the Protocol, is the principle of the penalization of all acts relating to trafficking in persons. The intention of the Protocol is also to have uniform domestic regulations concerning the identification of certain acts, and in this way, to facilitate the application of the provisions of the Protocol. At the same time, the Protocol also aims to create a high

---

[59] Adopted and opened for signature, ratification and accession by General Assembly resolution 55/25 of 15 November 2000.

standard of assistance to the victims of trafficking in persons. To achieve its goals, the Protocol has a number of articles which deal with different matters concerning prevention, elimination, penalization and protection.

Purposes

The Protocol has a close relation to the United Convention against Transnational Organized Crime. According to its provisions, it supplements the relevant Convention. Consequently, any interpretation of the Protocol should be in connection with the provisions of the Convention.[60] It also makes clear that all the provisions of the Convention are applicable unless otherwise provided herein.[61] The Protocol has also clarified that the offences stated in its content should also be regarded as offences that are established in the Convention. In this way the legislators of the Protocol have given a broader interpretation and application to the provisions of the Protocol.[62]

In the content of each article the Protocol expresses its purposes. To summarise, it has three chief purposes. These are: *a)* to prevent and combat various forms of trafficking in persons with a particular focus on women and children; *b)* to protect by various means and assist in different ways the victims of trafficking in persons with due regard to the fundamental human rights of the victims; *c)* to promote as much as possible the necessary cooperation among states parties in order to meet the objectives of the Protocol.[63]

All of the three main purposes of the Protocol must be respected and applied by states. A basic problem here is that the Protocol does not say that all these three purposes of the Protocol are interrelated, which means that a state may fulfil one purpose without exercising the other two. Although it would have been better to enter such a provision within the Protocol, a generous interpretation of the Protocol recognises the interrelations of all its purposes. Obviously, a state cannot choose one purpose and avoid another for different reasons. This is especially understandable when most parts of a case relating to trafficking in persons come, in one way or another, under its jurisdiction.

[60] Article 1 (1).
[61] Article 1 (2).
[62] Article 1 (3).
[63] Article 2.

Scope and Definitions

One of the helpful functions of the Protocol to Prevent, Suppress and Punish Trafficking in Persons is its policy for defining certain terms. The intention is here to put an end to different interpretations and to prevent contradictions in the application of the provisions of the Protocol. The aim is also to prevent the perpetrators of the crime of trafficking from escaping from prosecution and punishment. The Protocol applies, except as otherwise stated, to the prevention, investigation and prosecution of the offences established in the provisions of Article 5. The offences have to have a transnational nature and involve an organized criminal group. The scope of the Protocol also protects the victims of such offences.[64]

The definitions in the Protocol create a consistent legislative policy between different national systems. Although, the definitions are to be applied only in connection with the provisions of the Protocol, they are also useful in the application and implementation of other international instruments in the field. For instance, the Protocol reaffirms the international age of majority. According to it, a child is a person under 18 years old.[65]

The Protocol provides a wide definition of the term "trafficking in persons". According to it, the term means "the recruitment, transportation, transfer, harbouring or receipt of persons, by means of the threat or use of force or other forms of coercion, of abduction, of fraud, of deception, of the abuse of power or of a position of vulnerability or of the giving or receiving of payments or benefits to achieve the consent of a person having control over another person, for the purpose of exploitation." It goes further and defines the term "exploitation". It states that the term includes "at a minimum, the exploitation of the prostitution of others or other forms of sexual exploitation, forced labour or services, slavery or practices similar to slavery, servitude or the removal of organs"[66]

As is evident, the Protocol is apparently not fulfilled merely by following its definition covering the term "exploitation". This is because it uses the words "at a minimum". In this way, the legislators have tried to guarantee that the Protocol can fit any other situation to which the above definition is not sufficient to apply. Although, the Protocol does not aim to apply the principle of *ex post facto law,* it obviously places a responsibility on the states parties to make more serious and effective provisions within their legislations. Yet this problem is dealt with in other provisions of the

64 Article 4.

65 Article 3 (d).

66 Article 3 (a).

Protocol in order to minimize any wrongful interpretation.[67] The Protocol goes further and clarifies that the *consent of a victim* of trafficking in persons to the intended exploitation set forth in the Protocol is completely *irrelevant* where any of the means stated in the definition of trafficking in persons or exploitation is employed.[68]

Another significant part of the definition concerns the extension of the scope of the application of the term “trafficking in persons” to many acts that fall under the definition of exploitation. Accordingly, the recruitment, transportation, transfer, harbouring or receipt of a child for the purpose of exploitation shall be considered "trafficking in persons". This provision should also apply even if the conduct does not involve any of the means stated in the Protocol. The purpose is here to be sure that the definition of trafficking in persons is not limited and that the Protocol is applicable to all acts which are instrumental in the trafficking.

Criminalization

Trafficking in persons constitutes a crime against humanity. The legislators of the Protocol to Prevent, Suppress and Punish Trafficking in Persons have attempted throughout to criminalize all conduct relating to trafficking in persons. By this policy, they aim to prevent, prohibit, criminalize, prosecute and punish the perpetrators. But the Protocol has clearly stated that it applies to offences only if “those offences are transnational in nature and involve an organized criminal group.” Thus, other conducts of an illegal nature are not dealt with under the provisions of the Protocol. In other words, its provisions may not apply to offences which do not come under its definitions and scope. Since the Protocol is supplementary to the United Nations Convention against Transnational Organized Crime, the definition of the term “organized criminal group” has to be borrowed from the provisions of the Convention. According to it, "Organized criminal group" means “a structured group of three or more persons, existing for a period of time and acting in concert with the aim of committing one or more serious crimes or offences established in accordance with this Convention, in order to obtain, directly or indirectly, a financial or other material benefit.”[69]

---

[67] See the below paragraph.

[68] Article 3 (b).

[69] Article 2 of the Convention. United Nations Convention against Transnational Organized Crime, G.A. Res. 25, annex I, U.N. GAOR, 55th Sess., Supp. No. 49, at 44, U.N. Doc. A/45/49 (Vol. I) (2001).

In the light of the above, the Protocol declares it the responsibility of the states parties to take certain measures for the criminalization of the given offences within their respective legislations. It therefore demands the following:

1. Each State Party shall adopt such legislative and other measures as may be necessary to establish as criminal offences the conduct set forth in article 3 of this Protocol, when committed intentionally.
2. Each State Party shall also adopt such legislative and other measures as may be necessary to establish as criminal offences:
   (a) Subject to the basic concepts of its legal system, attempting to commit an offence established in accordance with paragraph 1 of this article;
   (b) Participating as an accomplice in an offence established in accordance with paragraph 1 of this article; and
   (c) Organizing or directing other persons to commit an offence established in accordance with paragraph 1 of this article.

Thus, the Protocol has taken into effective consideration different policies of criminalization for the application and implementation of the provisions of the Protocol. A significant provision within the above presentation concerns the term “intention”. This is because, according to the above provisions, all acts such as the recruitment, transportation, transfer, harbouring or receipt of adult persons, and the transfer, harbouring or receipt of a child for the purpose of exploitation, abduction, fraud or payment must have been carried out “intentionally” and not unintentionally for criminal responsibility to be recognized. This is at once one of the strongest and weakest aspects of the Protocol. This is because it will be very difficult in a court of criminal justice to prove the contrary if the perpetrator denies that the conduct in question has been carried out “intentionally”. In particular, the situation may be more difficult in the case of trafficking of children. The borderline of intention and non intention is indeed sometimes very difficult to prove, especially in the case of transnational crimes. For a crime to be transnational it must have been committed within two or several states, and although cooperation between the contracting parties is a necessary condition for the application of the provisions of the Protocol, this may not work for one reason or another. In particular, when a state is, due to certain circumstances of its legislation, obliged to prosecute an accused person who speaks a different language, its court translators can face the problem of different terminologies and other serious difficulties. Although we do not deny that a state cannot prosecute a person who did not have the intention to commit the crime, the proceedings of the court might very well be prolonged until it is proved beyond reasonable doubt that the accused had the intention of committing the crime. This is regardless of the assistance of the United Nations Office on Drugs and Crime to the states parties in order to implement properly the provisions of the Protocol.

Preventive Measures

As we have stated elsewhere, all relevant international instruments, dealing in one way or another with sex trafficking, attempt to prevent and criminalize certain acts or behaviour. This is also one of the main aims of the Protocol to Prevent, Suppress and Punish Trafficking in Persons, Especially Women and Children. The Protocol therefore makes certain significant provisions which encourage the states parties to take the necessary legislative measures for the prevention of sex trafficking or sexual exploitation of women and children. This policy of the Protocol may be carried out in one or several of the following ways:

i) They may establish comprehensive policies, programmes and other measures in order to prevent and combat trafficking in persons and also to protect the victims of trafficking in persons. This should be done with special consideration of the position of women and children with the purpose of also preventing re-victimization.[70] This is most crucial in the case of children who may again be the subject of sexual abuse. In other words, sexual re-victimization as a phenomenon of sex trafficking is the situation in which individuals who have been victims are at increased risk of again being in the position to be sexually exploited by others.

ii) Parties to the Protocol are also encouraged to undertake measures such as research, information and mass media campaigns in order to combat trafficking in persons. They should also take social and economic initiatives in order to strive for the purposes of the Protocol.[71]

iii) The third policy of prevention of trafficking in persons is based on programmes and other measures established in the Protocol. These policies and programmes should be carried out with appropriate consideration which may include cooperation with non-governmental organizations and any other relevant organization. It can also be carried out with other elements of civil society.[72]

iv) The Protocol has also encouraged states parties to adopt a policy of bilateral and multilateral cooperation with one another. They should also cooperate to improve the existing factors that can help persons, especially women and children, vulnerable to trafficking. Susceptibility

---

[70] Article 9 (1).
[71] Article 9 (2).
[72] Article 9 (3).

to trafficking may be based on poverty, underdevelopment and any lack of equal opportunity in society. The problem of this provision is that it will not be so easy to solve the problem of poverty faced by those who are victims of trafficking or sex trafficking. Yet, even if we accept that bilateral or multilateral cooperation between different states to prevent trafficking may be possible, this will again not be an easy task due to the fact that economic, social, political and other cultural factors are different between most states of the world.[73]

v) Another preventive measure demanded by the provisions of the Protocol is for the states parties to formulate and adopt legislative or any other measures, as they may deem necessary, for the application of its provisions. These may be educational, social or cultural measures. These can also be carried out through bilateral and multilateral cooperation. The aims of these policies and measures should be to discourage the demand that fosters all forms of exploitation of persons, with a special concentration on women and children.[74]

The five policies of the Protocol are an integral part of one another and generally speaking, all of them have a similar policy of application with the difference that one may lay stress on a unilateral policy of application while the other on a bilateral or multilateral policy for the prevention of trafficking in persons. This means that the application of the preventive provisions of the Protocol largely depends on the internal capacity of the state in question and to what extent the state wishes to improve the positions of women and children within its own borders or in other countries.

In order to strengthen the above preventive measures, the Protocol has also taken into consideration other defensive measures. These include border controls, transport measures, obligations of commercial carriers and particular sanctions for the violations of its provisions.[75] In addition, the

---

[73] Article 9 (4).

[74] Article 9 (5).

[75] For these purposes, the Protocol reads that: "1. Without prejudice to international commitments in relation to the free movement of people, States Parties shall strengthen, to the extent possible, such border controls as may be necessary to prevent and detect trafficking in persons. 2. Each State Party shall adopt legislative or other appropriate measures to prevent, to the extent possible, means of transport operated by commercial carriers from being used in the commission of offences established in accordance with article 5 of this Protocol. 3. Where appropriate, and without prejudice to applicable international conventions, such measures shall include establishing the obligation of commercial carriers, including any transportation company or the owner or operator of any means of transport, to ascertain that all passengers are in possession of the travel

Protocol has also taken certain measures that may be useful in preventing any type of falsification of the legal documents of the states parties. For instance, they should create such border documents that may be closed to the possibility of misuse and cannot readily be altered or replicated. Parties should also by all means ensure the security of travel and identity documents issued by their national authorities.[76] A state should also cooperate with the authorities of other states if the validity of the documents issued in its name is suspected to have been compromised for the purpose of trafficking in persons. Such a request by a state from another state for the verification of the legal validity of its documents should be responded to within a reasonable time.[77]

Protection of Victims

The system of international human rights law, including the international humanitarian law of armed conflict, as well as international criminal law and transnational criminal law, are moving radically and effectively towards the protection of all victims. This development not only applies to the protection of victims from unlawful activities during armed conflicts, but also their protection under any other circumstances. This includes also the protection of victims of the sale of persons, trafficking in persons, abduction and, not least of all, the sex trafficking and sexual exploitation of women and children. The legislators of many of these instruments dealing in one way or another with the questions of transnational crimes or international crimes have demanded the immediate protection of victims. This is what the Protocol to Prevent, Suppress and Punish Trafficking in Persons, Especially Women and Children, Supplementing the United Nations Convention against Transnational Organized Crime, has also taken into serious consideration.

---

documents required for entry into the receiving State. 4. Each State Party shall take the necessary measures, in accordance with its domestic law, to provide for sanctions in cases of violation of the obligation set forth in paragraph 3 of this article. 5. Each State Party shall consider taking measures that permit, in accordance with its domestic law, the denial of entry or revocation of visas of persons implicated in the commission of offences established in accordance with this Protocol.[75] 6. Without prejudice to article 27 of the Convention, States Parties shall consider strengthening cooperation among border control agencies by, inter alia, establishing and maintaining direct channels of communication." Article 11.

[76] Article 12.

[77] Article 13.

The Protocol has regulated a considerable number of useful provisions regarding the protection of victims which are more or less similar to other instruments of human rights law applicable to the protection of victims of crimes. The relevant provisions have generally attempted to protect all victims of trafficking in persons. This has been classified under seven principles which have similar legal values. All these measures of assistance to and protection of victims of trafficking in persons are applicable individually or collectively depending on the circumstances of the victims and the danger surrounding their position, such as vulnerability to re-victimization or the threat of physical or psychological harm.

Protection of Identity

The principle of protection of identity constitutes one of the important principles of the criminal justice system and is one of the significant principles within the system of human rights law applicable to sex trafficking or sexual exploitation of women or children. The principle is especially important regarding the protection of minors whose future well-being is seriously in danger and who are vulnerable to or at risk of being forced again into trafficking. For this reason the legislator provides that in appropriate cases, and to the extent possible under the national law of a state, sufficient protection should be given to the privacy and identity of victims of trafficking in persons. The protection of identity may be carried out in different ways including, *inter alia*, by taking the necessary measures in order to make legal proceedings concerning such trafficking confidential.[78] States must particularly be very careful concerning the protection of the identity of children, who are seriously harmed by the acts of trafficking and sexual exploitation.

Assistance in proceedings

The second principle of the protection of the victims of trafficking in persons is assistance of different kinds during the proceedings at court. This has been taken into recognition by the Protocol to Prevent, Suppress and Punish Trafficking in Persons. The parties should therefore ensure that their domestic or legal administrative systems fulfil the following requirements. These are information on relevant court and administrative procedures, and assistance to enable the views and concerns of victims to be presented and considered at appropriate stages of the criminal

[78] Article 6 (1).

proceedings against offenders. This should be carried out in a manner not prejudicial to the rights of defendants.[79] In any event, parties should give sufficient assistance during proceedings to the victims who are minors and cannot fully understand the power and authority of the court. They should particularly take into effective consideration the position of child victims who have been the object of serious violations of their rights by the offenders.

Recovery

The principle of recovery is one of the most important parts of the programmes protecting the victims of trafficking in persons, which includes, of course, sex trafficking and sexual exploitation of women and children. The Protocol to Prevent, Suppress and Punish Trafficking in Persons obliges each state party to take such measures as may seem necessary for the social, physical and psychological rehabilitation and recovery of victims of trafficking in persons. The implementation of these measures should also include, in appropriate cases, cooperation with relevant governmental or non-governmental organizations as well as other elements of civil society.

In particular, in the implementation of the above measures, states parties should take into serious consideration provisions regarding *a)* appropriate housing for the victims; *b)* counselling and information concerning their legal rights. This should be in a language that the victims of trafficking in persons can understand. *c)* They should receive also material, psychological and medical assistance; and *d)* Victims need also help with the matter of employment, educational and training.[80] Needless to say, the principle of recovery must be understood in its fullest form of application and productivity and not in isolation. This means that a victim may at the same time be given all the protection stated in the domestic legislation of a state such as psychological treatment, housing and necessary help for education and employment.

Special Need

The principle of special need implies to the legal duty of a state, with due consideration of the circumstances of a case, to find out the most essential needs of the victim. Thus, in the application of the provisions of the

---

[79] Article 6 (2).
[80] Article 6 (3).

Protocol regarding the protection of victims, states parties should take into consideration the age, gender and special needs of victims of trafficking in persons. This consideration must be focused on the needs of children, such as appropriate housing, education and care.[81] The principle of special need is, in particular, important in the case of children whose position is seriously in danger and who have no legal guardian for their protection.

Physical Safety

One of the significant principles of the Protocol to Prevent, Suppress and Punish Trafficking in Persons is the principle of physical safety. The principle protects the victims of trafficking in persons while they are, for one reason or another, residing within the jurisdiction of the state prosecuting the traffickers. Obviously, the principle protects victims from all threats to their physical safety. Although the principle constitutes one of the most significant principles for the protection of the victims of trafficking or sexual exploitation, it may easily be ignored in practice by the contracting parties because of the very vulnerable position of a victim of trafficking and the continuous instability of their social position. The parties should therefore put a heavy emphasis on the observation of this principle, especially in the case of children.

Compensation

The principle of the compensation of victims which is entered into the provisions of the Protocol to Prevent, Suppress and Punish Trafficking in Persons is taken from the most basic rules of civil legislation which can be found within all legislative systems of the world. The principle is also one of the core principles of general principles of law. The principle aims to provide victims of trafficking in persons, including sex trafficking and sexual exploitation, with the possibility of obtaining appropriate reparation for damages suffered. The general hope is that under the jurisdiction of different courts, the principle of the right to compensation should be treated seriously and should not be applied in a way which discriminates against certain victims.

Needless to say, all of the above principles including protection of identity, assistance in proceedings, recovery, special need, physical safety, and compensation should be legislated on and applied to all victims of trafficking in persons regardless of their sex, or ethnic, language, national,

[81] Article 6 (4).

cultural, educational, religious or social backgrounds. This should have been regarded as the first principle of the Protocol, although its general content implies this fact.

Victims in Receiving State

The seventh principle concerns the status of the victim in the receiving state. Therefore, provisions concerning assistance to and protection of victims of trafficking in persons have been enlarged with this principle. The purpose of the Protocol to Prevent, Suppress and Punish Trafficking in Persons is to harmonize the laws of states parties regarding victims of trafficking who come, for one reason or another, under the territorial jurisdiction of the receiving state.

Accordingly, each state party is under a conventional duty to adopt legislative or any other measures that are deemed necessary to permit the victims of trafficking in persons to stay in its territory "in appropriate cases". This can be fulfilled by different means and either temporarily or permanently.[82] Although the Protocol makes it the responsibility of governments to take certain necessary measures for the provision of permanent or temporary leave to remain for the victims of trafficking within their territory, it uses the term "in appropriate cases." This may be interpreted such that in all cases of trafficking victims have no legal right to demand residence within the territory of the receiving state. A state party may make decisions regarding their temporary or permanent residence according to the necessary requirements of each case, and this means in practice a right to choose between victims, including women and children. Article 14 of the Protocol attempts to reduce any possibility of a discriminatory decision. It reads that:

1. Nothing in this Protocol shall affect the rights, obligations and responsibilities of States and individuals under international law, including international humanitarian law and international human rights law and, in particular, where applicable, the 1951 Convention and the 1967 Protocol relating to the Status of Refugees and the principle of non-refoulement as contained therein.
2. The measures set forth in this Protocol shall be interpreted and applied in a way that is not discriminatory to persons on the ground that they are victims of trafficking in persons. The interpretation and application of those measures shall be consistent with internationally recognized principles of non-discrimination.

---

[82] Article 7 (1).

The legislators of the Protocol, in order to prevent the possible misapplication and misinterpretation of the above provisions, have made it the duty of a state party to give appropriate consideration to humanitarian and compassionate factors.[83] The legislators have thus attempted to prevent inconsistent and partial interpretations and applications of the Protocol. Yet, it is also obvious that "humanitarian and compassionate factors" should not have a degrading or humiliating effect on the victims of trafficking in persons. This is of particular importance in the case of the sex trafficking or sexual exploitation of women or children. Particular attention should also be given to child victims of sexual exploitation or sex trafficking. They should be received according to their age and their needs and the gravity of their case.

Repatriation of Victims

Having considered different situations concerning assistance to the victims and their status within the territorial jurisdiction of the receiving state, the Protocol also takes into consideration the position of the victims who will be returned to other states. The victims of trafficking in persons may therefore face different measures depending on their legal status, including in the legislation of the receiving state. Accordingly:

1. The State Party of which a victim of trafficking in persons is a national or in which the person had the right of permanent residence at the time of entry into the territory of the receiving State Party shall facilitate and accept, with due regard for the safety of that person, the return of that person without undue or unreasonable delay.
2. When a State Party returns a victim of trafficking in persons to a State Party of which that person is a national or in which he or she had, at the time of entry into the territory of the receiving State Party, the right of permanent residence, such return shall be with due regard for the safety of that person and for the status of any legal proceedings related to the fact that the person is a victim of trafficking and shall preferably be voluntary.
3. At the request of a receiving State Party, a requested State Party shall, without undue or unreasonable delay, verify whether a person who is a victim of trafficking in persons is its national or had the right of permanent residence in its territory at the time of entry into the territory of the receiving State Party.

---

[83] Article 7 (2).

4. In order to facilitate the return of a victim of trafficking in persons who is without proper documentation, the State Party of which that person is a national or in which he or she had the right of permanent residence at the time of entry into the territory of the receiving State Party shall agree to issue, at the request of the receiving State Party, such travel documents or other authorization as may be necessary to enable the person to travel to and re-enter its territory.

Yet, the above rules concerning the victims of trafficking in persons should be interpreted without any prejudice to any right afforded to the victims according to the provisions of the national law of the receiving state party.[84] Moreover, the above provisions should be applied without prejudice to any other applicable bilateral or multilateral agreement or arrangement which deals, in one way or another, with the question of the return of the victims of trafficking in persons.[85]

Justice

Without doubt the Protocol has a strong policy for the prevention of trafficking in persons. One problem of the Protocol may be its policy concerning the situation of victims of sex trafficking and sexual exploitation. This is in particular important when one realises that the situation and integrity of women and especially children is not treated equally well within the legislation of different states. Parties have, generally speaking, different attitudes towards the position of women and children. The boundary of the application of human rights principles governing the protection of women as well as children varies, not only, from one country to another, but also from one political party to another, and may vary further depending on the economic, social and religious context. This means that the victims of trafficking may not be properly protected by the provisions of the Protocol when there is such a possibility of discrimination between victims, or when the state decides whether children under the age of eighteen are to be treated as minors or as adults. Although the Protocol tries to resolve these problems and to prevent the possibility of discrimination its position may be controversial when put into practice. Of particular concern is the position of children who are the victims of trafficking in persons or who have been exploited across different territories by different nations. Whether such victims receive the spirit of justice is itself a serious question of law and morality.

[84] Article 8 (5).
[85] Article 8 (6).

CHAPTER EIGHT

PROSECUTION OF TRAFFICKING AT THE INTERNATIONAL CRIMINAL COURT (ICC)

Background

Although the perpetrators of sexual exploitation of children should be prosecuted in accordance with the principle of universality, the need for the prosecution of those who have committed crimes at an international level has long been one of the most serious questions within the international legal and political community. This question was especially strongly felt when the outbreak of the First World War demonstrated that there was no competent international criminal court which could bring the perpetrators of international crimes for prosecution and punishment under a single jurisdiction. The rivalries between the Great Powers at the time and the economic depression, as well as an arms race between various states, were some of the reasons for the start of the Second World War. At this time, those who engaged in the commission of war crimes, aggression, slavery, trafficking and pornography, could escape prosecution and punishment because of the non-existence of an international criminal court. The victims of both wars therefore went without any protection and a large number of these victims never received justice. The only reaction concerning the Second World War was the creation of the International Military Tribunal for the prosecution of major war criminals in Nuremberg and also the Tokyo Tribunal.[1] The accused were charged with the

[1] For consideration of Nuremberg Tribunal see Sheldon Glueck, 'By What Tribunal Shall War Offenders Be Tried?,' 56 *Harv.L.R.* 1059 (1942-3); Sheldon Glueck, *The Nuremberg Trial and Aggressive War* (New York, 1946); *The Judgment of the International Military Tribunal for the Trial of German Major War Criminals, Nuremberg 1946,* H.M. Stationary Office Cmd. 6964; Robert, H Jackson, 'Forward the Nürenberg Trial Becomes a Historical Precedent', 20 *Temple L.Q* (1946-7); Stimson, Henry, L, '*The Nuremberg, Trial, Landmark in*

commission of war crimes, crimes against humanity and crimes against peace. Both tribunals had many difficulties regarding several serious questions of law and morality. They realised that their laws were retroactive and that they were created according to a policy of non-impartiality by militarily powerful nations. In addition, it came about that they were only temporary tribunals and had no authority to exercise their power over other international crimes such as genocide, slave trafficking and exploitation of women and children. These problems had to be solved.

The process of the establishment of the United Nations, in particular between 1944 and 1945, raised many questions. One realisation was that the world needed the establishment of a permanent international criminal court which could have power over serious violations of international law. The International Law Commission was given the responsibility for dealing with this matter but it was not successful in the end because it faced the problem of the adoption and re-adoption of the principles of the Charter of the Nuremberg Tribunals. From this time on the international political situation deteriorated, and the Cold War led to the division of the world into two power blocs led by the United States and the Soviet Socialist Republic. The start of the Vietnam War also effectively pushed aside the idea of the establishment of an international criminal court. The only international court at this time was the International Court of Justice, or Cour Internationale de Justice, in The Hague which had no powers for dealing with international crimes.

In addition, the system of transnational criminal justice had no particular leverage in relations between states, and therefore, the significant questions of the prevention, prosecution, jurisdiction and punishment of the sex trafficking of women and children were mostly on paper and were not seriously enforceable. The problem of the application of justice was and is made more serious when one realises that there are

---

Law,' 25 *Foreign Affairs* 179 (1946-7); *Trials of War Criminals Before the Nuremberg Military Tribunals under Control Council Law* No. 10 (Nuremberg, 1946-1949; George Augustus Finch, *The Nuremberg Trial and International Law,* 41 AJIL 20 (1947); Hans Kelsen, 'Will the Judgement of the Nürenberg Trial Constitute a Precedent in International Law,' 1 *INT'L L.Q* 153 (1947); Arthur, K Kuhn, 'International Criminal Jurisdiction,' 41 *A.J.I.L.* 430 (1947); F.B. Schick, 'The Nuremberg Trial and the International Law of the Future,' 41 *A.J.I.L.* 770 (1947); Wright, Quincy, 'The Law of the Nuremberg Trial', 41 *A.J.I.L.* 38 (1947); *International Military Tribunal, Trial of the Major War Criminals Before the International Military Tribunal in Nuremberg* (1947); Hans Ehard, 'The Nuremberg Trial against the Major War Criminals and International Law,' 33 *A.J.I.L.* 223 (1949); *Trials of War Criminals Before the Nuremberg Military Tribunals under Control Council* (1951).

different perspectives on transnational justice. For instance, African, European or Asian have different views. These make the position of the victims of sexual exploitation of children or women much more complicated and controversial.

Ad hoc Tribunals

The outbreak of wars in the former Yugoslavia, Rwanda, Darfur and Sierra Leone raised many serious unsolved questions of justice for the United Nations General Assembly and Security Council. Both organs were prompted by the wars to create an international criminal court. In particular, the terrible sexual exploitation and rape of women and children during the war in the former Yugoslavia, and the use of forced sexual services during the other abovementioned wars, raised the question of what to do about violations of certain values of the international community as a whole. The level and degree of genocide in the former Yugoslavia and Rwanda[2] finally led to the establishment of the International Criminal Tribunal for the Former Yugoslavia (ICTY), the International Criminal Tribunal for the Rwanda (ICTR) and the hybrid tribunal, namely, the Special Court for Sierra Leone. All of these Courts

---

[2] Cosult J. E. Ackerman & E. O'Sullivan, *Practice and procedure of the International Criminal Tribunal for the Former Yugoslavia; with selected material from the International Criminal Tribunal for Rwanda* (2000); Michael N. Barnett, *Eyewitness to a Genocide: The United Nations and Rwanda* (2002); Belgian Senate, *Parliamentary Commission of Inquiry concerning Rwanda / Commission d'enquête parlementaire concernant les événements du Rwanda*, Report/Rapport, Brussels/Bruxelles, 6.12.1997. Laurence Burgorgue, Larsen (ed.), *La repression internationale du genocide rwandais,* (2003) ; Christopher Browning, *The path to genocide: Essays on launching the final solution* (2002); John A. Berry & Carol Pott Berry, (eds.), *Genocide in Rwanda* (1999); Howard Adelman, & Astri Suhrke, (eds.), *The path of a genocide: The Rwanda Crisis, from Uganda to Zaire* (1999); Colette Braeckman., *Rwanda: Histoire d'un génocide*, (1994) ; Colette Braeckman, *Terreurafricaine. Burundi, Rwanda, Zaïre: Les racines de la violence* (1996); Napoleon Abdulai, (ed.), *Genocide in Rwanda,* Africa Research & Information Centre, (1994); African Rights, *Rwanda: Death, Despair and Defiance* (1995); Amnesty International, *United Nations International Criminal Tribunal for Rwanda: Trials and tribulations*, AI Index IOR 40/03/98, (1998); Amnesty International, *Rwanda: The troubled course of justice*, AI Index AFR 47/10/00, (2000); Jacques Castonguay, *Les Casques Bleus au Rwanda*,(1998); Jean Pierre Chrétien, *Le défi de l'ethnisme: Rwanda et Buruni, 1990 - 1996,* (1997); Jean Pierre Chrétien., *The Great Lakes of Africa: Two thousand years of history*, (2003).

are still active and they deal with the concept of international crimes and violations of the rights of victims. They deal especially with the concept of the sexual exploitation of women and children during wartime.

Like the ICC, the constitutions of these three courts all deal, as we will demonstrate, with crimes against humanity and the sexual exploitation of women and children equivalent to enslavement. These principles may be examined within the provisions of Article 5 of the ICTY, Article 3 of ICTR and Article 2 of the Special Court for Sierra Leone. The term "enslavement" within the provisions of crimes against humanity in the constitutions of all the above tribunals and courts is also taken from Article 6 (c) of the Charter of the Nuremberg Tribunal. These tribunals/courts all differ from the ICC insofar as they have a temporary or *ad hoc* character. They will be terminated when their tasks have been accomplished.

Cases

One of the most well-known cases tried under the above tribunals/court is the case of Charles Taylor, the President of the Republic of Liberia, who was under investigation by the Special Court for Sierra Leone (SCSL), and whose trial was, because of security reasons, moved to The Hague in the Netherlands.[3] The permission to move was obtained from the United Nations. According to the evidence presented, inferiors and soldiers acting on his orders were engaged in the serious sexual violation and exploitation of women and children during the internal conflict. Some of the most important provisions of the Statute of the SCSL, which was drafted to prosecute and punish the perpetrators of war crimes or crimes against humanity, concern children's rights. They recognise the use of child soldiers or the sexual exploitation of children as serious infringements of the laws of the Statute and the international humanitarian law of armed conflict. Accordingly, "Conscripting or enlisting children under the age of 15 years into armed forces or groups or using them to participate actively in hostilities" were recognized serious crimes.[4] Article 5 of the Statute concerns crimes under Sierra Leonean law. It reads that:

---

[3] This was under the condition that if Charles Taylor were to lose the case, he would serve his term in another country; otherwise, the Dutch government would not have agreed to host his trial in its country. The jail term will be served in the United Kingdom.

[4] Article 4.

> The Special Court shall have the power to prosecute persons who have committed the following crimes under Sierra Leonean law:
> a. Offences relating to the abuse of girls under the Prevention of Cruelty to Children Act, 1926 (Cap. 31):
>   i. Abusing a girl under 13 years of age, contrary to section 6;
>   ii. Abusing a girl between 13 and 14 years of age, contrary to section 7;
>   iii. Abduction of a girl for immoral purposes, contrary to section 12.

Article 15 of the Statute of the SCSL relates to child victims of rape or various sexual abuses. It states that:

> 4. The Prosecutor shall be assisted by a Sierra Leonean Deputy Prosecutor, and by such other Sierra Leonean and international staff as may be required to perform the functions assigned to him or her effectively and efficiently. Given the nature of the crimes committed and the particular sensitivities of girls, young women and children victims of rape, sexual assault, abduction and slavery of all kinds, due consideration should be given in the appointment of staff to the employment of prosecutors and investigators experienced in gender-related crimes and juvenile justice.

Article 2 of the Statute concerns the concept of crimes against humanity. It provides that:

> The Special Court shall have the power to prosecute persons who committed the following crimes as part of a widespread or systematic attack against any civilian population:
> a. Murder;
> b. Extermination;
> c. Enslavement;
> d. Deportation;
> e. Imprisonment;
> f. Torture;
> g. Rape, sexual slavery, enforced prostitution, forced pregnancy and any other form of sexual violence;
> h. Persecution on political, racial, ethnic or religious grounds;
> i. Other inhumane acts.

According to Article 4 of the Statute, concerning other serious violations of international humanitarian law: "The Special Court shall have the power to prosecute persons who committed the following serious violations of international humanitarian law: [...] c. Conscripting or enlisting children under the age of 15 years into armed forces or groups or using them to participate actively in hostilities."

The Statute of the SCSL also makes various provisions concerning the prevention of sexual crimes against female children. For instance, Article 5 of the Statute borrowed from Sierra Leonean criminal legislation specifies that the Special Court shall have the power to prosecute persons who have committed the following crimes under Sierra Leonean law:

a. Offences relating to the abuse of girls under the Prevention of Cruelty to Children Act, 1926 (Cap. 31):
   i. Abusing a girl under 13 years of age, contrary to section 6;
   ii. Abusing a girl between 13 and 14 years of age, contrary to section 7;
   iii. Abduction of a girl for immoral purposes, contrary to section 12.

Article 15 of the Statute recognises the obligations of the prosecutor. It provides that:

> The Prosecutor shall be assisted by a Sierra Leonean Deputy Prosecutor, and by such other Sierra Leonean and international staff as may be required to perform the functions assigned to him or her effectively and efficiently. Given the nature of the crimes committed and the particular sensitivities of girls, young women and children victims of rape, sexual assault, abduction and slavery of all kinds, due consideration should be given in the appointment of staff to the employment of prosecutors and investigators experienced in gender-related crimes and juvenile justice.[5]

The Statute also adopts provisions protecting children in the Victims and Witnesses Unit which is set up by the Registry. Accordingly, the "Unit shall provide, in consultation with the Office of the Prosecutor, protective measures and security arrangements, counselling and other appropriate assistance for witnesses, victims who appear before the Court and others who are at risk on account of testimony given by such witnesses. The Unit personnel shall include experts in trauma, including trauma related to crimes of sexual violence and violence against children."[6]

Charles Taylor's trial was opened in The Hague on 4 June 2007. Brenda Hollis, a former US military attorney, was the prosecutor of the case. Witness testimony began on 7 January 2008. During the prosecution, live testimony from 94 prosecution witnesses was heard by the Court. The testimony of witnesses filled more than 50,000 pages. The Court also received written statements from 4 additional witnesses. A Motion for

[5] Article 15 (4).
[6] Article 16 (4).

Judgment Acquittal brought by the Defence was entirely dismissed by the Trial Chamber on 4 May 2009. In fact, the Defence presented their case on 13 July 2009 and after calling 21 witnesses, including Charles Taylor himself, concluded on 12 November, 2010. Charles Taylor was found guilty of 11 counts of crimes against humanity and war crimes. The charges against Charles Taylor are the following:

The Charges
Charles Taylor faces an 11-count indictment for crimes against humanity, violations of Article 3 Common to the Geneva Conventions and of Additional Protocol II, and other serious violations of international humanitarian law.
Crimes Against Humanity (CAH)
Violation of Article 3 Common to the Geneva Conventions and of
Additional Protocol II (war crimes) (WC)
Other serious violation of international humanitarian law (VIHL)

Terrorizing the civilian population and collective punishments
1. Acts of terrorism, WC

Unlawful killings
2. Murder, CAH
3. Violence to life, health and physical or mental well-being of persons, in particular murder, WC

Sexual violence
4. Rape, CAH
5. Sexual slavery and any other form of sexual violence, CAH
6. Outrages upon personal dignity, WC

Physical violence
7. Violence to life, health and physical or mental well-being of persons, in particular cruel treatment, WC
8. Other inhumane acts, CAH

Use of child soldiers
9. Conscripting or enlisting children under the age of 15 years into armed forces or groups, or using them to participate actively in hostilities, VIHL

Abductions and forced labour
10. Enslavement, CAH

Looting
11. Pillage, WC

Charles Taylor is the first head of state to be prosecuted and punished for several crimes including war crimes and crimes against humanity since the conclusion of the Nuremberg Tribunal for the prosecution and punishment of Major War Criminals of the Second World War.[7] Although one cannot deny that Charles Taylor was found not guilty of directly commanding crimes against humanity or war crimes, the judges of the SCSL were of the view that he had supplied soldiers and weapons to the Revolutionary United Front. Therefore, the Court concluded that Taylor was guilty of abetting and aiding war crimes during the relevant armed conflict. According to the Court, Charles Taylor had obtained clear knowledge that the Revolutionary United Front (RUF) was conducting atrocities against the general civilian population, such as by recruiting child soldiers, sexually exploiting children and mutilating victims. He was eventually convicted on 12 April and sentenced to 50 years imprisonment on 30 May, 2012. The SCSL has however delivered lengthier sentences than the one delivered to Charles Taylor, for instance, to Issa Sesay who was a commander in the RUF and was condemned to 52 years imprisonment.

The ICC

The developments concerning the establishment of various tribunals finally resulted in the formulation and ratification of one of the most important conventions in the world, namely, the Statute of the Permanent International Criminal Court (ICC)) in 1998. The Court was established in a very dramatic situation where the United States, constituting one of the five permanent members of the Security of Council of the United Nations, did not ratify the Statute and also officially withdrew its signature. The Court is set up to have jurisdiction over several international crimes. These are genocide, crimes against humanity, war crimes and, if possible, the crime of aggression. The Court is, contrary to the ICJ, an independent body from the United Nations Organization. This means it has an international legal personality and can engage in the writing of agreements with the United Nations or states of the world. Its relationship with the United Nations is already formulated within the provisions of a treaty.

According to the Statute of the Court, “It shall be a permanent institution and shall have the power to exercise its jurisdiction over persons for the most serious crimes of international concern, as referred to in this Statute, and shall be complementary to national criminal

[7] Of course one can also refer to the prosecution of Alberto Fujimori from Peru who was condemned to 25 years imprisonment for the killings and kidnappings which occurred during his Presidency and Saddam Hussein’s execution in Iraq.

jurisdictions."[8] The above statement makes it clear that the Court has jurisdiction over "the most serious crimes of international concern." Thus, all the crimes that are mentioned in the Statute of the Court are the most serious crimes and are to be prosecuted and punished whether by the Court or under national criminal jurisdictions. In other words, prevention of the crimes mentioned in the Court is important for the maintenance of those significant values of the international community as a whole. Again, the Statute of the Court makes it clear that the international legal community has a legal right to fight for the elimination of certain crimes that are seriously prejudicial to the integrity of human beings. Although the Statute has only mentioned four categories of international crimes, it may be applied more broadly to a number of other crimes that are listed within those four categories, such as apartheid, slavery, trafficking, and rape.

Crimes against Humanity

Among the crimes that are stated in the Statute of the ICC and are judged to be the most "serious crimes of international concern" are also listed sex trafficking, sexual exploitation, rape and sexual humiliation of women and children. The Statute of the Court recognizes the abovementioned crimes as constituting crimes against humanity. It states this important fact very clearly and leaves no doubt that the sex trafficking and sexual exploitation of women and children may come under its jurisdiction for prosecution and punishment. It says that

> Article 7
> Crimes against humanity
>
> 1. For the purpose of this Statute, "crime against humanity" means any of the following acts when committed as part of a widespread or systematic attack directed against any civilian population, with knowledge of the attack:
>   (a) Murder;
>   (b) Extermination;
>   (c) Enslavement;
>   (d) Deportation or forcible transfer of population;
>   (e) Imprisonment or other severe deprivation of physical liberty in violation of fundamental rules of international law;
>   (f) Torture;
>   (g) Rape, sexual slavery, enforced prostitution, forced pregnancy, enforced sterilization, or any other form of sexual violence of comparable gravity;

[8] Article 1.

(h) Persecution against any identifiable group or collectivity on political, racial, national, ethnic, cultural, religious, gender as defined in paragraph 3, or other grounds that are universally recognized as impermissible under international law, in connection with any act referred to in this paragraph or any crime within the jurisdiction of the Court;
(i) Enforced disappearance of persons;
(j) The crime of apartheid;
(k) Other inhumane acts of a similar character intentionally causing great suffering, or serious injury to body or to mental or physical health.

2. For the purpose of paragraph 1:

...

(c) "Enslavement" means the exercise of any or all of the powers attaching to the right of ownership over a person and includes the exercise of such power in the course of trafficking in persons, in particular women and children;

Article 7 thus has a very important value in the recognition of certain conducts as constituting crimes against humanity. The Statute of the ICC has in fact included trafficking in persons as a crime against humanity. An investigation into the provisions of Article 7 above demonstrates that crimes against humanity may, *inter alia*, be listed as “enslavement,” “sexual slavery,” “enforced prostitution,” and “any other form of sexual violence of comparable gravity.” This means that the Statute recognizes several actions or conducts which may be identified as crimes against humanity. Although the above identifications are independent of one another, they may yet be read in conjunction with one another because of their close connection as constituting crimes against humanity. It is here that the Statute of the ICC has defined the term “enslavement” which has not been defined within the constitutions of the preceding international tribunals/courts. It says that enslavement is *a)* the exercise of any ownership over a person or *b)* all of the powers attaching to the right of ownership over a person. According to the Statute of the ICC, enslavement also includes the exercise of such power in the course of trafficking in persons, in particular women and children. Consequently, the ICC explicitly defines the term “trafficking in persons” as constituting a crime against humanity. The interesting point here is that the formulation concerning enslavement has been borrowed from Article 7 (a) of the Supplementary Convention on the Abolition of Slavery, the Slave Trade, and Institutions and Practices Similar to Slavery formulated in 1956.[9] The relevant part of the Slavery Convention reads that enslavement is "the status or condition of a person over whom any or all of the powers attaching to the right of ownership are exercised." This means that the ICC puts a heavy emphasis on the recognition of the scope of the crimes against humanity as encompassing slavery and trafficking in persons, including the sex trafficking of women and children.

It is even more interesting to read closely the provisions of paragraph (h) in connection with various forms of sexual exploitation of women and children. The paragraph provides that "persecution against any identifiable group or collectivity on political, racial, national, ethnic, cultural, religious, gender" constitutes a crime against humanity. This means that the provisions of this paragraph are an integral part of law on sex trafficking since the act of sex trafficking may be designated and directed against a particular group whose race or culture may be different from the other side of the conflicting party. This was clearly demonstrated against the Muslim population of Herzegovina in the Yugoslavian conflict.

With the above introduction, the ICC creates the rights of prosecution and punishment of the crime of trafficking at a national level or, according to the principle of complementarity, either under the Court's jurisdiction or under the jurisdiction of its member states.[10] The principle of complementarity is rather a new expression in the system of international criminal justice, although the principle has been exercised to different degrees in the extradition, prosecution and punishment of criminals. In the contemporary system of international criminal justice, the principle helps in the identification, prevention, prosecution and punishment of the sexual exploitation of children and women in war or peacetime. Nevertheless, we do not deny that the principle has been rejected by many states and its value has sometimes been evaluated as zero. For instance, the Sudanese regime has not been willing to apply this principle

---

[9] Adopted by a Conference of Plenipotentiaries convened by Economic and Social Council resolution 608(XXI) of 30 April 1956 and done at Geneva on 7 September 1956. It was entered into force on 30 April 1957, in accordance with article 13.

[10] Consult J. Holmes, 'The Principle of Complementarity' in The International Criminal Court: The Making of Rome Statute – Issues, Negotiations, Results (R.S. Lee, ed., 1999), pp. 41-78; B.S. Bartram, 'Primacy or Complementarity: Reconciling the Jurisdiction of National Courts and International Criminal Tribunals,' 23 *Yale Journal of International Law* 383 (1998); L.A. Arbour, and M. Bergsmo., 'Conspicuous Absence of Jurisdictional Overreach' in *Reflections on International Criminal Court* (H.A.M. Von Hebel , J.G. Lammers, J. Schukking, eds, 1999); W. Schabas, An Introduction to the International Criminal Court (2001).

concerning its president Omar Hassan Ahmed Al-Bashir on charges of war crimes or crimes against humanity.[11]

Conditions for Prosecution

There are certain conditions required for the prosecution of trafficking in persons under the provisions of the Statute of the ICC. These are that *i)* the crimes are committed as part of a widespread attack, *ii)* they are committed as a systematic attack, *iii)* the crimes are directed against any civilian population and *iv)*with knowledge of that act. All these conditions are subject to discussion. Thus, there are several questions that must be resolved.

The first question is what the Statute of the ICC means by the use of the term "widespread." A reference to the decision of the ICTR illustrates the meaning of the term. The ICTR in its judgment defines the term as "massive, frequent, large-scale action carried out collectively with considerable seriousness and directed against a multiplicity of victims."[12]The ICTR also gives a definition for the term "systematic". According to it, systematic means "thoroughly organized and following a regular pattern on the basis of a common policy involving substantial public or private resources."[13] The definitions in the above have a very important message, i.e., there must be specific victims and there must have been a policy for the commission of the crime. They also make it clear that there must be a form of organization, or in the words of the ICTR, a "thoroughly organized" conduct. The judgment of the ICTR does not however say that the proof of both conditions - widespread and systematic - is necessary for the recognition of crimes against humanity.[14]

According to the above explanation, the ICC has clearly been authorized to have power over trafficking in persons under the definition of crimes against humanity. This means that it may prosecute cases of trafficking in persons, sexual slavery and forced prostitution. A concrete example is the enslavement of "comfort" women by the government of Japan during the Second World War.[15] These women were subject to

---

[11] See also *infra* section on complementarity.

[12] Prosecutor v. Akayesu, Judgement, No. ICTR-96-4-T (Sept. 2, 1998).

[13] Prosecutor v. Akayesu, Judgement, No. ICTR-96-4-T (Sept. 2, 1998).

[14] Consult Darryl Robinson, *Defining 'Crimes against Humanity' at the Rome Conference*," 93 The American Journal of International Law 43, 47 (1999).

[15] In pursuit of their criminal policy of aggression the Japanese Imperial Forces abducted and exploited approximately 200,000 very young females from 1937 to 1945. A large number of these women were about 12 years old. These females were captured in Asian countries with the purpose of exploiting them for sexual

various forms of violation including forced prostitution and other forms of sexual slavery.[16] Similarly, women and children were forced into sexual slavery and sexual exploitation in Rwanda and the Former Yugoslavia. The question of the sexual exploitation of young girls therefore became one of the serious questions during the proceedings of the ICTY or the ICTR. Both tribunals have thus clarified that sexual exploitation and rape of women or children during an armed conflict constitute crimes against humanity and are therefore punishable offences.[17]

Sexual Violence

There are, in fact, three terms which have occupied a significant and, at times, controversial space in the provisions of international criminal law, transnational criminal law, and the law of the statutes of the international criminal tribunals/courts. These are "sexual violence", "rape", and "sexual slavery". According to a United Nations report, sexual violence is "any violence, physical or psychological, carried out through sexual means or by targeting sexuality."[18] Therefore, a considerable number of acts can be recognised as constituting sexual violence, such as rape and attempted

---

services as sex slaves. This arrangement became an established institution in Japan and they became known as "comfort women". They were used by more than 2 million Japanese military troops including high-ranking officers. Comfort women were used in "comfort houses," after the Japanese invaded Manchuria in 1931. Comfort houses were created in countries that the Japanese invaded and occupied—from Manchuria to New Guinea. The comfort houses increased in number from 1937. The comfort women came from different states, but the majority of them (about 80-90%) were young women and teenaged girls from Korea who were taken using threats and force by Japanese troops. Between 10 to 20% of comfort women were Chinese, Dutch, Indonesian, Filippina or from other countries. Women who resisted were tortured in various ways and many were also killed through maltreatment and sexual abuse of their bodies. The Japanese government destroyed all of the comfort houses after the war and denied their existence. www.urbanstages.org/new/archive/comfortwomen/ - 14k.

[16] Consult Brook Sari Moshan, "*Women, War, and Words: The Gender Component in the Permanent International Criminal Court's Definition of Crimes Against Humanity*, 22 Fordham International Law Journal 154, 162 (1998).

[17] Several hundreds of children have been born as a consequence of rape in the former Yugoslavia.

[18] United Nations, *Contemporary Forms of Slavery: Systematic Rape, Sexual Slavery and Slavery-like Practices during Armed Conflict*, Final Report submitted by Ms. Gay J. McDougall, Special Rapporteur (New York: United Nations, 1998), E/CN.4/Sub. 2/1998/13, pp. 7-8.

rape, forcing two victims to perform sexual acts on each other, forcing a person to be naked in public and sexual slavery.

Rape

The word rape has not been so easy to define in the legal literature. In the *Foca* case, the Appeals Chamber Judgment of the ICTY defined rape in 2002[19] as an attack on the physical integrity of a female and not solely on her honour. Therefore, rape constitutes "the sexual penetration, however slight: (a) of the vagina or anus of the victim by the penis of the perpetrator or any other object used by the perpetrator; or (b) [of] the mouth of the victim by the penis of the perpetrator; where such sexual penetration occurs without the consent of the victim. Consent for this purpose must be consent given voluntarily, as a result of the victim's free will, assessed in the context of the surrounding circumstances. The *mens rea* is the intention to effect this sexual penetration, and the knowledge that it occurs without the consent of the victim."[20] According to the Chamber, the use of force does not constitute a necessary element for the recognition of rape. This is because the coercive circumstances presented in the *Foca* case made the victim's consent impossible. The coercive measures were similar to the crimes of sexual violence committed in Sierra Leone. Therefore, the idea that a genuine rape victim must manifest resistance under all conditions is impossible and impractical for many reasons, such as the physical strength and social power of the offender.[21]

In March 2009, Trial Chamber I of the SCSL issued its judgment in *Prosecutor v. Issa Hassan Sesay, Morris Kallon* and *Augustine Gbao*, known as the RUF.[22] The RUF committed many criminal acts, among them were also gender-based crimes such as widespread rape, sexual slavery and forced marriage. In fact the indictment charged the above persons with the following counts: rape as a crime against humanity;

---

[19] See also Human Rights Watch in www.hrw.org/sites/default/files/reports/sierleon0103.pdf.

[20] *Prosecutor v. DragoljubKunarac, RadomirKovac and ZoranVukovic*(*Foca*case), Appeals Chamber Judgement, June 12, 2002, IT-96-23 and IT-96-23/1, paras. 127-133.

[21] 1. Prosecutor v. Sesay, Kallon&Gbao, Case No. SCSL-04-15-T, Judgment (Special Court for Sierra Leone, Trial Chamber I, Mar. 2, 2009), *available at* http://www.scsl. org/LinkClick.aspx?fileticket=D5HojR8FZS4%3d&tabid=215.

[22] See also Valerie Oosterveld, 'The Gender Jurisprudence of the Special Court for Sierra Leone: Progress in the Revolutionary United Front Judgments', *Cornell International Law Journal Vol. 44, pp.49-74.*

sexual slavery as a crime against humanity; other inhumane acts, which included forced marriage, as a crime against humanity. It also listed outrages against personal dignity constituting a violation of Article 3 Common to the Geneva Conventions and of Additional Protocol II (count 9). They were finally convicted on the counts because of their participation in a joint criminal enterprise. The offenders' were found guilty of crimes including sexual slavery and forced marriage. According to the trial judgment, the RUF had committed rape crimes, and the three accused were found guilty of the commission of the crime against humanity of rape because their offences fitted the following description:

> (i) The Accused invaded the body of a person by conduct resulting in penetration, however slight, of any part of the body of the victim or of the Accused with a sexual organ, or of the anal or genital opening of the victim with any object or any other part of the body;
> (ii) The invasion was committed by force, or by threat of force or coercion, such as that caused by fear of violence, duress, detention, psychological oppression or abuse of power against such person or another person or by taking advantage of a coercive environment, or the invasion was committed against a person incapable of giving genuine consent;
> (iii) The Accused intended to effect the sexual penetration or acted in the reasonable knowledge that this was likely to occur; and
> (iv) The Accused knew or had reason to know that the victim did not consent.[23]

The term "rape" was similarly defined in the judgment of the *Akayesu* case by the ICTR. According to it, rape is constituted by a "a physical invasion of a sexual nature, committed on a person under circumstances which are coercive" and, therefore, the judgment clarifies that the scope of the definition of rape should not be restricted to the insertion of a penis into a victim's vagina or anus, neither should it be limited to the insertion of a penis into the mouth of the victim.[24]

A new case of rape is the barbarous rape of 126 women and children by the Congolese army troops in Minova in the Democratic Republic of Congo in November 2012. The army had lost a battle with the rebel M23 fighters in Goma before arriving in Minova. The United Nations and G8

---

[23] http://www.sc-sl.org/LinkClick.aspx?fileticket=XFkMHAERlnk%3d&. Visited on 14-09-2012.

[24] *Prosecutor v. Jean-Paul Akayesu*, Judgement, ICTR-96-4-T, September 2, 1998, para. 688. This definition was not however formulated into the ICC's Statute because of its broad definition of rape.

are now investigating as well as negotiating the way in which they should prevent impunity of Congolese soldiers.

Sexual Slavery

The third term relates to "sexual slavery".[25] As we have stated in the previous sections of this book, the definition of this can be found within the 1926 Slavery Convention and its 1953 Protocol amending the same Convention. It states that sexual slavery means the "status or condition of a person over whom any or all of the powers attaching to the right of ownership are exercised, including sexual access through rape or other forms of sexual violence."[26]

According to the above definition, sexual violence and rape both come under the provisions of laws on sexual slavery. This means that sexual violence or rape does not necessarily by itself imply the occurrence of sexual slavery, but that the crimes sexual violence and rape are both integrated into the definition of sexual slavery. In fact, sexual slavery constitutes the enslavement and degrading of a person to a very low condition which is combined with the deprivation of liberty. Thus, the legislator aims to emphasise that the term "sexual slavery" has a broad scope of applicability to sexual offences committed against women and children. The Elements of Crimes constituting an integral part of the Statute of the ICC is also relevant here. According to it, deprivation is also "any or all of the powers attaching to the right of ownership over one or more persons, such as by purchasing, selling, lending or bartering such a person or persons, or by imposing on them a similar deprivation of liberty."[27] It therefore continues that: "It is understood that such deprivation of liberty may, in some circumstances, include exacting forced labour or otherwise reducing a person to a servile status as defined in the Supplementary Convention on the Abolition of Slavery, the Slave Trade, and Institutions and Practices Similar to Slavery of 1956. It is also understood that the conduct described in this element includes trafficking

---

[25] See also the United Nations, *Contemporary Forms of Slavery: Systematic Rape, Sexual Slavery and Slavery-like Practices during Armed Conflict*, Final Report submitted by Ms. Gay J. McDougall, Special Rapporteur, E/CN.4/Sub. 2/1998/13, pp. 7-8.

[26] United Nations, *Contemporary Forms of Slavery: Systematic Rape, Sexual Slavery and Slavery-like Practices during Armed Conflict*, p. 9. The Slavery Convention was ratified by Sierra Leone on 13, March, 1962.

[27] Elements of Crimes, Article 7 (1) (g)-2 dealing with Crime against humanity of sexual slavery.

in persons, in particular women and children."[28] Obviously, with these provisions, the ICC aims to secure the position of children from any form of limitation of criminal responsibility.

The Geneva Conventions

There have been a large number of international agreements which deal with the regulation of armed conflicts. Their aims have been to minimize, as much as possible, criminal conduct during wartime, although one can scarcely deny the fact that most wars also have a criminal nature. The four Geneva Conventions of 1949 came into force for the regulation of armed conflicts and they are therefore formulated to secure the safety of civilians and their property from the unlawful conduct of combatants. According to the content of these four conventions, the contracting parties have undertaken to prevent their soldiers committing acts which are against the conventional and customary law of armed conflicts. They have therefore accepted a responsibility to inform all of their commanders and superiors about certain acts that are considered war crimes or grave violations of the international law of armed conflicts.

Of particular importance is the Geneva Convention IV relative to the Protection of Civilians in Time of War. Article 27 of the Convention reads that "Women shall be especially protected against any attack on their honour, in particular against rape, enforced prostitution, or any form of indecent assault." This means that women of all ages are protected by the Convention. The Convention clearly protects the dignity of women and criminalises all sexual misconduct against them. It is in fact an integral part of the obligations of states parties to take effective measures for the protection of children. The Convention has therefore clarified certain social rights of children within the provisions of its articles.

Cases

The Tribunals for both regions in Europe and Africa have taken very seriously the question of the sexual abuse of women and minors. The sexual enslavement of women during the war in the former Yugoslavia, especially against the Muslim population of Bosnia Herzegovina, was tried by the ICTY. According to the Tribunal, the sexual abuse of women and

---

[28] Footnote to the Elements of Crimes, Article 7 (1) (g)-2 dealing with the crime against humanity of sexual slavery.

young females constituted war crimes and crimes against humanity.[29] The ICTY prosecuted three former Serb soldiers who were heavily involved in the commission of sexual violence against the Muslim population of Herzegovina. They were found guilty of the rape of women and young girls. Two of these soldiers were also convicted by the ICTY for crimes of sexual enslavement. According to the Tribunal, they forcibly held thousands of Muslim young girls and women for over several months. They forced the prisoners to dance naked and to satisfy their sexual needs.[30] They were raped not once but several times until they were running with blood. Meanwhile, they would also be tortured if they refused to satisfy their requirements. Gang rape was therefore committed in many aspects. According to the ICTY, almost half of those prosecuted and convicted by the court have been found guilty of crimes involving elements of sexual violence. In the *Kunarac* case, the ICTY which was dealing with crimes committed during an armed conflict asserted that:

> ... forced or compulsory labour under enslavement as a crime against humanity. Under this definition, indications of enslavement include elements of control and ownership; the restriction or control of an individual's autonomy, freedom of choice or freedom of movement; and often, the accruing of some gain to the perpetrator. The consent of free will of the victim is absent. It is often rendered impossible or irrelevant by, for example, the threat or use of force or other forms of coercion; the fear of

---

[29] In one of its judgment, the ICTY concerning one of the accused stated that "In determining the appropriate sentence, the Chamber has assessed the gravity of Mr Zelenović's crimes, including the nature of the crimes of torture and rape as crimes against humanity, the particular circumstances of the case, and the form and degree of participation of Mr. Zelenović. The crimes to which Mr. Zelenović has pleaded guilty were part of a pattern of sexual assaults that took place over a period of several months, and in many different locations, and involved multiple victims. Mr. Zelenović took direct part in the sexual abuse of victims in a number of detention facilities, including multiple rapes of witness 75 and witness 87. … The women and girls in the detention centres lived in constant fear of repeated rapes and sexual assaults. Some became suicidal and others became indifferent to what happened to them. The victims at the detention centres in Foča suffered the unspeakable pain, indignity, and humiliation of being repeatedly violated, without knowing whether they would survive the ordeal. The scars left by the sexual assaults were deep and might never heal. This, perhaps more than anything, speaks about the gravity of the crimes in this case." http://www.un.org/icty/pressreal/2007/pr1152e-summary.htm.

[30] According to the United Nations's Special Representative on Sexual Violence in Conflict, 50,000 to 60,000 cases of rape have been reported. www.womenundersiegeproject.org/conflicts/profile/bosnia. Visited on 17-11-2012.

> violence, deception or false promises; the abuse of power; the victim's position of vulnerability; detention or captivity, psychological oppression or socio-economic conditions. Further indications of enslavement include exploitation; the exaction of forced or compulsory labour or service, often without remuneration and often, though not necessarily, involving physical hardship; sex; prostitution; and human trafficking.[31]

The importance of the above statement of the ICTY is that the enslavement was recognized as a crime against humanity and the crime can even be committed when there is no armed conflict. This means that sexual exploitation of women or children is not only a crime against humanity in wartime but also in peacetime.

Requirement for Identification

It is a question of significant importance, whether for the classification of trafficking in persons as a crime against humanity, there is any requirement of a *nexus* to war. Article 5 of the ICTY uses ambiguous language, but requires a *nexus* to an armed conflict. According to it, "The International Tribunal shall have the power to prosecute persons responsible for the following crimes when committed in armed conflict, whether international or internal in character, and directed against any civilian population…" However, the Appeals Chamber in its Decision on the Defence Motion for Interlocutory Appeal on Jurisdiction (*Tadic case*), rejected the interpretation that the relevant words of the Statute is only limited to the matter of armed conflict. In its opinion, such an interpretation is against the customary concept of crimes against humanity. Accordingly, with the exception of Article 5 of the Statute concerning crimes against humanity, no other statutory provision requires such a condition. Moreover, "it would however defeat the Security Council's purpose to read a similar international armed conflict requirement into the remaining jurisdictional provisions of the Statute. Contrary to the drafters' apparent indifference to the nature of the underlying conflicts, such an interpretation would authorize the International Tribunal to prosecute and punish certain conduct in an international armed conflict, while turning a blind eye to the very same conduct in an internal armed conflict."[32]In the *Tadic case*, it was also stated that the condition that crimes against

---

[31] *Prosecutor v Kunarac, Kovac and Vukovic*, Judgment of 22 Feb 2001, Case No IT-96-23-T and 23/1, para 541-542; See also www.cojite.org/tl.../Enslavement %20(reduction%20en%20esclavage).pdf.

[32] www.un.org/icty/tadic/appeal/decision-e/51002.htm - 216k.

humanity have to be committed in the time of armed conflict has also long since disappeared in other international documents which have been formulated after the Second World War. This is because:

> As the Prosecutor observed before the Trial Chamber, the nexus between crimes against humanity and either crimes against peace or war crimes, required by the Nuremberg Charter, was peculiar to the jurisdiction of the Nuremberg Tribunal. Although the nexus requirement in the Nuremberg Charter was carried over to the 1948 General Assembly resolution affirming the Nuremberg principles, there is no logical or legal basis for this requirement and it has been abandoned in subsequent State practice with respect to crimes against humanity. Most notably, the nexus requirement was eliminated from the definition of crimes against humanity contained in Article II (1)(c) of Control Council Law No. 10 of 20 December 1945.[33]

After the above explanation the Appeals Chamber continues that:

> . . . It is by now a settled rule of customary international law that crimes against humanity do not require a connection to international armed conflict. Indeed, as the Prosecutor points out, customary international law may not require a connection between crimes against humanity and any conflict at all. Thus, by requiring that crimes against humanity be committed in either internal or international armed conflict, the Security Council may have defined the crime in Article 5 more narrowly than necessary under customary international law. There is no question, however, that the definition of crimes against humanity adopted by the Security Council in Article 5 comports with the principle of *nullumcrimen sine lege.*[34]

For confirmation of the above point, one can simply examine the content of the conventions relating to genocide and apartheid. Both of these documents apply to both war and peacetime. According to the provisions of Article 1 of the Genocide Convention, states parties "confirm that genocide, whether committed in time of peace or in time of war, is a crime

---

[33] The Prosecutor v. DuskoTadic A/K/A "Dule", Decision on the Defence Motion for Interlocutory Appeal on Jurisdiction, Appeal Chamber's Judgment (1995), no.140. www.un.org/icty/tadic/appeal/decision-e/51002.htm - 216k. See Control Council Law No. 10, Control Council for Germany, Official Gazette, 31 January 1946, at p. 50.

[34] The Prosecutor v. DuskoTadic A/K/A "Dule", Decision on the Defence Motion for Interlocutory Appeal on Jurisdiction, Appeal Chamber's Judgment (1995), no.141.

under international law which they undertake to prevent and to punish." The provisions of most documents applicable to the crime of apartheid refer also to the fact that the crime constitutes a crime against humanity. The preamble of the Convention on apartheid states that "*Observing* that the General Assembly of the United Nations has adopted a number of resolutions in which the policies and practices of apartheid are condemned as a crime against humanity." Article 1 of the Convention, without specificifying any requirement for the necessity of armed conflict, states that "The States Parties to the present Convention declare that apartheid is a crime against humanity and that inhuman acts resulting from the policies and practices of apartheid and similar policies and practices of racial segregation and discrimination, as defined in article II of the Convention, are crimes violating the principles of international law, in particular the purposes and principles of the Charter of the United Nations, and constituting a serious threat to international peace and security." With these provisions, the article clearly emphasises that crimes against humanity can also be committed in peacetime.

Moreover, Article 3 of the ICTR does not require a *nexus* to an armed conflict and it omits such a requirement. The article reads that "The International Tribunal for Rwanda shall have the power to prosecute persons responsible for the following crimes when committed as part of a widespread or systematic attack against any civilian population on national, political, ethnic, racial or religious grounds…"

The abovementioned policy is also employed within the provisions of the Statute of the ICC which has omitted the vocabulary of the ICTY. The ICC in Article 7, as we have demonstrated above, formulates that for the purpose of its Statute, the term "crime against humanity" "means any of the following acts when committed as part of a widespread or systematic attack directed against any civilian population, with knowledge of the attack."

The examination of some of the most important instruments of international criminal law proves that the provisions of the ICC governing crimes against humanity are not restricted to wartime. In other words, the ICC has complementary jurisdiction over all crimes which may come under the category of crimes against humanity. This means that the crimes listed within Article 7, such as murder, extermination, enslavement, torture, rape, sexual slavery and apartheid all constitute crimes against humanity and are prosecutable and punishable by the law of the Court. The jurisdiction of the Court also applies to trafficking in persons, sexual exploitation and, not least of all, sexual abuse of children in various ways for the purposes of trafficking.

Complementarity Jurisdiction

Within the system of conventional international law, there are different ways to achieve the proper prosecution and punishment of perpetrators of crimes. These may be achieved by national, regional or international courts. The content of most international conventions applicable to trafficking in persons or sex trafficking and sexual exploitation of children require states parties to take the necessary legislative measures in order to bring those who have committed sex offences under an appropriate jurisdiction for the purpose of prosecution and punishment.

Whilst the Statute of the ICC also concerns the prosecution and punishment of those who have committed crimes against humanity, its power of jurisdiction is rather different from the power of national criminal courts. This is because the provisions of the ICC governing crimes against humanity and its jurisdiction do not apply automatically whether the trafficking in persons or sex slavery has been committed within a national or international context. The crimes have to meet certain conditions. These conditions are *inter aliaa*) a criminal investigation does not begin in the state in which the crime is committed, or the state is protecting the criminals. *b*) The state in which a person has been the victim of the relevant international crimes concerning trafficking in persons does not require extradition of the accused persons for the purpose of prosecution and punishment. *c*) The states which have, by one means or another, been affected by the consequence of the crimes are not interested in prosecuting the accused persons. *d*) The extradition of offenders has, for one reason or another, been prevented. *e*) There is an unjustified delay in the proceedings. *f*) A state prosecuting the offences has not been impartial in the proceedings of justice or *g)*A state is unable to prosecute the offenders.

All of the above principles denote the priority of jurisdiction of national courts in order to begin judicial proceedings over crimes of trafficking in persons. Whenever the ICC considers that the prosecution of offenders is not taking place in the appropriate countries as detailed above, it can, according to the principle of complementarity, begin its investigation. This principle means that the ICC bears responsibility for exercising its jurisdiction over persons for the most serious crimes of international concern. It also means that all national remedies for the prosecution of criminals must have been exhausted, and it is at this stage that the ICC will function as an international Court, or as a mandatory to national criminal courts, in order to prosecute and punish the perpetrators of trafficking in persons. The preamble of the ICC also states this fact. It reads that “the International Criminal Court established under this Statute shall be complementary to national criminal jurisdictions.” These words of the Statute are also strengthened by the provisions of its Article 1. The function of the ICC becomes clear with the reading of those provisions. The article states that “An International Criminal Court ("the Court") is hereby established. It shall be a permanent institution and shall have the power to exercise its jurisdiction over persons for the most serious crimes of international concern, as referred to in this Statute, and shall be complementary to national criminal jurisdictions.”

One reason why the Court has received only a complementarity function is that the states parties wanted to have effective control over the concept of international crimes, although the crimes are already defined within the provisions of the Statute. Another reason is that the prosecution and punishment of certain offenders are considered to be the primary right of a state and states do not want to diminish this right. The Statute of the ICC grants the exercise of jurisdiction to the Court and the Court is responsible for extending its jurisdiction wherever it is necessary, but under the condition of state sovereignty. This means that although the Court can exercise jurisdiction over enslavement, which includes trafficking in persons or sexual exploitation of women and children, the trafficking cannot be effectively prevented under the limited rights of the Court, unless the states parties positively contribute to the resolving of the question of whether the crime should be tried under their own legislation or the ICC Statute. Yet whether states recognise trafficking in persons as a crime against humanity within their legislation is another question of the motivation of justice and morality.

That is why one of the functions of the principle of complementarity is to support and encourage the relevant states parties if they do not give the Court the right of investigation. States should take into practical recognition the implementation of the Statute. This means that although the principle of complementarity implies a weakness in the application of international jurisdiction over serious international crimes, it makes it clear that states are under recognized international obligations not to ignore the rights of victims in any circumstances, in particular the sexual exploitation of children. Here it is the willingness or unwillingness of a state which calls for or dismisses the principle of complementarity.

CHAPTER NINE

REACHING EFFECTIVE CRIMINALIZATION

Protection of Values

The rapid development of technology and means of transportation since the establishment of the United Nations Organization, and access to new computerized systems such as the internet over recent decades, have seriously broadened the scope of the prostitution of women and children. Trafficking in persons has become one of the most serious problems in the world. Furthermore, increasing poverty in different parts of the world leads to sex trafficking and the sexual exploitation of children, in particular, is becoming more and more an international epidemic which is harming the fundamental values of the international community as a whole.

Sex trafficking and exploitation of women and children have fundamentally a commercial purpose. In fact, commercial sex is extracted from women or children through different methods, such as debt bondage, deception, fraud, abduction, false promises, coercion, and violent assault on their physical integrity. Women and children are exposed to psychological and physical violence from all the parties involved. The traffickers treat them as cargo and the persons for whom they are forced to work or to serve treat them like slaves. The term "consent" appears to have no relevance at all in the whole system of trafficking in persons.

Sex trafficking and sexual exploitation of women and children are not only dealt with within the fundamental international human rights instruments, but also, within the system of international criminal conventions and international humanitarian law. All these instruments imply the fact that trafficking in persons, including sex trafficking in women and children, constitutes a crime and is therefore prosecutable and punishable according to the process of law. They oblige the states parties to take serious measures for the implementation of their provisions in order to prevent or eliminate sex trafficking. They have also required the contracting parties to take serious national measures for the protection of victims and their future welfare in order to prevent their re-victimization.

Throughout this work we have tried to prove that the provisions governing trafficking in persons in general, and sex trafficking as well as the sexual exploitation of women and children in particular, constitute some of the most significant norms of the international law of *jus cogens* or the peremptory norms of general international law. Consequently, they call upon all states to adopt certain legislative and procedural measures for the prevention and elimination of trafficking. The conclusions in different sections of this work have also proved that these norms are considered obligation *erga omnes* and are to be fulfilled by all states of the world without regard to their acceptance of certain norms within their national legislation. The fundamental reason for this principle is the fact that the maintenance of certain values of the international community is so important and vital that they are to be respected and protected by all states of the world with no derogation of these values permitted. This is also based partly on the provisions of the Vienna Convention on the law of treaties and partly on the provisions of the Charter of the United Nations which make it the duty of all states of the world including members or non-members and their nationals to protect certain fundamental values of the international community as a whole.

In any event, the precise relevance of fundamental values is not easy to express, because they are interwoven with many other values basic to human nature. Their original significance is reflected within the fundamental principles of natural and positive law. Generally, they protect those important principles related to the integrity of mankind as a whole, which constitute an integral part of each individual personality. Any violation of these fundamental values equates to the violation of the basic rights of children, women and men and establishes a legal duty, according to the provisions of international human rights law and other international instruments, for the states of the world to protect the victims and prosecute and punish the organizers of the criminal behaviour. The reason is that the values endangered by traffickers are of global concern and do not have a limited scope of application.

The legal examination of a large number of conventional provisions proves that the sex trafficking and sexual exploitation of women and children cannot be solved in isolation. This is generally understood in the light of the increasing extension of the forced immigration of women and children from one country to another by the traffickers. In order to prevent, as much as possible, the sex trafficking and sexual exploitation of children, there must be a process of balancing up all the pertinent conventions and an appropriate weight has to be given to the various principles and factors surrounding the circumstances of each case.

Underlying Reasons

Based on the examination of various intentions within the provisions of different international instruments and due to the existence of various norms criminalizing the sex trafficking and sexual exploitation of children, the following reasons and measures may be useful for the recognition and prevention of the relevant crimes:

Poverty The effect of increasing poverty, economic stagnation, economic sanctions, or political repression within some parts of the world like North Korea, Latin America, some parts of Africa, Russia and Iran, to give a very few examples. This economic depression can also be seen within some of the countries of Europe and Asia. This means that the United Nations relevant organs have to work with this problem in order to improve the economic situation for women and children in poor countries.

Integration strategies Some states or regions also have a problem with the implementation of strategies for suppression, prevention and integration in order to counter the rapid proliferation of trafficking in persons, including the sex trafficking and sexual exploitation of women and children. The United Nations has to actively encourage the relevant countries to initiate preventative measures for the protection of women and children who are particularly vulnerable to trafficking for the sex trade. Approaches taken by states may consist of monitoring the trends and developments of sex trafficking, creating of anti sex trafficking policy, taking into recognition the questions of criminological factors, imposing measures to be implemented within the scope of states organs for the prevention of sex trafficking and protection of vulnerable victims and encouraging of common knowledge concerning the crime. Each of the above strategies describes the way in which a state may take actions against sex trafficking of women and children.

Non-incorporation A considerable number of states in the world, such as Iran, Russia, Guatemala, Costa Rica, Dominican Republic, Honduras, El Salvador, Argentina, Panama, Nicaragua, Ukraine and the Baltic states, have not yet acknowledged the seriousness of the sex trafficking of children and women within their programmes. The women and gradually the children of these regions suffer deeply from unemployment without any effective financial support from their governments.

Tourist Attraction The sexual exploitation of children has become one of the most lucrative sources of income in tourist ports. The problem has become so serious that children have been transported to these areas to provide services for tourists. This problem has to be resolved by each state within its own territories, and effective machinery for prevention has to be created with the assistance of the relevant organs of the United Nations.

Criminalization Many states in the world have criminalized sex trafficking and various forms of sexual exploitation of children under their national legislations but this criminalization is sometimes very weak and scarcely sufficient for the prevention of the crime. This problem has to be solved by each state of the world and sex trafficking as well as the sexual exploitation of children must be recognized as grave violations of the law of the international community as a whole.

Prostitution Non-prohibition of sex purchasing within many countries in the world, many of them in Europe, encourages, by one means or another, the development of sex trafficking and the sexual exploitation of women and children. However, there are also a few states in Europe, such as Iceland, Norway and Sweden, the laws of which prohibit the purchasing of sex but do not criminalize the prostitute.[1]This means that states which permit prostitution and which are also struggling against sex trafficking should re-examine the question of prostitution. This is in order not to increase, in one way or another, the problem of sex trafficking into their own or other countries. They should formulate certain rules or obligations for the deterrent of purchasers of sex services and also for the direct support of those who are exploited in prostitution.

Support by governments Although many governments demand that sex trafficking should be prohibited and their laws have taken measures against the sex trafficking and exploitation of young girls, the practice of these government is sometimes in contradiction with international rules and trafficking is directly or indirectly permitted in certain circumstances under their internal laws. This is the case in Germany, Greece, and France.

Artificial prohibition There are also countries, including Islamic states such as Iran, the constitutions of which prohibit trafficking and apparently

---

[1] Max Waltman, 'Prohibiting Sex Purchasing and Ending Trafficking: The Swedish Prostitution Law', *33 Michigan Journal of International Law* (2011),pp.133-157.

punish its perpetrators. But the fact is that they permit it under other names using religious reasoning.

Corrupted justice The administration of justice within many states of the world which have problems with sex trafficking and sexual exploitation of women and children is very weak and can easily be corrupted by the traffickers.

Dignity Although the fundamental principles of the United Nations, international human rights law, and many other direct and indirect instruments, such as conventions dealing with the ILO, state the equality of both sexes, the reality is rather different. In many countries in the world, men are still attributed much more value and integrity than women or children and this can be felt in most aspects of daily relations.

Social degradation One serious obstacle to preventing the development of sex trafficking in women and children is the degradation of their social conditions within different cultural activities and modalities. In many countries in the world, women are not welcome to take part in civil and political life, and this is even the case in permanent members of the United Nations such as Russia and China and also other members such as Iran or Afghanistan.

Armed conflicts One of the serious causes of the increase in sex trafficking and sexual exploitation of women and children is the waging of war. A considerable number of wars have increasingly resulted in the development of prostitution, sex slavery, sex trafficking, rape and the sexual exploitation of young girls and boys. The term "comfort women" became known as a consequence of the Second World War. The very prolonged Vietnam War, armed conflict in Rwanda, nationalist war in the territories of the former Yugoslavia, and ten years of war between Iraq and Iran are a few examples of conflicts increasing the development of prostitution and trafficking at a national and international level.

False promises Smuggling of families, women and children from one part of the world to another part by people smugglers has not always ended as they intended. This is especially true in the case of females who have been given false promises by their carriers. For instance, North Korean women, with the hope of finding a job and establishing a better standard of living in China, have placed themselves in the hands of smugglers only to find themselves forced to work in brothels.[2]

Neighbourhood markets The existence of neighbourhood markets is another reason for the spread of the sex trafficking and sexual exploitation of children. These are, for instance, from Russia to Finland and Sweden, from Honduras in Latin America to Belize, Guatemala, El Salvador, Mexico and the United States, and North Korea into China.

Lack of implementation The United Nations Security Council does not implement effective sanctions for the prevention of the crimes. Therefore, the body of international legal instruments suffers from the lack of the effective implementation of its machinery. This means that if the illegal and inhuman practice of trafficking is going to decrease, the application or implementation of the relevant instruments must take priority over other interests of states. Obviously, the Security Council system must be modified and until this has been done sex trafficking will remain one of the dominant forms of commerce in the world.

Jus cogens and* obligation *erga omnes There can be no doubt that the law governing the prevention and elimination of trafficking in human beings is an integral part of *jus cogens* norms or general international law and it is therefore a duty of states to respect and implement these norms. One can therefore strongly assert that the provisions of the relevant international conventions relating to women and children constitute an integral part of international customary law and are also a significant part of the general principles of international law which have to be respected and tolerated. Furthermore, it is true that since the creation of the United Nations and the adoption of the Universal Declaration of Human Rights, the international legal system has so far tended to establish individual rights and protections. This is especially evident concerning the rights of women and

[2] It is stated that for "the past nearly twenty years, North Korean women have waded through the muddy waters of the Tumen River to cross the North Korean border into China. In fact, the majority of refugees who flee North Korea for food or for hope of better economic opportunities are women.[2] Yet, for many of these women, neither food nor better economic opportunities materialize: North Korean refugee women are frequently lured by traffickers into performing sex work in karaoke bars or brothels or are forced into illegal 'marriages' to older, rural Chinese farmers." The Creation of the *Living Dead*: North Korean Refugee Women in China Jeannie Chung, Feminist Legal Theory Workshop December 22, 2009, p.1. blogs.law.columbia.edu/.../Jeannie-Chung-Fall-2009-FLTW-Final-Paper.doc.

children. In particular, they have received special protection under the United Nations Charter and also other related documents of human rights law formulated in accordance with the Universal Declaration of Human Rights. All these imply the effective consolidation of provisions relating to the prohibition of trafficking and the international norms compulsory within the jurisdiction of states. This means that there exists a legal duty for all states to provide effective legislative measures for the prevention and elimination of sex trafficking and sexual exploitation of children in order to guarantee the individual's rights and protection.[3]

Cooperation There is no doubt that the international legal machinery cannot work effectively as long as there is a lack of effective cooperative system between various states of the world for the prevention, elimination and prosecution of sex trafficking. This means that states of the world have to give particular attention to the questions of cooperation between their judicial administration, police and prosecution departments and also other relevant organs or authorities.

Victims Social integration of victims has often been considered important within different international conventions. Although protecting victims is vital for the practical prevention and elimination of sex trafficking, it is a fact that victims will not be recognized as victims if the legislative machinery of states has not sufficient efficiency to protect them from the very beginning. In particular, states have to realise that developing the awareness of their population concerning the harmful effects of sex trafficking will help individuals not to end up as victims of trafficking in the future. They should definitely have programmes to help vulnerable groups through social and financial support for this end.

---

[3] In any event, there are a considerable number of international cases which denote the tendency of states in the General Assembly or the Security Council to respond to *erga omnes* breaches. Some of the cases in which states have joint other states' enforcement actions through various sanctions are the apartheid practices in South Africa, the Iraq invasion of Kuwait, events of genocide and rape in the former Yugoslavian, the genocide and rape in Rwanda as well as recent rape cases in Congo. Although sanctions may have been taken against serious *erga omnes* violations, we do not deny the fact that respond to *erga omnes* breaches may be prevented because of political interests of super military or political parties. A clear example is the serious *erga omnes* violations in Chile between 1973 and 1990 and the support of the terrorist activities of Pinochet by the United States agent namely the 'CIA activities in Chile.'

Children One of the most serious features of trafficking is the sexual exploitation of children. This takes various forms including pornography, sexual penetration of their bodies, selling them as slaves, and their actual murder in the production of illicit video. Additionally, they may be very young with the age of victims varying from a few months to 18 years old. This means that traffickers may seek out their victims between different ages. Obviously, the legal machinery of the world does not properly function and this has to be strengthened by the creation of national and international courts which have legal expertise from different bodies concerning the questions and issues of children.

The United Nations should commit to raising awareness among member states that the sexual exploitation of children or young people is a horrific form of sexual abuse that affects millions of children.

The ICC Our examination of the constitution of the permanent International Criminal Court, the ICC, indicates that trafficking in persons is criminalized by its provisions and constitutes a prosecutable crime within the Court's jurisdiction. Trafficking in persons is dealt with under crimes against humanity as it is also formulated under the constitutions of ICTY, ICTR and the Special Court for Sierra Leone. All these imply that the crime of sex trafficking and sexual exploitation of children must be brought before the jurisdiction of the Court by states parties or the Security Council of the United Nations according to the provisions of the Statute of the ICC. In other words, the recognition of the trafficking in persons should be taken seriously by all states and organizations dealing in one way or another with its prevention.

Conclusion

Sexual exploitation of children may be a crime against humanity,[4] war crime[5] and also a serious violation of human rights law.[6] It is therefore a violation of international criminal law, international humanitarian law, and

[4] *Prosecutor v Kunarac, Kovac and Vukovic*, Judgment of 22 Feb 2001, Case No IT-96-23-T and 23/1, para 541-542.

[5] *Prosecutor v Krnojelac,* ICTY, Judgment of 15 Mar 2002, Case No IT-97-25-T, para 356.

[6] Piotrowicz, Ryszard., 'States' Obligations under Human Rights Law towards Victims of Trafficking in Human Beings: Positive Developments in Positive Obligations', Vol. 0, No.0 *International Journal of Refugee Law*, pp. 3-4.

transnational criminal law.[7] As the Report of the Working Group on Contemporary Forms of Slavery points out 'transborder trafficking of women and girls for sexual exploitation is a contemporary form of slavery and constitutes a serious violation of human rights' law.[8]

The whole philosophy behind the criminalization of trafficking in persons including the sex trafficking and sexual exploitation of children is to protect the international integrity of children, women and men. This has to be achieved by all available means. States of the world should realise that organized criminality, in particular sex trafficking, will not be ended by legislative measures. Traffickers remain successfully engaged in this business, even though there have been international conventions prohibiting it since the establishment of the League of Nations. The trade in this business is much stronger than was thought in the beginning. The problem is getting more serious due to the fact that the contemporary economic system of the world is dramatically affecting the social structures of most nations, in particular poor countries and rich countries which do not pay any attention to democratic principles. A considerable degree of caution must be exercised in evaluating the sex trafficking of women and children from developing states. Strong legislative measures within different countries of the world should not result, by one means or another, in the exploitation or even death of the victims of trafficking. There must be a balance between the means and the end and the proper application of economic, social and cultural norms.

---

[7] See also Farhad Malekian and Kerstin Nordlöf., 'International Legal Status of Children' in the Encyclopaedia of Criminology & Criminal Justice (Jay S. Albanese, editor, 5 voles, 2013).

[8] Report of the Secretary-General on Slavery, the Slave Trade and Other Forms of Servitude', para. 536, n 1323. Cited in ibid., pp.3-4. See *also* Farhad Malekian., 'The Law Governing Crimes against Women Constituting *Obligatio Erga Omnes' in Crimes Against Women* (David Pike, 2010), pp.3-22.

APPENDIX ONE

OPTIONAL PROTOCOL TO THE CONVENTION ON THE RIGHTS OF THE CHILD ON THE SALE OF CHILDREN, CHILD PROSTITUTION AND CHILD PORNOGRAPHY

Adopted and Opened for Signature, Ratification and Accession by General Assembly Resolution A/RES/54/263 of 25 May 2000, Entered into Force on 18 January 2002

The States Parties to the present Protocol,

Considering that, in order further to achieve the purposes of the Convention on the Rights of the Child and the implementation of its provisions, especially articles 1, 11, 21, 32, 33, 34, 35 and 36, it would be appropriate to extend the measures that States Parties should undertake in order to guarantee the protection of the child from the sale of children, child prostitution and child pornography,

Considering also that the Convention on the Rights of the Child recognizes the right of the child to be protected from economic exploitation and from performing any work that is likely to be hazardous or to interfere with the child's education, or to be harmful to the child's health or physical, mental, spiritual, moral or social development,

Gravely concerned at the significant and increasing international traffic in children for the purpose of the sale of children, child prostitution and child pornography,

Deeply concerned at the widespread and continuing practice of sex tourism, to which children are especially vulnerable, as it directly promotes the sale of children, child prostitution and child pornography,

Recognizing that a number of particularly vulnerable groups, including girl children, are at greater risk of sexual exploitation and that girl children are disproportionately represented among the sexually exploited,

Concerned about the growing availability of child pornography on the Internet and other evolving technologies, and recalling the International Conference on Combating Child Pornography on the Internet, held in Vienna in 1999, in particular its conclusion calling for the worldwide criminalization of the production, distribution, exportation, transmission, importation, intentional possession and advertising of child pornography, and stressing the importance of closer cooperation and partnership between Governments and the Internet industry,

Believing that the elimination of the sale of children, child prostitution and child pornography will be facilitated by adopting a holistic approach, addressing the contributing factors, including underdevelopment, poverty, economic disparities, inequitable socio-economic structure, dysfunctioning families, lack of education, urban-rural migration, gender discrimination, irresponsible adult sexual behaviour, harmful traditional practices, armed conflicts and trafficking in children,

Believing also that efforts to raise public awareness are needed to reduce consumer demand for the sale of children, child prostitution and child pornography, and believing further in the importance of strengthening global partnership among all actors and of improving law enforcement at the national level,

Noting the provisions of international legal instruments relevant to the protection of children, including the Hague Convention on Protection of Children and Cooperation in Respect of Intercountry Adoption, the Hague Convention on the Civil Aspects of International Child Abduction, the Hague Convention on Jurisdiction, Applicable Law, Recognition, Enforcement and Cooperation in Respect of Parental Responsibility and Measures for the Protection of Children, and International Labour Organization Convention No. 182 on the Prohibition and Immediate Action for the Elimination of the Worst Forms of Child Labour,

Encouraged by the overwhelming support for the Convention on the Rights of the Child, demonstrating the widespread commitment that exists for the promotion and protection of the rights of the child,

Recognizing the importance of the implementation of the provisions of the Programme of Action for the Prevention of the Sale of Children, Child Prostitution and Child Pornography and the Declaration and Agenda for Action adopted at the World Congress against Commercial Sexual Exploitation of Children, held in Stockholm from 27 to 31 August 1996, and the other relevant decisions and recommendations of pertinent international bodies,

Taking due account of the importance of the traditions and cultural values of each people for the protection and harmonious development of the child,

Have agreed as follows:

Article 1

States Parties shall prohibit the sale of children, child prostitution and child pornography as provided for by the present Protocol.

Article 2

For the purposes of the present Protocol:

(a) Sale of children means any act or transaction whereby a child is transferred by any person or group of persons to another for remuneration or any other consideration;

(b) Child prostitution means the use of a child in sexual activities for remuneration or any other form of consideration;

(c) Child pornography means any representation, by whatever means, of a child engaged in real or simulated explicit sexual activities or any representation of the sexual parts of a child for primarily sexual purposes.

Article 3

1. Each State Party shall ensure that, as a minimum, the following acts and activities are fully covered under its criminal or penal law, whether such offences are committed domestically or transnationally or on an individual or organized basis:
   (a) In the context of sale of children as defined in article 2:
      (i) Offering, delivering or accepting, by whatever means, a child for the purpose of:
         a. Sexual exploitation of the child;
         b. Transfer of organs of the child for profit;
         c. Engagement of the child in forced labour;
      (ii) Improperly inducing consent, as an intermediary, for the adoption of a child in violation of applicable international legal instruments on adoption;
   (b) Offering, obtaining, procuring or providing a child for child prostitution, as defined in article 2;

(c) Producing, distributing, disseminating, importing, exporting, offering, selling or possessing for the above purposes child pornography as defined in article 2.

2. Subject to the provisions of the national law of a State Party, the same shall apply to an attempt to commit any of the said acts and to complicity or participation in any of the said acts.
3. Each State Party shall make such offences punishable by appropriate penalties that take into account their grave nature.
4. Subject to the provisions of its national law, each State Party shall take measures, where appropriate, to establish the liability of legal persons for offences established in paragraph 1 of the present article. Subject to the legal principles of the State Party, such liability of legal persons may be criminal, civil or administrative.
5. States Parties shall take all appropriate legal and administrative measures to ensure that all persons involved in the adoption of a child act in conformity with applicable international legal instruments.

Article 4

1. Each State Party shall take such measures as may be necessary to establish its jurisdiction over the offences referred to in article 3, paragraph 1, when the offences are committed in its territory or on board a ship or aircraft registered in that State.
2. Each State Party may take such measures as may be necessary to establish its jurisdiction over the offences referred to in article 3, paragraph 1, in the following cases:
   (a) When the alleged offender is a national of that State or a person who has his habitual residence in its territory;
   (b) When the victim is a national of that State.
3. Each State Party shall also take such measures as may be necessary to establish its jurisdiction over the aforementioned offences when the alleged offender is present in its territory and it does not extradite him or her to another State Party on the ground that the offence has been committed by one of its nationals.
4. The present Protocol does not exclude any criminal jurisdiction exercised in accordance with internal law.

Article 5

1. The offences referred to in article 3, paragraph 1, shall be deemed to be included as extraditable offences in any extradition treaty existing

between States Parties and shall be included as extraditable offences in every extradition treaty subsequently concluded between them, in accordance with the conditions set forth in such treaties.

2. If a State Party that makes extradition conditional on the existence of a treaty receives a request for extradition from another State Party with which it has no extradition treaty, it may consider the present Protocol to be a legal basis for extradition in respect of such offences. Extradition shall be subject to the conditions provided by the law of the requested State.
3. States Parties that do not make extradition conditional on the existence of a treaty shall recognize such offences as extraditable offences between themselves subject to the conditions provided by the law of the requested State.
4. Such offences shall be treated, for the purpose of extradition between States Parties, as if they had been committed not only in the place in which they occurred but also in the territories of the States required to establish their jurisdiction in accordance with article 4.
5. If an extradition request is made with respect to an offence described in article 3, paragraph 1, and the requested State Party does not or will not extradite on the basis of the nationality of the offender, that State shall take suitable measures to submit the case to its competent authorities for the purpose of prosecution.

Article 6

1. States Parties shall afford one another the greatest measure of assistance in connection with investigations or criminal or extradition proceedings brought in respect of the offences set forth in article 3, paragraph 1, including assistance in obtaining evidence at their disposal necessary for the proceedings.
2. States Parties shall carry out their obligations under paragraph 1 of the present article in conformity with any treaties or other arrangements on mutual legal assistance that may exist between them. In the absence of such treaties or arrangements, States Parties shall afford one another assistance in accordance with their domestic law.

Article 7

States Parties shall, subject to the provisions of their national law:

(a) Take measures to provide for the seizure and confiscation, as appropriate, of:

(i) Goods, such as materials, assets and other instrumentalities used to commit or facilitate offences under the present protocol;
(ii) Proceeds derived from such offences;

(b) Execute requests from another State Party for seizure or confiscation of goods or proceeds referred to in subparagraph (a);
(c) Take measures aimed at closing, on a temporary or definitive basis, premises used to commit such offences.

Article 8

1. States Parties shall adopt appropriate measures to protect the rights and interests of child victims of the practices prohibited under the present Protocol at all stages of the criminal justice process, in particular by:
   (a) Recognizing the vulnerability of child victims and adapting procedures to recognize their special needs, including their special needs as witnesses;
   (b) Informing child victims of their rights, their role and the scope, timing and progress of the proceedings and of the disposition of their cases;
   (c) Allowing the views, needs and concerns of child victims to be presented and considered in proceedings where their personal interests are affected, in a manner consistent with the procedural rules of national law;
   (d) Providing appropriate support services to child victims throughout the legal process;
   (e) Protecting, as appropriate, the privacy and identity of child victims and taking measures in accordance with national law to avoid the inappropriate dissemination of information that could lead to the identification of child victims;
   (f) Providing, in appropriate cases, for the safety of child victims, as well as that of their families and witnesses on their behalf, from intimidation and retaliation;
   (g) Avoiding unnecessary delay in the disposition of cases and the execution of orders or decrees granting compensation to child victims.
2. States Parties shall ensure that uncertainty as to the actual age of the victim shall not prevent the initiation of criminal investigations, including investigations aimed at establishing the age of the victim.
3. States Parties shall ensure that, in the treatment by the criminal justice system of children who are victims of the offences described in the

present Protocol, the best interest of the child shall be a primary consideration.

4. States Parties shall take measures to ensure appropriate training, in particular legal and psychological training, for the persons who work with victims of the offences prohibited under the present Protocol.
5. States Parties shall, in appropriate cases, adopt measures in order to protect the safety and integrity of those persons and/or organizations involved in the prevention and/or protection and rehabilitation of victims of such offences.
6. Nothing in the present article shall be construed to be prejudicial to or inconsistent with the rights of the accused to a fair and impartial trial.

Article 9

1. States Parties shall adopt or strengthen, implement and disseminate laws, administrative measures, social policies and programmes to prevent the offences referred to in the present Protocol. Particular attention shall be given to protect children who are especially vulnerable to such practices.
2. States Parties shall promote awareness in the public at large, including children, through information by all appropriate means, education and training, about the preventive measures and harmful effects of the offences referred to in the present Protocol. In fulfilling their obligations under this article, States Parties shall encourage the participation of the community and, in particular, children and child victims, in such information and education and training programmes, including at the international level.
3. States Parties shall take all feasible measures with the aim of ensuring all appropriate assistance to victims of such offences, including their full social reintegration and their full physical and psychological recovery.
4. States Parties shall ensure that all child victims of the offences described in the present Protocol have access to adequate procedures to seek, without discrimination, compensation for damages from those legally responsible.
5. States Parties shall take appropriate measures aimed at effectively prohibiting the production and dissemination of material advertising the offences described in the present Protocol.

Article 10

1. States Parties shall take all necessary steps to strengthen international cooperation by multilateral, regional and bilateral arrangements for the prevention, detection, investigation, prosecution and punishment of those responsible for acts involving the sale of children, child prostitution, child pornography and child sex tourism. States Parties shall also promote international cooperation and coordination between their authorities, national and international non-governmental organizations and international organizations.
2. States Parties shall promote international cooperation to assist child victims in their physical and psychological recovery, social reintegration and repatriation.
3. States Parties shall promote the strengthening of international cooperation in order to address the root causes, such as poverty and underdevelopment, contributing to the vulnerability of children to the sale of children, child prostitution, child pornography and child sex tourism.
4. States Parties in a position to do so shall provide financial, technical or other assistance through existing multilateral, regional, bilateral or other programmes.

Article 11

Nothing in the present Protocol shall affect any provisions that are more conducive to the realization of the rights of the child and that may be contained in:

(a) The law of a State Party;
(b) International law in force for that State.

Article 12

1. ach State Party shall, within two years following the entry into force of the present Protocol for that State Party, submit a report to the Committee on the Rights of the Child providing comprehensive information on the measures it has taken to implement the provisions of the Protocol.
2. Following the submission of the comprehensive report, each State Party shall include in the reports they submit to the Committee on the Rights of the Child, in accordance with article 44 of the Convention, any further information with respect to the implementation of the

present Protocol. Other States Parties to the Protocol shall submit a report every five years.

3. The Committee on the Rights of the Child may request from States Parties further information relevant to the implementation of the present Protocol.

Article 13

1. The present Protocol is open for signature by any State that is a party to the Convention or has signed it.
2. The present Protocol is subject to ratification and is open to accession by any State that is a party to the Convention or has signed it. Instruments of ratification or accession shall be deposited with the Secretary- General of the United Nations.

Article 14

1. The present Protocol shall enter into force three months after the deposit of the tenth instrument of ratification or accession.
2. For each State ratifying the present Protocol or acceding to it after its entry into force, the Protocol shall enter into force one month after the date of the deposit of its own instrument of ratification or accession.

Article 15

1. Any State Party may denounce the present Protocol at any time by written notification to the Secretary- General of the United Nations, who shall thereafter inform the other States Parties to the Convention and all States that have signed the Convention. The denunciation shall take effect one year after the date of receipt of the notification by the Secretary-General.
2. Such a denunciation shall not have the effect of releasing the State Party from its obligations under the present Protocol in regard to any offence that occurs prior to the date on which the denunciation becomes effective. Nor shall such a denunciation prejudice in any way the continued consideration of any matter that is already under consideration by the Committee on the Rights of the Child prior to the date on which the denunciation becomes effective.

Article 16

1. Any State Party may propose an amendment and file it with the Secretary-General of the United Nations. The Secretary-General shall thereupon communicate the proposed amendment to States Parties with a request that they indicate whether they favour a conference of States Parties for the purpose of considering and voting upon the proposals. In the event that, within four months from the date of such communication, at least one third of the States Parties favour such a conference, the Secretary-General shall convene the conference under the auspices of the United Nations. Any amendment adopted by a majority of States Parties present and voting at the conference shall be submitted to the General Assembly of the United Nations for approval.
2. An amendment adopted in accordance with paragraph 1 of the present article shall enter into force when it has been approved by the General Assembly and accepted by a two-thirds majority of States Parties.
3. When an amendment enters into force, it shall be binding on those States Parties that have accepted it, other States Parties still being bound by the provisions of the present Protocol and any earlier amendments they have accepted.

Article 17

1. The present Protocol, of which the Arabic, Chinese, English, French, Russian and Spanish texts are equally authentic, shall be deposited in the archives of the United Nations.
2. The Secretary-General of the United Nations shall transmit certified copies of the present Protocol to all States Parties to the Convention and all States that have signed the Convention.

Appendix Two

Protocol to Prevent, Suppress and Punish Trafficking in Persons Especially Women and Children, supplementing the United Nations Convention against Transnational Organized Crime[1]

Preamble

The States Parties to this Protocol,

Declaring that effective action to prevent and combat trafficking in persons, especially women and children, requires a comprehensive international approach in the countries of origin, transit and destination that includes measures to prevent such trafficking, to punish the traffickers and to protect the victims of such trafficking, including by protecting their internationally recognized human rights,

Taking into account the fact that, despite the existence of a variety of international instruments containing rules and practical measures to combat the exploitation of persons, especially women and children, there is no universal instrument that addresses all aspects of trafficking in persons,

Concerned that, in the absence of such an instrument, persons who are vulnerable to trafficking will not be sufficiently protected,

Recalling General Assembly resolution 53/111 of 9 December 1998, in which the Assembly decided to establish an open-ended intergovernmental ad hoc committee for the purpose of elaborating a comprehensive international convention against transnational organized crime and of

---

[1] Adopted and opened for signature, ratification and accession by General Assembly resolution 55/25 of 15 November 2000

discussing the elaboration of, inter alia, an international instrument addressing trafficking in women and children,

Convinced that supplementing the United Nations Convention against Transnational Organized Crime with an international instrument for the prevention, suppression and punishment of trafficking in persons, especially women and children, will be useful in preventing and combating that crime,

Have agreed as follows:

I. General Provisions

Article 1

Relation with the United Nations Convention against Transnational Organized Crime

1. This Protocol supplements the United Nations Convention against Transnational Organized Crime. It shall be interpreted together with the Convention.
2. The provisions of the Convention shall apply, mutatis mutandis, to this Protocol unless otherwise provided herein.
3. The offences established in accordance with article 5 of this Protocol shall be regarded as offences established in accordance with the Convention.

Article 2

Statement of purpose

The purposes of this Protocol are:

(a) To prevent and combat trafficking in persons, paying particular attention to women and children;

(b) To protect and assist the victims of such trafficking, with full respect for their human rights; and

(c) To promote cooperation among States Parties in order to meet those objectives.

Article 3

Use of terms

For the purposes of this Protocol:

(a) "Trafficking in persons" shall mean the recruitment, transportation, transfer, harbouring or receipt of persons, by means of the threat or use of force or other forms of coercion, of abduction, of fraud, of deception, of the abuse of power or of a position of vulnerability or of the giving or receiving of payments or benefits to achieve the consent of a person having control over another person, for the purpose of exploitation. Exploitation shall include, at a minimum, the exploitation of the prostitution of others or other forms of sexual exploitation, forced labour or services, slavery or practices similar to slavery, servitude or the removal of organs;

(b) The consent of a victim of trafficking in persons to the intended exploitation set forth in subparagraph (a) of this article shall be irrelevant where any of the means set forth in subparagraph (a) have been used;

(c) The recruitment, transportation, transfer, harbouring or receipt of a child for the purpose of exploitation shall be considered "trafficking in persons" even if this does not involve any of the means set forth in subparagraph (a) of this article;

(d) "Child" shall mean any person under eighteen years of age.

Article 4

Scope of application

This Protocol shall apply, except as otherwise stated herein, to the prevention, investigation and prosecution of the offences established in accordance with article 5 of this Protocol, where those offences are transnational in nature and involve an organized criminal group, as well as to the protection of victims of such offences.

Article 5

Criminalization

1. Each State Party shall adopt such legislative and other measures as may be necessary to establish as criminal offences the conduct set forth in article 3 of this Protocol, when committed intentionally.
2. Each State Party shall also adopt such legislative and other measures as may be necessary to establish as criminal offences:
   (a) Subject to the basic concepts of its legal system, attempting to commit an offence established in accordance with paragraph 1 of this article;
   (b) Participating as an accomplice in an offence established in accordance with paragraph 1 of this article; and

(c) Organizing or directing other persons to commit an offence established in accordance with paragraph 1 of this article.

II. Protection of Victims of Trafficking in Persons

Article 6

Assistance to and protection of victims of trafficking in persons

1. In appropriate cases and to the extent possible under its domestic law, each State Party shall protect the privacy and identity of victims of trafficking in persons, including, inter alia, by making legal proceedings relating to such trafficking confidential.
2. Each State Party shall ensure that its domestic legal or administrative system contains measures that provide to victims of trafficking in persons, in appropriate cases:
   (a) Information on relevant court and administrative proceedings;
   (b) Assistance to enable their views and concerns to be presented and considered at appropriate stages of criminal proceedings against offenders, in a manner not prejudicial to the rights of the defence.
3. Each State Party shall consider implementing measures to provide for the physical, psychological and social recovery of victims of trafficking in persons, including, in appropriate cases, in cooperation with non-governmental organizations, other relevant organizations and other elements of civil society, and, in particular, the provision of:
   (a) Appropriate housing;
   (b) Counselling and information, in particular as regards their legal rights, in a language that the victims of trafficking in persons can understand;
   (c) Medical, psychological and material assistance; and
   (d) Employment, educational and training opportunities.
4. Each State Party shall take into account, in applying the provisions of this article, the age, gender and special needs of victims of trafficking in persons, in particular the special needs of children, including appropriate housing, education and care.
5. Each State Party shall endeavour to provide for the physical safety of victims of trafficking in persons while they are within its territory.
6. Each State Party shall ensure that its domestic legal system contains measures that offer victims of trafficking in persons the possibility of obtaining compensation for damage suffered.

Article 7

Status of victims of trafficking in persons in receiving States

1. In addition to taking measures pursuant to article 6 of this Protocol, each State Party shall consider adopting legislative or other appropriate measures that permit victims of trafficking in persons to remain in its territory, temporarily or permanently, in appropriate cases.
2. In implementing the provision contained in paragraph 1 of this article, each State Party shall give appropriate consideration to humanitarian and compassionate factors.

Article 8

Repatriation of victims of trafficking in persons

1. The State Party of which a victim of trafficking in persons is a national or in which the person had the right of permanent residence at the time of entry into the territory of the receiving State Party shall facilitate and accept, with due regard for the safety of that person, the return of that person without undue or unreasonable delay.
2. When a State Party returns a victim of trafficking in persons to a State Party of which that person is a national or in which he or she had, at the time of entry into the territory of the receiving State Party, the right of permanent residence, such return shall be with due regard for the safety of that person and for the status of any legal proceedings related to the fact that the person is a victim of trafficking and shall preferably be voluntary.
3. At the request of a receiving State Party, a requested State Party shall, without undue or unreasonable delay, verify whether a person who is a victim of trafficking in persons is its national or had the right of permanent residence in its territory at the time of entry into the territory of the receiving State Party.
4. In order to facilitate the return of a victim of trafficking in persons who is without proper documentation, the State Party of which that person is a national or in which he or she had the right of permanent residence at the time of entry into the territory of the receiving State Party shall agree to issue, at the request of the receiving State Party, such travel documents or other authorization as may be necessary to enable the person to travel to and re-enter its territory.
5. This article shall be without prejudice to any right afforded to victims of trafficking in persons by any domestic law of the receiving State Party.

6. This article shall be without prejudice to any applicable bilateral or multilateral agreement or arrangement that governs, in whole or in part, the return of victims of trafficking in persons.

III. Prevention, Cooperation and Other Measures

Article 9

Prevention of trafficking in persons

1. States Parties shall establish comprehensive policies, programmes and other measures:
   (a) To prevent and combat trafficking in persons; and
   (b) To protect victims of trafficking in persons, especially women and children, from revictimization.
2. States Parties shall endeavour to undertake measures such as research, information and mass media campaigns and social and economic initiatives to prevent and combat trafficking in persons.
3. Policies, programmes and other measures established in accordance with this article shall, as appropriate, include cooperation with non-governmental organizations, other relevant organizations and other elements of civil society.
4. States Parties shall take or strengthen measures, including through bilateral or multilateral cooperation, to alleviate the factors that make persons, especially women and children, vulnerable to trafficking, such as poverty, underdevelopment and lack of equal opportunity.
5. States Parties shall adopt or strengthen legislative or other measures, such as educational, social or cultural measures, including through bilateral and multilateral cooperation, to discourage the demand that fosters all forms of exploitation of persons, especially women and children, that leads to trafficking.

Article 10

Information exchange and training

1. Law enforcement, immigration or other relevant authorities of States Parties shall, as appropriate, cooperate with one another by exchanging information, in accordance with their domestic law, to enable them to determine:
   (a) Whether individuals crossing or attempting to cross an international border with travel documents belonging to other persons or without

travel documents are perpetrators or victims of trafficking in persons;

(b) The types of travel document that individuals have used or attempted to use to cross an international border for the purpose of trafficking in persons; and

(c) The means and methods used by organized criminal groups for the purpose of trafficking in persons, including the recruitment and transportation of victims, routes and links between and among individuals and groups engaged in such rafficking, and possible measures for detecting them.

2. States Parties shall provide or strengthen training for law enforcement, immigration and other relevant officials in the prevention of trafficking in persons. The training should focus on methods used in preventing such trafficking, prosecuting the traffickers and protecting the rights of the victims, including protecting the victims from the traffickers. The training should also take into account the need to consider human rights and child- and gender-sensitive issues and it should encourage cooperation with non-governmental organizations, other relevant organizations and other elements of civil society.
3. A State Party that receives information shall comply with any request by the State Party that transmitted the information that places restrictions on its use.

Article 11

Border measures

1. Without prejudice to international commitments in relation to the free movement of people, States Parties shall strengthen, to the extent possible, such border controls as may be necessary to prevent and detect trafficking in persons.
2. Each State Party shall adopt legislative or other appropriate measures to prevent, to the extent possible, means of transport operated by commercial carriers from being used in the commission of offences established in accordance with article 5 of this Protocol.
3. Where appropriate, and without prejudice to applicable international conventions, such measures shall include establishing the obligation of commercial carriers, including any transportation company or the owner or operator of any means of transport, to ascertain that all passengers are in possession of the travel documents required for entry into the receiving State.

4. Each State Party shall take the necessary measures, in accordance with its domestic law, to provide for sanctions in cases of violation of the obligation set forth in paragraph 3 of this article.
5. Each State Party shall consider taking measures that permit, in accordance with its domestic law, the denial of entry or revocation of visas of persons implicated in the commission of offences established in accordance with this Protocol.
6. Without prejudice to article 27 of the Convention, States Parties shall consider strengthening cooperation among border control agencies by, inter alia, establishing and maintaining direct channels of communication.

Article 12

Security and control of documents

Each State Party shall take such measures as may be necessary, within available means:

(a) To ensure that travel or identity documents issued by it are of such quality that they cannot easily be misused and cannot readily be falsified or unlawfully altered, replicated or issued; and

(b) To ensure the integrity and security of travel or identity documents issued by or on behalf of the State Party and to prevent their unlawful creation, issuance and use.

Article 13

Legitimacy and validity of documents

At the request of another State Party, a State Party shall, in accordance with its domestic law, verify within a reasonable time the legitimacy and validity of travel or identity documents issued or purported to have been issued in its name and suspected of being used for trafficking in persons.

IV. Final Provisions

Article 14

Saving clause

1. Nothing in this Protocol shall affect the rights, obligations and responsibilities of States and individuals under international law, including international humanitarian law and international human rights law and, in particular, where applicable, the 1951 Convention

and the 1967 Protocol relating to the Status of Refugees and the principle of non-refoulement as contained therein.

2. The measures set forth in this Protocol shall be interpreted and applied in a way that is not discriminatory to persons on the ground that they are victims of trafficking in persons. The interpretation and application of those measures shall be consistent with internationally recognized principles of non-discrimination.

Article 15

Settlement of disputes

1. States Parties shall endeavour to settle disputes concerning the interpretation or application of this Protocol through negotiation.
2. Any dispute between two or more States Parties concerning the interpretation or application of this Protocol that cannot be settled through negotiation within a reasonable time shall, at the request of one of those States Parties, be submitted to arbitration. If, six months after the date of the request for arbitration, those States Parties are unable to agree on the organization of the arbitration, any one of those States Parties may refer the dispute to the International Court of Justice by request in accordance with the Statute of the Court.
3. Each State Party may, at the time of signature, ratification, acceptance or approval of or accession to this Protocol, declare that it does not consider itself bound by paragraph 2 of this article. The other States Parties shall not be bound by paragraph 2 of this article with respect to any State Party that has made such a reservation.
4. Any State Party that has made a reservation in accordance with paragraph 3 of this article may at any time withdraw that reservation by notification to the Secretary-General of the United Nations.

Article 16

Signature, ratification, acceptance, approval and accession

1. This Protocol shall be open to all States for signature from 12 to 15 December 2000 in Palermo, Italy, and thereafter at United Nations Headquarters in New York until 12 December 2002.
2. This Protocol shall also be open for signature by regional economic integration organizations provided that at least one member State of such organization has signed this Protocol in accordance with paragraph 1 of this article.

3. This Protocol is subject to ratification, acceptance or approval. Instruments of ratification, acceptance or approval shall be deposited with the Secretary-General of the United Nations. A regional economic integration organization may deposit its instrument of ratification, acceptance or approval if at least one of its member States has done likewise. In that instrument of ratification, acceptance or approval, such organization shall declare the extent of its competence with respect to the matters governed by this Protocol. Such organization shall also inform the depositary of any relevant modification in the extent of its competence.
4. This Protocol is open for accession by any State or any regional economic integration organization of which at least one member State is a Party to this Protocol. Instruments of accession shall be deposited with the Secretary-General of the United Nations. At the time of its accession, a regional economic integration organization shall declare the extent of its competence with respect to matters governed by this Protocol. Such organization shall also inform the depositary of any relevant modification in the extent of its competence.

Article 17

Entry into force

1. This Protocol shall enter into force on the ninetieth day after the date of deposit of the fortieth instrument of ratification, acceptance, approval or accession, except that it shall not enter into force before the entry into force of the Convention. For the purpose of this paragraph, any instrument deposited by a regional economic integration organization shall not be counted as additional to those deposited by member States of such organization.
2. For each State or regional economic integration organization ratifying, accepting, approving or acceding to this Protocol after the deposit of the fortieth instrument of such action, this Protocol shall enter into force on the thirtieth day after the date of deposit by such State or organization of the relevant instrument or on the date this Protocol enters into force pursuant to paragraph 1 of this article, whichever is the later.

Article 18

Amendment

1. After the expiry of five years from the entry into force of this Protocol, a State Party to the Protocol may propose an amendment and file it with the Secretary-General of the United Nations, who shall thereupon communicate the proposed amendment to the States Parties and to the Conference of the Parties to the Convention for the purpose of considering and deciding on the proposal. The States Parties to this Protocol meeting at the Conference of the Parties shall make every effort to achieve consensus on each amendment. If all efforts at consensus have been exhausted and no agreement has been reached, the amendment shall, as a last resort, require for its adoption a two-thirds majority vote of the States Parties to this Protocol present and voting at the meeting of the Conference of the Parties.
2. Regional economic integration organizations, in matters within their competence, shall exercise their right to vote under this article with a number of votes equal to the number of their member States that are Parties to this Protocol. Such organizations shall not exercise their right to vote if their member States exercise theirs and vice versa.
3. An amendment adopted in accordance with paragraph 1 of this article is subject to ratification, acceptance or approval by States Parties.
4. An amendment adopted in accordance with paragraph 1 of this article shall enter into force in respect of a State Party ninety days after the date of the deposit with the Secretary-General of the United Nations of an instrument of ratification, acceptance or approval of such amendment.
5. When an amendment enters into force, it shall be binding on those States Parties which have expressed their consent to be bound by it. Other States Parties shall still be bound by the provisions of this Protocol and any earlier amendments that they have ratified, accepted or approved.

Article 19

Denunciation

1. A State Party may denounce this Protocol by written notification to the Secretary-General of the United Nations. Such denunciation shall become effective one year after the date of receipt of the notification by the Secretary-General.

2. A regional economic integration organization shall cease to be a Party to this Protocol when all of its member States have denounced it.

Article 20

Depositary and languages

1. The Secretary-General of the United Nations is designated depositary of this Protocol.
2. The original of this Protocol, of which the Arabic, Chinese, English, French, Russian and Spanish texts are equally authentic, shall be deposited with the Secretary-General of the United Nations.
   In witness whereof, the undersigned plenipotentiaries, being duly authorized thereto by their respective Governments, have signed this Protocol.

Appendix Three

European Parliament Resolution on the Trafficking of Women and Children in Cambodia (2005)

Official Journal 247 E , 06/10/2005 P. 0161 - 0163

The European Parliament,

- having regard to its previous resolutions on Cambodia, and in particular those of 13 March 2003 [1] and 12 February 2004 [2],

- having regard to the cooperation agreement between the European Community and the Kingdom of Cambodia [3], which entered in force on 1 November 1999,

- having regard to the 2000-2003 EC-Cambodia Strategy Document and the 2005-2006 National Indicative Programme,

- having regard to the statement made by the Local Presidency of the European Union on behalf of the EU Heads of Missions in Phnom Penh on the attack on a shelter for victims of human trafficking operated by the Association "Agir Pour les Femmes en Situation Précaire" (Afesip),

- having regard to the UN Convention on the Rights of the Child and to the Convention on the Elimination of All Forms of Discrimination against Women, ratified by Cambodia and by all EU Member States,

- having regard to the UN Protocol to Prevent, Suppress and Punish Trafficking in Persons, especially Women and Children, and the UN Convention against Organised Crime,

- having regard to the EU guidelines on the protection of human rights activists approved by the European Council in July 2004,

- having regard to the agreement between UN and Cambodia on a budget for a special Cambodia war crimes tribunal,

- having regard to Rule 115(5) of its Rules of Procedure,

A. having regard to the attack on the Srey Khan Center of the Afesip Association where 91 women and young girls were staying, 83 of whom had been freed the day before by officials working for the Department for

Trafficking in Human Beings and Juvenile Protection from a hotel where prostitution was being practised,

B. whereas the fate of these 91 women and girls is unknown,

C. whereas eight people were arrested during the police operation and freed the following day,

D. having regard to the death threats received by Somaly Mam, an activist working for children forced into prostitution and for whom the Cambodian government cannot guarantee protection,

E. whereas trafficking in humans beings and sexual exploitation are a form of modern day slavery and constitute flagrant violations of fundamental human rights carried out by organised criminal networks operating across international borders; whereas this is a lucrative business for the traffickers,

F. whereas trafficking in human beings is increasing because of poverty, unemployment, the vulnerability of women and children, deteriorating social conditions in the countries of origin, the high profits and low risks experienced by traffickers, and the demand for women and children for purposes of prostitution and other forms of sexual exploitation,

G. whereas efforts still need to be made in the fight against organised crime and trafficking in human beings,

H. whereas during the 7th Consultative Group (CG) meeting on Cambodia of 6 and 7 December 2004 participants agreed on a series of common indicators, including enacting domestic violence and antitrafficking laws, to help the government of Cambodia and development partners alike to monitor performance in the coming year,

I. considering the creation of an Interministerial Committee by the government of Cambodia which will investigate the attack on the Afesip centre,

1. Denounces the sexual exploitation of minors as a crime "erga omnes" and an attack on the fundamental rights of children which must be fought at all levels;

2. Stresses its preoccupation with child prostitution in Cambodia and with the trafficking in human beings both to and from Cambodia, with the objective of using them for forced labour, prostitution and begging and in illegal adoptions;

3. Recalls the principles of the Charter of Human Rights and especially the rights of girls, in the case of sexual exploitation of minors in Asia and in the rest of the world;

4. Condemns the attack of 8 December 2004 on the Afesip shelter for victims of human trafficking in Phnom Penh and the abduction of 91 women and girls, some of them minors;

5. Condemns the sex tourism industry in Cambodia and the other countries where it occurs, and requests that EU Member States enact and apply the necessary legislation needed to bring to justice all those involved in sex tourism with minors;

6. Insists that the Commission takes into account the rights of children and women who are victims of trafficking in the programming of its human rights policy, within the framework of the European Initiative for Democracy and Human Rights;

7. Requests that the Commission supports human rights organisations in Cambodia, especially those dedicated to the protection of victims of trafficking and sexual exploitation;

8. Welcomes the decision of the Government of Cambodia to establish an interministerial committee including representatives of the foreign missions and national and international non-governmental organisations, as observers to witness, further investigate and personally interview the women concerned;

9. Is confident of a positive and fair result from the Interministerial Committee which has just been set up, and recognises that the Cambodian authorities have made efforts to combat trafficking in women and children; underlines, however, the need to increase the number of prosecutions and convictions of traffickers so to put an end to trafficking in women and child prostitution;

10. Calls on the Cambodian authorities to guarantee the safety of child protection organisations and their workers, especially for those organisations working to help trafficking and sexual exploitation victims;

11. Calls on the Cambodian authorities to guarantee the safety of Somaly Mam, whose life is in danger;

12. Calls on the Government of Cambodia to ratify the UN Protocol to Prevent, Suppress and Punish Trafficking in Persons, especially Women and Children, and the UN Convention against Organised Crime;

13. Calls on the EU Member States to act together in the fight against organised crime and trafficking in human beings, especially trafficking in minors;

14. Instructs its President to forward this resolution to the Council, the Commission, the Government of Cambodia, and the Governments of the ASEAN Member States.

[1] OJ C 61 E, 10.3.2004, p. 417.
[2] P5_TA(2004)0101.
[3] OJ L 269, 19.10.1999, p. 18.

BIBLIOGRAPHY

Abd-el-Malek, al-Saleh Osman., 'The Right of the Individual to Personal Security in Islam' in Bassiouni, *The Islamic Criminal Justice System*, pp.55-90.

Abdulai, Napoleon, (ed.)., *Genocide in Rwanda, Africa Research & Information Centre*, (1994).

Abraham, Shailaja., *Going nowhere: Trafficking of Women & Children in International Sex Trade* (2001).

Adelman Howard & Astri Suhrke, (eds.)., *The path of a genocide: The Rwanda Crisis, from Uganda to Zaire* (1999).

Akanda, Latifa., *Trafficking and Prostitution* (1997).

Allain, Jean, Slavery in International Law (2012).

Arbour, L.A. and Bergsmo M.., 'Conspicuous Absence of Jurisdictional Overreach' in *Reflections on International Criminal Court* (H.A.M. Von Hebel , J.G. Lammers, J. Schukking, eds, 1999).

Bachrach, Michael., 'The Protection and Rights of Victims under International Criminal Law,' 34(1) *The International Lawyer* (2000).

Barnett, Michael N., *Eyewitness to a Genocide: The United Nations and Rwanda* (2002).

Bassiouni, M. Cherif., 'International Recognition of Victims' Rights,' in Bassiouni (ed.), *International Criminal Law,* vol. III, 635-701 (2008).

—. (ed.), *International Criminal Law* (3 vols., 1999).

—. (ed.), *The Islamic Criminal Justice System* (1982).

—. 'The Discipline of International Criminal Law,' in M. Cherif Bassiouni (ed.), *International Criminal Law*, vol. 1 (2008) pp.3-40.

—. 'The Subjects of International Criminal Law: Ratione Personae' in M. Cherif Bassiouni (ed.), *International Criminal Law*, vol. 1 (2008) pp.41-70.

—. *Introduction to International Criminal Law* (2003).

Berry, John A. & Carol Pott Berry, (eds.), *Genocide in Rwanda* (1999).

Bosworth, Smith R., *Mohammed and Mohammedanism* (1889).

Braeckman, Colette., *Rwanda: Histoire d'un Génocide*, (1994).

Brown, Bartram., 'Primacy or Complementarity: Reconciling the Jurisdiction of National Courts and International Criminal Tribunals,' 23 *Yale Journal of International Law* 383 (1998).

Browning, Christopher., *The path to genocide: Essays on launching the final solution* (2002).

Burgorgue-Larsen Laurence., (ed.)., *La répression internationale du génocide rwandais,* (2003) .

Commonwealth Secretariat, London, *Report of the Expert Group on Strategies for Combating the Trafficking of Women and Children* (2003)

Conny, Rijken., *Trafficking in Persons: A Prosecution from a European Perspective* (2003).

Cryer, Robert., 'The Doctrinal Foundations of International Criminalization,' in *International Criminal Law*, Vol.1 (M. Cherif Bassiouni, ed. 2008) pp. 107-128.

Van Dam Cees, *European Tort Law* (2007).

Dinstein, Yoram., *'International Criminal Law,'* 20 *Israel Law Review* 206 (1985).

Duffy, Helen., 'HadijatouMani Koroua v Niger: Slavery Unveiled by the ECOWAS Court', *Human Rights Law Review* (2008), pp.1-20.

Ehard, Hans., 'The Nuremberg Trial against the Major War Criminals and International Law,' 33 *A.J.I.L.* 223 (1949).

Finch, George Augustus., *The Nuremberg Trial and International Law,* 41 AJIL 20 (1947).

Friedlander, Robert A., 'The Foundations of International Criminal Law: A Present-Day Inquiry,' 15 *Case Western Reserve Journal of International Law*13 (1983).

Gathia, Joseph., *Child Prostitution in India* (1998).

Gideon, Boas and William A. Schabas (eds.), *International Criminal Law Developments in the Case Law of the ICTY* (2003).

Glueck, Sheldon., 'By What Tribunal Shall War Offenders Be Tried?,' 56 *Harv.L.R.* 1059 (1942-3).

—. *The Nuremberg Trial and Aggressive War* (New York, 1946).

Grant, David and Beth Grant., *Beyond the Soiled Curtain: Project Rescue's Fight for the Victims of the Sex-Slave Industry* (2007).

Haroon, Khan Sharwani., *Studies in Muslim Political Thought and Administration* (1959).

Holmes, J., 'The Principle of Complementarity' in The *International Criminal Court: The Making of Rome Statute – Issues, Negotiations, Results* (R.S. Lee, ed., 1999), pp. 41-78.

Human Trafficking (2006).

Husain, Mazhar., *Immoral Traffic (Prevention) Act, 1956* (1997).

Ibrahim, Shihata., *Islamic Law and the World Community*, I, No.4 Harvard International Club Journal (1962).

International Military Tribunal, Trial of the Major War Criminals Before the International Military Tribunal in Nuremberg (1947).

Jackson, Robert, H., 'Forward the Nürenberg Trial Becomes a Historical Precedent', 20 *Temple L.Q* (1946-7).

Kara, Siddharth, *Sex Trafficking: Inside the Business of Modern Slavery* (2008).

Kelly, Robert J & MAGHAN, Jess Ors., *Illicit Trafficking* (2005).

Kelsen, Hans., 'Will the Judgement of the Nürenberg Trial Constitute a Precedent in International Law,' 1 *INT'L L.Q* 153 (1947).

Kempadoo, Kamala, Jyoti Sanghera, and Bandana Pattanaik., *Trafficking and Prostitution Reconsidered: New Perspectives on Migration, Sex Work, and Human Rights* (2005).

Kempadoo, Kamala, Sanghera, Jyoti & Pattanaik, Bandana (eds.)., *Trafficking and Prostitution Reconsidered* (2005).

Kendall, Virginia M. and T. Markus Funk., *Child Exploitation and Trafficking: Examining the Global Chanllenges and U.S. Responses* (2011).

Khadduri Majid., (translator), *THE ISLAMIC LAW OF NATIONS: SHAYBANI'S SIYAR* (1966).

—. (ed)., *Law in the Middle East,* (1955).

—. War and Peace in the Law of Islam (1955).

—. *'Islam and the Modern Law of Nations',* 50 *American Journal of International Law* (1956), pp.358-72.

—. *The Islamic Theory of International Relations and Its Contemporary Relevance* in Proctor, 24-ff.

Khalafalla, Ahmad., 'Muhammed Islamic Law, Civilization and Human Rights,' 12 *Egyptian Review of International Law* (1956).

Krishnamurthy, K., *Trafficking in Human Beings* (2005).

Kuhn, Arthur, K., 'International Criminal Jurisdiction,' 41 *American Journal of International Law* 430 (1947).

Laczko, Frank & Gozdziak Elzbieta (Eds.)., *Data and Research on Human Trafficking* (International Organization for Migration, Switzerland, 2005).

Lee, Maggy., *Human Trafficking* (2007).

—. Trafficking and Global Crime Control (2010).

Lippman, Matthew., Sean McConville, and Mordechai Yerushalmi, *Islamic Criminal Law and Procedure: An Introduction (1988).*

Mahmud Brevli., *Islam and the Contemporary Faiths* (1965).

Malekian, Farhad and Kerstin Nordlöf., *Confessing the International Rights of Children* (2012).

—. *Principles of Islamic International Criminal Law: A Comparative Search* (2011).
—. 'The Miserable Wedding of Naturalism into Positivism,' *ID EST Journal* (2009), pp. 139-151.
—. *Documents on the Principles of International Human Rights* (2007).
—. 'Emasculating the Philosophy of International Criminal Justice in the Iraqi Special Tribunal,' 38:3 *Cornell International Law Journal* (2005) 673-723.
—. 'International Criminal Responsibility' in M. Cherif Bassiouni (ed.), *International Criminal Law*, (1999).
—. The Law Governing Crimes against Women Constituting *Obligatio Erga Omnes' in Crimes Against Women* (David Pike, 2010), pp.3-22.
—. *The Monopolization of International Criminal Law in the United Nations: A Jurisprudential Approach* (1993, 1 ed., 2 ed, 1995).
—. *International Criminal Law: The Legal and Critical Analysis of International Crimes* (2 vols. 1991).
—. (eds.), *The Sovereignty of Children in Law* (2012).
—. 'Judging International Criminal Justice in the Occupied Territories', 12 *International Criminal Law Review* (2012) 827–869.
Maulvi, Muhammad Ali., *Islam the Religion of Humanity* (1926).
Muhammad Salim, Al-'Awwa, '*The Basis of Islamic Penal Legislation'* in Bassiouni, The Islamic Criminal Justice System, pp.127-47.
Nair, Sankar Sen P.M., *Trafficking In Women and Children in India* (2005).
National Human Rights Commission, *New Delhi, From Bondage to Freedom: An analysis of International Legal Regime on*
Nordlöf, Kerstin., (see also Malekian)
Nordlöf, Kerstin., 'Economic Raison d'être of Trafficking in Children' *in Rätten i den Ekonomiska Krisen* (2012), pp.191-214.
O'Sullivan J. E. Ackerman & E., *Practice and Procedure of the International Criminal Tribunal for the Former Yugoslavia with Selected Material from the International Criminal Tribunal for Rwanda* (2000).
Obakata, Tom., *Trafficking of Human Beings from a Human Rights Perspective* (2006).
Pike, David., *Crimes Against Women* (2010).
Piotrowicz, Ryszard., 'States' Obligations under Human Rights Law towards Victims of Trafficking in Human Beings: Positive Developments in Positive Obligations', Vol. 0, No.0 *International Journal of Refugee Law*, pp. 1–21 .

Posner, Eric A., Erga Omnes Norms, Institutionalization, and Constitutionalism in International Law 1 (The Law School, the University of Chicago, 2008), Johan M. Olin Law and Economics Working Paper No. 419 (2d Series), Public Law and Legal Theory Working Paper No.224, Electronic copy available at: http://ssrn.com/abstract=1211424.

Proctor J. Harris (ed.)., *Islam and International Relations* (1965).

Proctor, J. Harris., (ed.), *Islam and International Relations* (1965).

Quincy Wright., 'The Law of the Nuremberg Trial', 41 *American journal of International Law* 38 (1947).

Ragazzi, Maurizio., *The Concept of International Obligations Erga Omnes* (2000).

Rishmawi Mervat., 'The Revised Arab Charter on Human Rights: A Step Forward?' *5 (2) Human Rights Law Review* (2005), pp.361-376.

Saarc, Secretariat Kathmandu., *SAARC Convention on preventing and combating trafficking in women & children for prostitution* (SAARC Secretariat, Kathmandu, 2002).

Sadat, Leila Nadya., *The International Criminal Court and the Transformation of International Law: Justice for the New Millennium*, (2002).

Schabas W., *An Introduction to the International Criminal Court* (2001).

Schabas, William A., 'Reservations to the Convention on the Elimination of All Forms of Discrimination Against Women and the Convention on the Rights of the Child,' *3 William & Mary Journal of Women and the Law (1997),* 79-112.

Schabas, William A., 'Reservations to the Convention on the Rights of the Child', *Human Rights Quarterly* 18.2 (1996), pp. 472-491.

Schick F.B., 'The Nuremberg Trial and the International Law of the Future,' 41 *American Journal of International Law* 770 (1947).

Schwarzenberger Georg, 'The Problem of an International Criminal Law,' 3 *Current Legal Problems* (1950) 263.

Selj, Helen J., *Prostitution, Women and Misuse of the Law* (2003).

Stimson, Henry, L., 'The Nuremberg, Trial, Landmark in Law,' 25 *Foreign Affairs* 179 (1946-7).

Tams, J., *Enforcing Obligations Erga Omnes in International Law* (2005).

Terreur africaine, *Burundi, Rwanda, Zaïre: Les racines de la violence* (1996).

Trials of War Criminals Before the Nuremberg Military Tribunals under Control Council Law No. 10 (Nuremberg, 1946-1949).

Trials of War Criminals Before the Nuremberg Military Tribunals under Control Council (1951).

Vervaele, J., "The Transnational *ne bis in idem* Principle in the EU: Mutual Recognition and Equivalent Protection of Human Rights", 1 *Utrecht Law Review* (2005).

Waltman, Max., 'Prohibiting Sex Purchasing and Ending Trafficking: The Swedish Prostitution Law', 33 *Michigan Journal of International Law* (2011), pp.133-157.

Wise, Edward M.., 'Prolegomenon to the Principles of International Criminal Law,' 16 *New York University Law Review* 562 (1970).

Zemanek, Karl., 'The New Trends in the Enforcement of Era Omnes Obligations,' 6 *Max Planck Yearbook of United Nations Law* (2000), pp.1-52.